Small Business

6th Australian Edition

by Veechi Curtis

Small Business For Dummies®, 6th Australian Edition

Published by

John Wiley & Sons Australia, Ltd

42 McDougall Street

Milton, Qld 4064

www.dummies.com

Copyright © 2021 John Wiley & Sons Australia, Ltd

The moral rights of the author have been asserted.

ISBN: 978-0-730-38484-7

 A catalogue record for this book is available from the National Library of Australia

All rights reserved. No part of this book, including interior design, cover design and icons, may be reproduced or transmitted in any form, by any means (electronic, photocopying, recording or otherwise) without the prior written permission of the Publisher. Requests to the Publisher for permission should be addressed to the Contracts & Licensing section of John Wiley & Sons Australia, Ltd, 42 McDougall Street, Milton, Qld 4064, or email auspermissions@wiley.com.

Cover image: © Carlina Teteris/Moment/Getty Images

Typeset by SPi

LIMIT OF LIABILITY/DISCLAIMER OF WARRANTY: THE PUBLISHER AND THE AUTHOR MAKE NO REPRESENTATIONS OR WARRANTIES WITH RESPECT TO THE ACCURACY OR COMPLETENESS OF THE CONTENTS OF THIS WORK AND SPECIFICALLY DISCLAIM ALL WARRANTIES, INCLUDING WITHOUT LIMITATION, WARRANTIES OF FITNESS FOR A PARTICULAR PURPOSE. NO WARRANTY MAY BE CREATED OR EXTENDED BY SALES OR PROMOTIONAL MATERIALS. THE ADVICE AND STRATEGIES CONTAINED HEREIN MAY NOT BE SUITABLE FOR EVERY SITUATION. THIS WORK IS SOLD WITH THE UNDERSTANDING THAT THE PUBLISHER IS NOT ENGAGED IN RENDERING LEGAL, ACCOUNTING, OR OTHER PROFESSIONAL SERVICES. IF PROFESSIONAL ASSISTANCE IS REQUIRED, THE SERVICES OF A COMPETENT PROFESSIONAL PERSON SHOULD BE SOUGHT. NEITHER THE PUBLISHER NOR THE AUTHOR SHALL BE LIABLE FOR DAMAGES ARISING HEREFROM. THE FACT THAT AN ORGANISATION OR WEBSITE IS REFERRED TO IN THIS WORK AS A CITATION AND/OR A POTENTIAL SOURCE OF FURTHER INFORMATION DOES NOT MEAN THAT THE AUTHOR OR THE PUBLISHER ENDORSES THE INFORMATION THE ORGANISATION OR WEBSITE MAY PROVIDE OR RECOMMENDATIONS IT MAY MAKE. FURTHER, READERS SHOULD BE AWARE THAT INTERNET WEBSITES LISTED IN THIS WORK MAY HAVE CHANGED OR DISAPPEARED BETWEEN WHEN THIS WORK WAS WRITTEN AND WHEN IT IS READ.

Trademarks: Wiley, the Wiley logo, For Dummies, the Dummies Man logo, A Reference for the Rest of Us!, The Dummies Way, Making Everything Easier, dummies.com and related trade dress are trademarks or registered trademarks of John Wiley & Sons, Inc. and/or its affiliates in the United States and other countries, and may not be used without written permission. All other trademarks are the property of their respective owners. John Wiley & Sons Australia, Ltd is not associated with any product or vendor mentioned in this book.

Printed in Singapore

M WEP234171 191023

Contents at a Glance

Table of Contents

Introduction

Every once in a while, I work as a mentor for start-up businesses. I find it fascinating to sit in a room with half a dozen people, and listen to the hopes, dreams and business ideas of each person. Many people are planning to start businesses that others have done before, such as opening a hairdressing salon or a lawn mowing business; other people have ideas that are new in some way, such as a business specialising in making homes safe for toddlers, or a start-up delivering mental wellbeing training to corporates.

I've realised that no matter what the idea, every new business benefits from strategic thinking. If you're starting a business that others have done many times before, such as hairdressing or lawn mowing, strategic thinking helps define your point of difference and how you can set yourself apart from others. If your new business involves an entrepreneurial idea that nobody else has done before, strategic thinking is the key to safeguarding your business idea, and transforming creativity into practical action.

Despite the challenges of Australia's rapidly changing business environments, with the pace picking up ever faster, I believe that most people are capable of running their own business. With the right software in place, you don't need to be an accountant in order to understand your finances; with a decent product or service and an understanding of what makes you different, you don't need to be a marketing guru in order to make a sale. Instead, all you need is some capital, a willingness to work hard and lots of straightforward advice. This book provides the straightforward advice bit — in bucketloads.

I find small business exciting. For me, being self-employed is about helping other people, having flexibility in my working life, and making a few dollars to boot. I hope you enjoy the journey too, and I wish you the very best of luck.

About This Book

Despite the branding, I don't think you're a 'dummy' — far from it. For me, *For Dummies* books are about a 'can-do' attitude. No matter how inexperienced you are, if you're ready to give something a go, this book is here to help.

The whole *For Dummies* outlook helps me a great deal when I'm writing, reminding me to stay creative and think positive. I can be a little risk-averse at times, worrying more about profit margins and making enough to pay the mortgage, and sometimes, I need that push of encouragement to let my entrepreneurial side flourish. Hopefully, I find a balance between practicality and creativity throughout this book, and you can benefit from that, too.

This book (all 20 bite-sized chunks of it) is designed so you can pick it up at any point and just start reading. Perhaps you want to know about hiring your first employee (Chapter 13) but you're not the least interested in legal structures (Chapter 7). That's fine — just skip the first 12 chapters and start off from where you want to be.

One more thing. Throughout this book you'll see *sidebars* — text that sits in a separate box with grey shading. Think of sidebars in the same way as you might do about designer brands: Nice to have, but not essential. Feel free to skip these bits.

Foolish Assumptions

When you work with small business, you learn to assume nothing. I see everything from clients who time all strategic decisions to fit with the stars (no kidding!) to multimillion-dollar enterprises that have grown out of nothing in a matter of months.

So, in this book I try to assume very little about you. You don't need to know anything about bookkeeping, business planning, marketing or tax, and I try to explain all concepts in the simplest possible way. I focus on the kinds of things I reckon most small businesses are concerned about, combining positive advice about promoting your business and planning for success with practical guidance about the really tricky stuff — such as dealing with unhappy employees or digging yourself out of financial difficulties.

Icons Used in This Book

AHEAD OF THE PACK

Want to be streets ahead of the competition? Look for this handy icon.

MONEY STUFF

Get out your calculator and start doing those sums. This icon flags money stuff, highlighting vital information for anyone with an eye for making a dollar or two.

REMEMBER

Tie a knot in your hankie, pin an eggtimer to your shirt but, whatever you do, don't forget . . .

TECHNICAL STUFF

This icon flags tricky, slightly nerdy stuff that's nice to have, but that you can probably live without!

TIP

This icon indicates handy advice or insights into how to improve your business or make life easier.

TRUE STORY

If you can't learn from history, you're doomed to repeat your mistakes. Real-life stories from businesses and people who've been there provide all the history lessons you could ever want.

WARNING

A pitfall for the unwary. Read these warnings carefully (and then you can't say no-one told you . . .).

Where to Go from Here

Small Business For Dummies is no classic work of literature (one day, I promise myself!), and so you don't need to start reading from page one and plough through to the end. Instead, jump in and start reading from whatever section is most relevant to you:

>> New to business? I suggest you read Chapters 1, 2 and 3 before doing much else. Chapter 1 asks if you're ready to run your own business, Chapter 2 looks at how you're going to stand out from the rest of the pack, and Chapter 3 looks at whether to start a business from scratch, buy an existing business, or go for a franchise.

>> If you think you're ready to start, Chapters 4 to 7 are about developing your entrepreneurial spirit — thinking about how big you want this business to be, what risks lie ahead, creating a business plan and choosing a legal structure that best fits your needs.

» Chapters 8 to 11 talk about planning for profit, covering everything from pricing your goods and services, building your first budget, checking the financial sense of your business idea and establishing your very first marketing plan.

» You don't get anywhere in business without people skills so, in Chapters 12 to 14, I share lots of advice about developing an exceptional customer service ethos, and talk about being an employer (including knowing your legal obligations and understanding how to recruit good staff) and an effective manager.

» Need help with money? Chapters 15 to 18 delve into the nitty-gritty, looking at financing your business idea, bookkeeping systems, budgets and grotty subjects such as GST and income tax.

» Finally, my favourite part of any Dummies title: The Part of Tens. Chapter 19 offers ten tips for what to do if you hit hard times, and Chapter 20 provides a few handy pointers of what to do when you're ready to move on and sell your business.

Thank you, dear reader, for taking the time to read *Small Business For Dummies*. I hope you find something along the way that helps you and your business to grow.

1

Getting Started

IN THIS PART . . .

Find out whether you're ready to be a small business owner.

Uncover where your winning tactic lies.

Decide whether to buy an existing business, start from scratch, or purchase a franchise.

IN THIS CHAPTER

» Working for yourself — the good things that make it all worthwhile

» Working for yourself — the bad things that no-one wants to talk about

» Making sure the time is right (now, where *is* my crystal ball?)

» Figuring out your business strategy

» Digging up government advice, free of charge

Chapter **1**

Is Small Business for You?

love small business. For me, small business is about believing in yourself, being passionate about what you do and creating opportunities. Our culture of getting up, getting out and giving it a go fits perfectly with this entrepreneurial existence, explaining why so many Australians are hooked on the self-employed way of life.

Although starting your own business can be daunting at first, the everyday challenges don't leave you with much time to regret your decision. Besides, being self-employed is a pretty addictive thing: Working your own hours, being responsible for your decisions and raking in handsome profits (here's hoping) are just some of the attractions of being your own boss.

In this chapter, I talk about what it means to start your own business. I take you on a roller-coaster ride over the highs and lows of small business terrain (for every upside to being out there on your own, a downside exists, too), through to making the decision *when* to actually 'open shop'. After all, the success of any venture depends on timing — the best time for the business, the best time for the economy and the best time for you.

So, put on your Stackhat, hold on tight and get ready for the trip of a lifetime . . .

Working for Yourself — A Dream Come True?

If you ask most small business people what they like the best about working for themselves, you're likely to get a pretty cynical reply — something about the delights of working for peanuts and the thrills of doing bookwork in the wee hours of the night. But dig a little deeper, and most self-employed people warm to the question.

Doing what you love to do

Doing what you're passionate about has a lot going for it. If you want to play the trumpet day and night, you're likely to be happiest as a professional musician. If you love hanging off cliffs on the end of a rope, you're going to dig being a climbing instructor. And if you've never quite gotten over your LEGO phase, you probably need to go and build houses.

Happy people love what they do for a living. Besides, being self-employed is often the only way you can get to do just that. (Nine-to-five jobs tend to be rather thin on the ground for trumpet players or climbing instructors!)

Earning pots of money (here's hoping)

With many trades and professions, your income always has a pre-defined upper limit, no matter how hard you work — teachers, carpenters or nurses on the regular payroll, for example, are limited in the amount of pay they can get. However, by setting up your own business, whether you're tutoring private students, building house extensions or doing private home nursing, your earning potential immediately increases.

MONEY STUFF

Statistics that compare the taxable income of self-employed individuals with those of employees working in similar industries or professions are hard to come by. However, if you start up a low-risk kind of business — home-tutoring, for example — the financial benefits of becoming self-employed are small but relatively guaranteed. On the other hand, if you start up a high-risk business — say, launching a new invention — you could end up losing everything you have. Or, you could just wind up a millionaire.

Being your own boss

No-one is going to dispute being your own boss is *fantastic*. And no matter how much you stuff things up, no-one can give you the boot — except perhaps your customers — leaving you with a feeling of security that's hard to beat. Here are some other reasons being your own boss feels so good:

>> **You get to set your own rules:** Your rules may involve anything from setting enormously high standards, to declaring mufti days seven days a week.

>> **You choose when (and how often) you work:** Of course, choosing when you work often means working 24 hours a day, seven days a week. However, in theory you can pick and choose which hours you work and when you take holidays.

>> **You follow your own instincts:** You can do what you think is right, as opposed to doing what someone else thinks is right. I know firsthand how frustrating it is to be forced to do stuff the wrong way, or the slow way, just because the person who is giving the orders happens to be your boss.

>> **You can use your conscience:** You can afford to make decisions that may not be the best from an economic point of view, but are good decisions in terms of your own conscience. For example, a business colleague of mine who recently purchased an electric car was acting according to her principles, rather than seeking to save dollars.

>> **You can take risks:** When you're self-employed, you can take risks that you may not be able to otherwise take. Thousands of successful businesses have been started by former employees who went out on their own because their employers didn't believe in the viability of their new ideas.

>> **You can provide employment for family members:** Being in a business team with your family, and being able to provide employment when it's needed, can be one of life's most satisfying experiences. (Of course, it can also be one of life's most frustrating experiences, but I'm not going there right now.)

>> **You can realise your dreams:** No business book is complete unless it mentions dreams. Nothing beats putting your heart and soul into what you believe in.

Staying home

I confess that working from home somewhat lost its shine for me during the COVID-19 lockdown. However, over the years I've really appreciated the flexibility that working from home affords. Generally, I love walking to my 'office', ten seconds down the hallway, rather than commuting two hours by train to the city.

GRAB SOME INSPIRATION

A whole business community is out there for you to lean on. These links and sites may have changed by the time you're reading this, but here are some of my favourite sources of inspiration:

- www.flyingsolo.com.au is not just a website for 'micro businesses', but a community as well, with over 120,000 members, hundreds of articles, lots of free tips and tools, and a busy bunch of forum boards.

- www.entrepreneur.com is a website as well as a magazine, and has more of a start-up, corporate bent. I find many of the articles helpful and a bit of nudge to keep my thinking fresh.

- With an upbeat feel and great info, www.smartcompany.com.au is an Australian site dedicated to free news and resources for small- to medium-sized businesses.

- A favourite of mine when I'm in the car is the Goal Digger podcast, hosted by entrepreneur Jenna Kutcher (podcast.jennakutcher.com). This show is all about setting and managing goals, whether for your side-hustle (how I love that term!) or for your main game.

- When I'm in the mood to refresh my marketing, I enjoy the Strategy Hour podcast, facilitated by Think Tank collective hosts (bossproject.com/podcast). These practical podcasts help with the nitty-gritty details of business, with hundreds of episodes covering all kinds of different topics.

REMEMBER

According to the Australian Bureau of Statistics (ABS), home-based businesses make up over half of all the small businesses in Australia, reflecting part of an international trend towards more businesses operating from home (a trend presumably partly fuelled by improvements in technology). Home business is the spawning ground from which larger businesses are born, including iconic brands such as AirTasker, Billabong, Canva and Salt Gypsy.

Working for Yourself — Reality Strikes

An acupuncturist once said to me: 'When you work for yourself, you work for a real bastard. No holiday pay, no sick pay, no bonuses — long hours, filthy pay and no promotion.' As I lay on the couch, needles sticking out of my ears and my navel, I reflected on my 60-hour weeks and wobbly bank balance. I had to agree with him.

Teetering on the edge

As the years have passed by, I've developed a sniffer-dog instinct for which businesses are likely to succeed, which are going to struggle and which are doomed to fail. Although I usually wish I wasn't so chillingly accurate (especially when I predict failure), occasionally life delivers a surprise — the success of an overpriced French restaurant with a mad chef, for example, or the survival of a bed and breakfast in the back of beyond.

WARNING

Running a business is an inherently risky game. Sometimes, this risk makes things exciting and, other times, just plain old scary. Of course, business success is a fantastic feeling but, on the other hand, failure can be quite catastrophic. You can lose your house, your job, even your family, all in the one hit, not to mention the disillusionment of having precious dreams crushed by harsh reality.

How well you cope with risk depends on your age, personality and health. Certainly, investing your life's savings in a new venture is infinitely scarier when you're 60 than when you're 30. I recommend you always minimise risk by keeping a tight control on your finances, a topic I explore in detail in Chapters 15 to 18.

Working night and day for little pay

Unfortunately (or maybe fortunately), the brilliant business ideas that earn $10 million in the first year are very few and far between. For many people, the only sure-fire way to succeed is to work loooong hours in the first year or so, taking on the roles of bookkeeper, marketing consultant, salesperson and managing director all in one.

These long hours do tend to settle down as your business becomes established, however, and the ABS reports that the average self-employed owner-operator works 42 hours per week. And, at the other end of the spectrum, many people choose to only work part-time in their business, content to choose lifestyle and flexibility over income.

WARNING

One of the hardest things about being self-employed is staying motivated. Not just in the first year, where everything is interesting and different, but year after year after year. Of course, as your business grows, you can hopefully employ staff to help. (Chapters 13 and 14 talk more about becoming an employer and building an effective team.) Ideally, you can arrive at a point where your business earns money, even if you're not working in it every day of the week.

Weathering feast and famine

Sometimes, the highs and lows of small business profits make even Melbourne's weather look reliable. A bumper year, and the bank account is rosy. Then you lose a client or two, interest rates go up, and before you know it, you're wondering how to pay the rent.

MONEY STUFF

In Chapter 15, I talk about creating budgets for business set-up expenses, and share tips for securing business finance. Some consultants advise you not to expect to make any money at all in your first year of business, and to have savings put aside to pay for your living expenses during this time. Such advice is prudent, but the truth is that sometimes businesses take even longer than a year before they make a profit, and even businesses that have been cruising along happily for years can strike hard times.

I used to find the feast and famine of running my own business very stressful, but I'm getting better at managing this dichotomy as time goes by, even managing to put money aside when things go well. How you cope with the effect of this insecurity depends not only on your personality, but on your family commitments as well.

Getting the Timing Right

Weighing up the good and the bad about being self-employed is tricky enough, but when you add the 'you' factor into the mix, you may decide to rethink some issues. You have to consider not only your own skills and expertise, but also whether you have the timing right: The right timing for the business idea, the right timing for you and your family, and the right timing for the business environment.

Timing it right for your idea

An experienced entrepreneur once said to me: 'If real estate is all about position, position, position, then business is all about timing, timing, timing.' He's right, of course. If you were selling fondue sets in the 1970s, chances are your business would be successful. Try to sell the same fondue sets for a living these days, and it would be slim pickings indeed (although my mother does have very fond memories of cheese and chocolate fondue dinner parties).

If you're not sure whether now's the right time to start your business, consider the following:

WARNING

>> **Fickle fashions:** Humans are capricious creatures and what's hot today may be ice-cold tomorrow. Whether the latest craze is kids going nuts about a Disney action doll or adults getting worked up about a big sporting event, make sure you're not the one who suffers when everyone gets bored and tired. Try to jump on the bandwagon near the beginning or during the build-up — don't leap in at the peak.

>> **Industry trends:** The difference between a trend and a craze may seem hard to pick at first, but the difference is both real and important. Be aware of trends in your industry and capitalise on opportunities. For example, the long-term and growing interest in low-carbon and energy-efficient building supplies is a positive trend that indicates a whole host of business opportunities.

TRUE STORY

>> **Lead times:** If you've got a long lead time for your project, research the project well. I remember a client who decided to build storage units in a busy country town. The demand seemed guaranteed, because there weren't any at that time. Three years later (after prolonged development applications through council and a $350,000 construction), the units were ready. The only snag was two other developers opened units that same year, creating a glut of supply and fierce price wars.

>> **Bleeding edge or cutting edge?** You may love being leader of the pack, but creating a product or service that customers aren't ready for yet is pointless.

>> **Seasonal variations:** If you're planning a business that is highly seasonal, factor this aspect carefully into your timing when making your business plan. Give yourself time to plan carefully for the peak season so you can take full advantage of that period.

TIP

My last comment about timing is that Australia's business environment is shifting faster than ever, and what might seem to be perfect timing right now could end up being horrendous timing in hindsight. Evaluate how robust your business idea might be in the face of natural disasters, pandemics, recessions or changes in government policy, and how you can design your new business to be as agile and responsive as possible. A business that responds quickly to change will be much better positioned to thrive than one that isn't.

Timing it right for you

Of course, good timing is not just a question of whether the outside world is ready and eager for what you have to offer. Good timing is also about how ready you are, personally. Consider the following:

>> **Experience:** For example, if you're looking at buying a nursery, do you have horticulture training as well as hands-on retail experience? If you're

considering going freelance as a consultant, do you have enough consulting experience behind you? In Chapter 3, I explore how you might compensate for a lack of experience, and why buying an existing business or purchasing a franchise may be preferable to starting a business from scratch.

>> **Planning:** I recommend you don't even consider starting a new business without first drawing up a business plan. In fact, planning for your business is so important that I dedicate Chapters 4 to 7 to this very topic.

MONEY
STUFF

>> **Capital:** Don't start a business without enough capital behind you. (I talk lots more about how much money is enough in Chapter 15.) Starting a business with insufficient capital is like competing in a marathon when you didn't sleep the week before.

>> **Age, health and stamina:** Age can be a factor at both ends of the spectrum. Most 18 year olds are unlikely to have enough experience to cope with running their own business. On the other hand, a 65 year old may be short on motivation, ambition and energy, especially for new ventures requiring long hours and huge input.

TIP

>> **Your family life:** Don't start a new venture without consulting your family and enlisting their support. The backing of your partner is vital during this time. (Resigning from your regular job to become a self-employed mural painter the week before your partner is due to deliver twins isn't likely to go down well.)

Timing it right for the economy

No business is an island but, rather, functions as an organic part of the world around it. Imagine owning a fantastic, go-ahead cafe in the Pilbara region of Western Australia. However cleverly managed, this café is at the mercy of whether local mines expand or shut down, whether the economy is booming or in recession and, further still, world commodity prices. Be aware of the following economic influences:

AHEAD OF
THE PACK

>> **Industry-specific events:** Be alert for changes in your industry that may affect the viability of your business, such as additional licensing requirements, new government regulations or major shifts in available technology. For example, with the changes in financial planning regulations, many accountants are now restricted in the types of advice they can supply to clients.

>> **Tax or government policy reform:** Many a good business has been sent to the dogs because of tax reform. Think of a political football such as the solar industry, which has been subject to major government funding changes every year or so for the last 15 years in Australia. Keep your ear to the ground and listen out for these changes within your industry network and via the media, before they happen.

>> **Interest rates and currency exchange:** Some businesses are more affected by interest rate and currency exchange fluctuations than others. Importing, exporting, construction and real estate are just some of the businesses that can be affected, as well as any business with large borrowings. If you're likely to be affected by interest rate or currency exchange fluctuations, look carefully at economic indicators and plan accordingly.

>> **Recessions:** Even the most successful business can sometimes have a bad year, or a couple of bad years, especially in times of recession. Such businesses rely on profits built up over previous years to see them through. However, if you start a new business in the middle of a recession, ask yourself whether you're going to be able to finance it until the good times arrive.

REMEMBER

Stay abreast of current economic trends and how they may affect your business plan.

TIP

GO BACK TO SCHOOL

Just as you wouldn't expect to drive a car without ever having lessons, I recommend that you don't plunge into a new business venture without any practice or instruction. Instead, check out what courses are available.

Probably the most practical approach is your local TAFE. Although the courses on offer vary from campus to campus, look for a particular small business course that focuses on getting a business started, and which includes formulating your very first business plan.

Similarly, you may find something relevant through your local community college, but be aware that the quality of these courses varies. (Community colleges don't always stick to curriculums in the same way as TAFEs do, so the quality of their courses depends on the individual tutors, and whether or not the course is working towards a particular certification.)

If business management is what turns you on (and this doesn't necessarily mean working for yourself), an undergraduate course at university may be your best bet. For example, I completed a joint major in Accounting and Business Management, and the subjects provided a great all-round understanding for all kinds of things.

If you have a university degree under your belt in a different area, a Master of Business Administration (MBA) is another option. But, be aware — while an MBA is an impressive achievement, it isn't a hugely practical option if you're thinking of running a small one-person enterprise, because the overall emphasis of such courses is on larger enterprises and organisations, rather than on small business.

Staying Safe or Inventing the Wheel?

Businesses fall into three broad categories. The first type of business is one that has been done before, and therefore, has been tried and tested. The second type of business is one that finds its own niche, thereby doing something especially tailored to a small group of customers. The third type of business is one that launches an entirely new concept on the world.

Playing it safe

Probably the safest and most reliable approach is to go for an *established* kind of business; one that lots of people have tried and succeeded in before you. Most retail shops and many service businesses fall into this category — for example, bookshops, florists or hairdressers, builders, electricians or plumbers.

One good thing about going into the kind of business that many others have done before you is that you can find out what to expect in terms of sales, profit margins, expenses and more. With this kind of business, success depends not so much on the strength of your original idea, but more on good business sense and your ongoing capacity to differentiate yourself from your competitors. If possible, this difference should capitalise on your skills and resources, so that this difference is hard for competitors to imitate.

WARNING

Do bear in mind that changes in technology are shaking up even the most traditional kinds of businesses. For example, bookshops used to offer solid business profits, so long as you selected a good location and you knew your trade. However, the changes brought about by ebooks and online distribution mean that, nowadays, opening a bookshop would be a very different proposition indeed. Similarly, a bookkeeping business may have been a safe bet in the past, but cloud technology and new accounting software solutions are rendering many bookkeeping services obsolete.

If you choose to go with an established kind of business, you may prefer to purchase an existing business, rather than starting from scratch. For many kinds of established businesses, franchising is also an option. Skip to Chapter 3 to find out more.

Finding your own niche

The next type of business is called a *niche* business. Developing a niche means doing something specialised and catering to a small but (hopefully) dedicated market. A niche business can cover anything from manufacturing custom guitars to producing hand-stitched silk lingerie, or from designing permaculture gardens to cooking special food for diabetics.

The best thing about niche businesses is that you can start off on a small scale. Starting small means low risk, less expense setting up and an opportunity to try out your idea and test the response. The best way to promote a niche business is usually through online advertising, where developing your own e-commerce site along with a social media presence can mean generating business all around the globe. For lots more about social media and building your marketing plan, check out Chapter 11.

Going out on a limb

The last type of business is called the *entrepreneur* type, reserved for new inventions or new market concepts. Untested and unknown, this type of business can occasionally experience resounding success but (sadly), more often, spectacular failure. (I still feel a pang whenever I remember my friend's invention of a solar-powered windmill-hat, a great idea but scarcely a hot fashion item.)

With the entrepreneur type of business, you're taking a gamble. Though the chance of failure is high, if you do succeed (and success is always possible), the rewards can be huge. I talk about market research, and how to find the products or services that customers *really* want, in Chapters 2, 5 and 11.

Assessing your chances of survival

Australians are a pretty entrepreneurial bunch. With a population of 25 million (give or take a few), almost 2.4 million businesses are alive and kicking. Impressive, don't you reckon? Almost 10 per cent of the population run their own business.

But what about business survival? Are all these businesses fly-by-nighters, that start up one year and are gone the next? Not so long ago, a business coaching franchise advised a client of mine that 80 per cent of businesses go bust in the first year, and only 8 per cent of businesses survive five years or more.

Pish tosh. Business is tough, but it's not a suicidal mission. The ABS reports that half of new businesses without employees, and 30 to 40 per cent of new businesses with employees, cease trading within the first three years. However, these figures don't shed light on how many businesses chose to cease trading (as opposed to going broke or 'failing'), and how many businesses actually experienced financial loss upon closing their business. In my experience, very few business people rate their overall experience as a negative one.

A QUICK QUIZ FOR SUCCESS

So, you're not sure if you're cut out for the world of business? Then don't leave your steady (but mind-numbingly boring) government job quite yet. Instead, complete this illuminating questionnaire to see how you rate in the success stakes.

Your most recent power bill is unreal (as is your newest love). You know you can't pay the bill on time. Do you . . .

A. Think 'what the hell' — this is what love is all about.

B. Stay awake at night wondering where you're going to find the readies.

C. Contact the power company and ask for a fortnight's extension.

D. Live on Vegemite sandwiches and take cold showers until you're flush with cash again.

It's horror hour. Dinner needs cooking, the kids need help with homework and your mobile is ringing. What do you do?

A. Have a beer and ignore everyone.

B. Scream at the dinner, stir the homework and pour soy sauce on the kids.

C. Cook, call out instructions to the kids and take the phone call. All at the same time, of course.

D. Do one thing at a time, logically one after the other.

How are you with maths?

A. Okay, so long as you can make figures up whenever you have to.

B. Just the thought of maths makes you feel inadequate.

C. You can use Excel and don't mind doing simple stuff.

D. Fine, especially if the maths has a practical application that's relevant to you.

You're playing Pictionary with your partner at a local fundraiser. How do you behave?

A. You act the goat. It's a game, after all.

B. You get cranky and wish it weren't so slow.

C. Relaxed. You're naturally good at Pictionary.

D. You play with dogged concentration and a will to win.

Describe your relationship with bureaucracy.

A. You chuck bill reminders and letters from the government in the recycling bin as soon as they arrive. They're not even worth reading.

B. You feel anxious about completing forms correctly, and anxious that if you get something wrong, you might get fined.

C. This kind of stuff is okay. You whiz through most forms pretty quickly.

D. You enjoy the orderliness of completing forms and having everything in order.

It's Sunday afternoon, you're painting the verandah and some old friends drop by unexpectedly. Do you . . .

A. Ask them in and let them help themselves to tea. Shame that there's no milk.

B. Pull up a chair and talk until the cows come home.

C. Get them to help you paint the verandah. Free labour!

D. Feel irritated they didn't ring to tell you they planned to come by.

How important is it for you to have a regular, steady income?

A. You couldn't care less. You don't need much to live on anyway.

B. You dream about a regular income but life doesn't usually work out that way.

C. It's important in the long term, but you can do without it right now.

D. You want more than a regular income. You aim to succeed and make your first million within the next five years.

It's midnight and your new online ordering system has crashed. What do you do?

A. Switch off your computer and give up.

B. Swear, curse, and blame everyone including the cat.

C. Ring your night-owl IT friend and offer homemade chocolates in exchange for their help.

D. Work steadily till dawn, solving the problem.

(continued)

(continued)

Mostly *A*s

It's good to be laid-back, but you may not get much done lounging in that hammock all day. Being in business is hard work and you need to be inspired and motivated. If 60-hour weeks aren't your cup of tea, you're best to start a part-time business where you can pick and choose your hours, have lots of fun, and make a modest amount of money.

Mostly *B*s

You may be a bit of a stress-bucket, but your creative talents are there for expressing. Being your own boss may suit you well, although financial success may be elusive, especially at first. Do be careful: If you lack business experience and you already have significant financial commitments, the stress of starting out on your own may take its toll.

Mostly *C*s

Aha. You're not only super-cool and enterprising, but you're also resourceful and a natural multi-tasker, making the perfect personality for the small business person. When you can be web designer, manager, salesperson and bookkeeper all in the one day, and stay calm and collected to boot, you know you're on your way to success.

Mostly *D*s

Slow and steady wins the race, and a bit of dogged persistence along with a healthy dose of ambition helps, too. These qualities all help in running your own business, although you may need to choose a business that matches your conservative personality. A strong network of advisers and business associates are particularly important to your business success.

However, I am a realist when it comes to recognising that many small businesses face significant challenges from time to time. In Chapter 19, I share lots of tips for carrying your business through tough times, and in Chapter 20, I take the more optimistic perspective of how to sell your business and how to ensure you get the best price when you do.

STICK TO THE KNITTING

TRUE STORY

I recall a client of mine, a highly experienced business manager, who purchased two hairdressing salons as an investment. Despite relatively sound business practices, both salons floundered, simply because my client didn't have any experience in the hairdressing industry: He failed to understand that most customers didn't come to the salon looking for value for money, but came looking for a chat and a confidence boost; he didn't appreciate that several of the hair stylists in this particular salon expected 'cash' wages as part of their weekly pay (something the previous owner had offered); and he had difficulties maintaining hygiene and dealing with money going missing out of the till.

My client made an elementary mistake in that he didn't stick to doing what he did best.

My point? If you've been a musician all your life, you're going to be much better starting a music school than opening a florist shop. If you've always worked as a landscape gardener, you're probably ill advised to open a bookshop.

Stick to what you're good at: Business is competitive enough without trying to do something that you have little or no experience in.

Getting the Government to Help You

You're paying out all these taxes, so you may as well get something back. The quality of available government advice is luck of the draw: Some advisers are great, others are a bit dodgy. However, most government advice is free and can often be just what the doctor ordered. Here's a summary of what advice is available and where to find it:

>> **The Wild West:** The Small Business Development Corporation is a government agency focused on developing the small business sector. They offer advice on finance, marketing, business planning and regulations. Visit www.smallbusiness.wa.gov.au.

>> **Tassie tigers:** Business Tasmania has a good portal for small businesses at www.business.tas.gov.au.

>> **The Top End:** Head to www.nt.gov.au/industry for territory-specific planning advice, business licence information, and business support. This website also links to business advisory centres across the territory, known as Small Business Champions.

- » **Brash and brazen:** www.business.nsw.gov.au is a good resource, and I can recommend the Business Connect program. This heavily subsidised (and indeed, often free) service provides face-to-face support and expert advice to help develop your business.

- » **Eureka and Ned:** Business Victoria is a central organisation based in Melbourne offering information and referral services for small businesses. An excellent website at www.business.vic.gov.au offers links to a whole load of business services, including business mentoring and workshops.

- » **Don't you worry about that!** The best source of info in Queensland is www.business.qld.gov.au. Here you can find a whole range of resources, plus access to training seminars and workshops.

- » **The lost city:** ACT Innovation, Industry and Investment (www.cmtedd.act.gov.au) offers small business advice and administers a range of business support and development programs.

- » **Home of the white pointer:** For South Australian business advice, start at www.business.sa.gov.au. They offer great small business support and advice, including several Business Enterprise Centres and Regional Development units.

- » **National Business Enterprise Centres:** In addition to the state government business development departments listed here, a national network of Business Enterprise Centres is available to help you get your business going in the right direction. Go to www.becaustralia.org.au to find a BEC near you.

For more about business planning, and other business resources, skip ahead to Chapter 6.

Setting Yourself Up for Success

I talk a lot about the pros and cons of small business in this chapter and, as you've probably gathered by now, I speak from a somewhat conservative standpoint because I know both how tough small business can be and also the amount of commitment required.

However, don't imagine for a minute that you're not capable of success. With careful research, willpower, financial backing and a healthy dose of inspiration, you're going to be hard-pressed to think of a reason you can't succeed in the way many others have done before you. (And, of course, that's what the rest of *Small Business For Dummies* is all about!)

IN THIS CHAPTER

» Identifying what gives you an edge

» Ensuring your business idea is strong enough to fly

» Understanding the relationship between risk and gain

» Analysing your competitors (complete with cloak and dagger)

» Matching competitive strategy to strategic advantage

Chapter **2**

Figuring Out What's So Special about You (And Your Business)

Whalt is it that makes you, or your business, so special?

Even if you have a business that's similar to thousands of others — maybe you mow lawns, have a hairdressing salon or tutor high school students — I still recommend you come up with an idea that makes your business different from others in some way, or that provides you with a competitive edge.

Similarly, if your business caters for a very specific niche — maybe you sell gluten-free cookies or baby clothes made from organic cottons — you need to identify what it is about your skills or circumstances that enables you to service this niche better than others.

In this chapter, I help you define the essence of what makes your business special, or more likely to succeed than others. This quality is called your *strategic advantage* and is the single most important ingredient for ongoing business success.

Understanding Strategic Advantage

Many business people use the terms competitive advantage and strategic advantage synonymously. However, to be really precise, you could argue that these two terms relate to slightly different aspects of your business.

A *competitive advantage* is something that's different from, better than, or not offered by your competitors. For example, if a town has two hairdressing salons and one offers a mobile service but the other doesn't, the first salon has a competitive advantage because they're providing something their competitors aren't.

A *strategic advantage* is something that stems from capabilities within your business that are hard for others to copy. These capabilities tend to be a unique blend of assets, knowledge, people networks, skills or technology. For example, imagine the owner of the salon with the mobile haircutting service has a background in nursing, and so has a natural understanding of the needs of her many elderly housebound clients. Imagine also that the owner's husband is a mechanic, which means the vehicle used for providing the salon's mobile service is kept on the road at minimal cost. This unique blend of skills and cost efficiency forms part of this salon's strategic advantage.

Having said all this, competitive and strategic advantages tend to overlap so much that I try to avoid getting bogged down in arguing about the distinction. I use the term strategic advantage in most of this chapter (because, after all, a true strategic advantage should ultimately result in a competitive advantage — an idea I return to at the end of this chapter) but if you'd rather use the term competitive advantage, that's just fine.

Identifying your secret weapon

How can your business beat the competition, and what benefits can you provide that the competition can't? Here are some ways that your business may be able to secure a strategic advantage against others in the same industry:

**AHEAD OF
THE PACK**

>> **Added value:** Can you offer added value in comparison to your competitors? Think 24-hour delivery, locally sourced product, a mobile service, or a quality of product or service that's beyond industry norms.

- **Exclusive distribution rights:** Do you have exclusive distribution rights to a sought-after product or service?

- **First cab off the rank:** Do you have a new idea that nobody else has tried before? Or a new way of doing something that makes the product or service better, quicker or cheaper?

- **Intellectual property:** Do you have unique intellectual property (IP) that customers want and that's hard to copy? IP includes copyright, patents and trademarks. If you're just getting started with your business, your IP could be as simple as a clever business name, an eye-catching logo or a well-chosen domain name (that is, a web address).

- **Location:** If you're a retailer, do you have a great location in a central shopping area? (Location is often *the* prime strategic advantage for retailers.) Or are you the only business providing a service in a particular suburb or region? Are the demographics of your location ideally matched to your business, or are you located in a central spot for freight and transport?

- **Lower costs:** Do you have an innovative way of doing things that reduces costs, creates economies of scale or significantly improves business processes?

- **Obsession and drive:** Do you have exceptional vision or drive? Is this drive connected with a particular obsession? (For example, think of Steve Jobs and his obsession about design.)

- **Perfectly matched team:** If you're in a business partnership of some kind, do you have a unique combination of skills and do you work well together as a team? (The synergy created by two or more people who have complementary skills and who work well together can be a force to be reckoned with, and something that's hard for competition to copy.)

- **Specialist skills:** Are you a specialist who has an insight into a particular industry that nobody else is likely to have? Maybe you can see a gap in the industry that nobody else is catering to, or maybe you can see a way to do something better.

TIP

Think of a business that you know that has been really successful (maybe a local business or a friend's business, or even a big name such as The Body Shop, McDonald's or Microsoft). Go through the list of different strategic advantages and think about which of these advantages could apply to these businesses.

Focusing on real-life examples

Try to deepen your understanding of strategic advantage (refer to the preceding section) by applying the concept to a few real-life situations that are easy to imagine. Picture yourself sitting in a room with four people and each of these people sharing their idea for a new business:

>> Leila plans to start a business mowing lawns in her local neighbourhood.

>> Tess has recently qualified as an acupuncturist and plans to start up a practice specialising in children's health.

>> Dave has an idea to provide a mobile home-safety service, installing devices such as gates, cupboard latches and electrical safety switches to make homes toddler-proof. His partner is in real estate and has great marketing skills.

>> Shayne, who is a fashion designer with a large Instagram following, has partnered with a friend with photography skills to sell his services as a market influencer.

Referring to the strategic advantages listed in the preceding section, have a think about which of these advantages could be relevant to the example businesses. You can see how I've rated the strategic advantage potential for each of the four businesses in Table 2-1.

Have a look at Table 2-1 and see if you agree with my assessment of potential advantages. For example, can you think of ways that someone with a lawn mowing business could get an edge over competition with added value services, location or lower costs?

TABLE 2-1   **Rating Businesses According to Potential Strategic Advantage**

	Lawn Mowing	Acupuncturist	Toddler Safety	Market Influencer
Added value	Maybe		Yes	
Exclusive distribution				
First cab off the rank			Yes	
Intellectual property				Maybe
Location	Maybe	Maybe	Maybe	
Lower costs	Maybe			
Obsession and drive				Yes
Perfectly matched team		Maybe	Maybe	Maybe
Specialist skills		Yes		

Justifying Why You Can Succeed

In this chapter's preceding sections, I explore the concept of strategic advantage in relation to a range of possible businesses. I like to work with examples in this way because the different business scenarios help to highlight how this concept changes so much depending on the context.

In this section, I help you to apply the concept of strategic advantage to your business. If you're struggling to come up with anything that's special about your business — maybe you haven't stumbled on that winning idea quite yet — please do persist. The process of identifying your strategic advantage is even more important for you.

Uncovering your inner mojo

One good way to broaden your sense of where your strategic advantage may lie is to look at your existing customers and their buying patterns. (Or, if you haven't started your business yet, imagine what these answers might be.) Ask yourself these questions:

>> When customers come to me, why is that?

>> When potential customers go to my competitors instead, why is that?

>> When potential customers make an enquiry but end up not purchasing my goods or services, why is that?

>> Are the benefits I offer (or intend to offer) to my customers unique?

I like asking these questions because getting the answers usually means engaging in some market research. This naturally crosses over with competitor analysis, which I talk about later in this chapter.

AHEAD OF THE PACK

Honest, ongoing market research that compares the benefits your business provides to customers against the benefits your competitors provide is essential to business success.

Asking three key questions

For a strategic advantage to be really worth something — in terms of the goodwill of your business or your likely financial success — this advantage has to be something that you can sustain over the long term.

I like to think that any really strong strategic advantage should have three attributes:

>> **The advantage can't be easily copied by others.** The ideal strategic advantage is one that's really tricky for your competition to copy. Examples are a winning recipe or flavour (think Coca-Cola), a unique synergy of skills within your organisation, or expert knowledge that few others have.

>> **The advantage is important to customers.** Think of the farmers who switched to growing organic produce in the early 1990s, before organics became more mainstream. Many of these farmers did really well because organics were so important to particular customers. (And although the advantage was relatively easy to copy, many authorities required a seven-year lead time with no chemicals before a farm could be officially certified.)

>> **The advantage can be constantly improved.** If you can identify the thing that gives you an edge and constantly work this advantage, you have a strategic advantage that is potentially sustainable in the long term.

TRUE STORY

When Steve Jobs and Steve Wozniak started Apple, one key strategic advantage was their match of skills (Wozniak's knowledge of electronics and Jobs' marketing skills), along with a mutual interest in great design. The synergy of their skills was hard for others to copy, the beautiful design was something that customers really wanted, and Apple was in a position to continually improve and develop this advantage.

WARNING

Don't fall into the trap of thinking that because you're cheaper than everyone else, this is a strategic advantage. Being cheaper than everyone else usually means one of two things: Either your business isn't as profitable as it should be, or your competitors can grab your strategic advantage at any moment just by dropping their prices, too. Usually, being cheaper than others is only a strategic advantage if you have some special skills, technology or volume of production that enables you to be cheaper.

Growing your advantages over time

Sometimes your strategic advantage isn't something that's blindingly clear from the moment you set out in business, but instead grows over time. Your skills grow as you develop in business, and your understanding of how you're different from the competition consolidates as well.

From time to time, you can review your strategic advantage by asking yourself these questions:

>> What am I naturally good at? (Or what is my team good at?) Where do I feel I have been particularly successful in my business?

>> What do I offer to my customers that's either cheaper than my competitors, better value or unique in some way?

>> Does a point exist where what I'm naturally good at connects with what I do better than my competitors? If so, how can I build and develop this?

TRUE STORY

When our local osteopath first started out in business, he didn't really have anything that separated him from the competition. The only thing that was really different about him was that he was an elite rock climber in his spare time. However, as his business grew, he became expert at treating other climbers for their injuries. His business developed, and now he treats climbers who not only live locally, but also come from interstate. He even does some international consultations (and, yes, if you're wondering, some parts of an osteopathic consultation can be conducted via Zoom!). This combination of skills — being a natural climber and a highly trained osteopath — is hard to beat, and a true strategic advantage.

Making sure a demand really exists

One common mistake people make when starting a new business is that they're overly optimistic about the demand or interest in their product or services. A sunhat with a solar-powered fan on top may seem a good idea, but is anyone going to be seen dead wearing such a thing? In the ideal world, find a way to test the demand for your business idea before you invest too much capital or time in its development.

TRUE STORY

A friend of mine had an idea to start a business selling handmade timber beds. He decided to test this idea by running a stall once a month at the local markets. The response seemed good at first, but he soon found that people were reluctant to pay the extra dollars for his products, with people comparing his prices against the mass-manufactured timber beds made from poor-quality pine and available from large discount furniture chains. His profits were also lower than expected, and the time required to liaise with customers about their individual orders was higher. The result was that he decided not to pursue this business idea, but to explore other ways of making money instead.

Understanding How Risk Relates to Gain

In most situations, the business with the highest potential strategic advantage is going to be the business that requires the most capital or involves the most risk of failure. For example, in Table 2-1 earlier in this chapter, the business with the highest number of yeses in the strategic column is the toddler safety business. This business has the advantages of being a new idea, and something that clearly adds value for customers, but involves fairly substantial risks. Because this is a new service, people aren't going to look around thinking to hire someone to make their home toddler-proof. This business will have to invest significantly in marketing to make consumers aware of its services and may yet find that demand is so weak that the business idea is unsustainable.

In contrast, lawn mowing has few potential strategic advantages but probably the lowest risk of all. (The cost for Leila to set up her business could be as low as placing an ad on Facebook Marketplace.) The reason that strategic advantages are hard to find for Leila's business is that a lawn is only ever a lawn, and Leila is limited in what she can offer that others can't.

However, I still include 'maybe' against three possible strategic advantages for Leila's lawn mowing business:

>> **Added value:** Maybe Leila has some specialist horticultural knowledge that could differentiate her from her competitors.

>> **Location:** Maybe Leila would be providing the only service in her suburb, or maybe she lives in a very exclusive suburb with lots of high-income earners.

>> **Lower costs:** Maybe Leila's teenage son works for her at low hourly rates, enabling Leila to afford very competitive prices.

REMEMBER

If your business is very similar to many others, you may find it's tricky to identify strategic advantages and to stand out from your competitors. The upside of a business that's very similar to many others is that the risks are usually lower; the downside of a low-risk business is that it's always going to be tricky to charge premium rates or make above-average profits.

Figuring Out Who Your Competitors Really Are

I like to organise competitors into three broad groups, and I suggest you try to do so too:

>> **Head-to-head competitors** provide exactly the same service or exactly the same product as you do.

>> **'Sometimes' competitors** provide a slightly different service or product, or are in a different location.

>> **Left-field competitors** don't normally compete with you but, if circumstances were to change, could possibly do so.

WARNING

When you're thinking about the competition for your proposed business, don't be too literal — think about where both your business and its industry are headed. For example, a watchmaker repairing and selling watches 30 years ago would have probably thought that the main competition was other watchmakers. The idea that the mobile phone could almost completely annihilate this industry would seem a long shot.

Also, don't be hesitant to compare your business against big-time competitors such as supermarket chains or large franchises. While you may find it hard to imagine how your fledgling business could ever compete, the mass-market nature of these competitors often leaves niches that are underserviced, providing opportunities for smaller players.

Understanding why you need to do this

Here are five reasons I recommend you spend time analysing your competitors:

>> **You can get fresh inspiration:** Your competition can be a source of inspiration, showing you where to gain a possible edge. Pricing specials, weekend packages, discount offers, creative advertising and clever sales techniques are just some of the things you may decide to copy. After all, imitation is the greatest form of flattery (although your competitors may not see it that way!).

>> **You can avoid terrible mistakes:** Competitor analysis may provide the reality check that prevents you from taking unnecessary risks and losing your savings. For example, in my local town a whole strip of cafes come and go with every change in season. If I were thinking about starting a cafe, a competitor analysis may quickly reveal that the rents in this strip are hideously high, the landlords are difficult, and nobody is making enough profits to survive, let alone thrive.

>> **You can capitalise on others' weaknesses:** Interacting with competitors can also point to potential opportunities. For many people, the seed of a winning business idea is sown by not being able to receive good enough service or quite the right product. So they think, *I can do better than that*, and a new business idea or marketing strategy is born.

>> **You can set your prices just right:** If you're going to compete head-on with another business, you want to be right across the services that business

provides, and the prices it charges. Unless a massive undersupply exists, charging $20 more per hour is probably pointless if you're providing an identical service to a close competitor.

>> **You can identify your point of difference:** Unless you know exactly what your competitors provide, you won't know how to sell your differences.

Grouping competitors

One of the purposes of identifying competitors is so you can develop a competitive strategy to deal with each one. However, when you create a list of head-to-head competitors, this can sometimes be a long list. For example, if you're starting up a business as an electrician, you may find 50 other electricians are working in your local area. You don't want to have to come up with 50 different competitive strategies, so your best tactic is to try to group these competitors in some way.

Try this process:

1. **List your competitors in a small number of groups based on similarities.**

   For example, the electrician may split their list of 50 other electricians according to size of the business, focus of the business (maybe some focus more on repairs, others on hot water, others on new buildings), or by locality or suburb.

2. **Think about how you've organised these groups. Will a customer looking for your kind of business use these same criteria?**

   For example, if a customer is searching online for an electrician, are they going to search by suburb, by specialty, or by services provided (such as 24-hour call outs)?

3. **Have a think about where you belong in the scheme of things.**

   For example, the electrician may decide they want to focus on solar systems but within a 50-kilometre radius only.

4. **Think to the future. Do you want to be in this same group in five years' time?**

   For example, maybe the electrician has a vision to offer not just solar installations, but home-energy consultations also.

TIP

By organising your competitors into groups, you can build a clearer idea about how to develop different competitive strategies, depending on what kind of competitor you're dealing with.

Profiling your competitors

When investigating your competitors, don't limit yourself to visiting your competitor's website but, instead, try to dig a little deeper. The time has come for you to don your dark sunglasses, felt hat and fake moustache. Talk to your competitors' suppliers or distributors, or quiz customers who have defected to your side of the fence. You may even have to go undercover and pose as a customer (or ask a family member to do so) — I know that such clandestine activity can feel a bit weird, but the results are usually worth it.

Table 2-2 shows a detailed competitive analysis where the owner of a copywriting business does a comparison with three other copywriting businesses also offering services online, rating competitors according to what they do better (or worse).

TABLE 2-2   **Rating Head-to-Head Competitors**

Does this competitor . . .	ABC	CopytoGo	WriteNow
Have cheaper pricing than me?	Yes	No	No
Offer a faster turnaround time?	No	No	Yes
Offer specific services that I don't?	No	Yes	No
Offer onsite services, not just online?	No	No	No
Offer a larger variety of pricing packages?	No	No	Yes
Have more expertise/a higher level of skill?	No	No	No
Service different niches?	No	No	No
Have more testimonials than me?	Yes	No	No
Have a more active social media presence?	No	No	Yes
Have a stronger online marketing strategy?	No	No	Yes
Have more capital and power to expand?	No	No	Yes

Thinking about future competitors

In Chapter 5, I talk about your vision for the future, and how important it is to keep your eyes open to trends in the economy, the environment and in your industry. This macro way of thinking is also useful at the early planning stages of your business, particularly if you spend a while thinking not just who your competitors are right now, but also who your competitors could be in one, two or five years' time.

Ask yourself questions relating to the following areas:

>> **Automation potential:** Could any existing competitors automate their processes using advanced technology and, therefore, become more of a threat than they already are?

>> **Big players coming to town:** Could a franchise chain or large company move into your village, suburb or town and take lots of your customers? (In my village, the longstanding boutique wine store struggled when two big liquor chains moved within 3 kilometres.)

>> **Buyout of minor competitors by a larger competitor with more capital and muscle:** Could one of your existing competitors be bought out by someone with more capital and better distribution and, in the process, become a very formidable competitor? (Think about how some smaller gourmet food brands have been purchased by supermarket chains and suddenly appear in every store.)

>> **Changes in technology:** Could changes in technology mean your product or service becomes obsolete? (Think of the long-lost corner video store, the appliance repair technician or the 24-hour photo lab.)

>> **Cheaper imports:** Could the goods you provide be substituted by imported goods if the exchange rate changes?

>> **Customers doing it themselves:** Could your main customer or customers decide creating your product or providing your service in-house makes more sense? (Think of the big supermarket chains that now manufacture their own generic food lines.)

>> **Life cycle of business idea:** Is the life cycle of your business reaching maturity or beyond, meaning numerous competitors and fewer profits to go around? (Think of the mobile coffee vans that were once a clever niche business but are now a dime a dozen.)

>> **Offshoring of labour:** Could the services you provide be performed offshore instead? (Almost anything that's mostly labour and can be done on a computer is vulnerable to offshoring.)

>> **Service offered online:** Could the service you provide be sold online and, therefore, open to international competition? (Even some things that I would never have imagined could go online have done so. I don't go to my local yoga class any more, but instead log onto a yoga website that offers hundreds of pre-recorded classes to fit any duration, level or style of yoga.)

AHEAD OF
THE PACK

WHY YOU CAN SOMETIMES BEAT THE BIG GUYS

When you're checking out competitors, you may come across lots of factors that make it tough for you to compete with the big guys in town, such as high capital costs, expensive IT systems or huge distribution networks. These factors are called *entry barriers*.

The flipside of entry barriers can be *exit barriers*. Sometimes competitors have invested so much in expensive rentals or specialised equipment, or sometimes competitors can be so management top-heavy, that they can't get easily out of the less profitable parts of their business, and also can't act quickly when opportunities arise.

For smaller businesses, these exit barriers sometimes point to opportunities. Maybe you can distribute product much more cheaply using the internet, while the competition is wedded to expensive retail rentals. Similarly, maybe you can act quickly in response to new fads or fashions, creating and promoting products in a fraction of the time a big company takes to do the same thing.

Choosing Your Competitive Strategy

Any business, including yours, is faced with these three possible competitive strategies.

Pick one, and only one, competitive strategy

Don't try to be all things to all people. Pick one of these strategies, and only one, and run with it:

>> **Be the cheapest.** With a *cost leadership strategy*, you're not necessarily the cheapest across all products you offer, or the cheapest for every service but, in general, you're aiming to compete on price. Price leadership can be a tempting strategy — after all, customers are always looking for a bargain — but is risky over the long term. Unless you have a strategic advantage that enables you to deliver your product or service more cheaply than your competitors, competing on price can mean weak profitability. (On the other hand, if you're just getting started, choosing to be cheapest may be a good strategy for gaining clients and building up experience.)

>> **Create a point of difference.** With a *differentiation strategy*, you set out to differentiate yourself in some way other than price. For example, an electrician could seek to make response time and punctuality a point of difference ('We'll arrive within 30 minutes of the agreed time or the first hour is free'), or could make availability a point of difference ('24-hour call-out service, 7 days a week'.)

REMEMBER

Ideally, if you choose differentiation as your competitive strategy, you want to find a synergy between this differentiation and the strategic advantage you identified earlier in this chapter. For example, maybe a strategic advantage for this electrician is that his partner also has a trade license. Between them, they can offer a 24-hour service without worrying about leaving the kids unattended at home, and they don't have to pay the penalty rates that other businesses would normally have to pay if sending an employee out on a job in the middle of the night on a Sunday.

>> **Find a particular focus or niche:** With a *niche strategy*, your aim is to serve a specific market segment rather than deal with the whole market. In *We Are All Weird*, written by Seth Godin and published by Brilliance Corporation, Godin argues that people are seeking choices more than ever, and that this competitive strategy is an increasingly smart pathway for business.

REMEMBER

Always try to pursue a clear strategy. If you choose to muddle along not doing anything that's clearly different from others, you will find it difficult to both compete and establish a clear strategic advantage in the market.

DON'T BE AFRAID TO PIKE OUT

I sometimes find that when people do an honest appraisal of their business idea and the competition, the resulting business proposal is found to be quite weak. Sometimes this is because the person starting up in business has limited skills or minimal capital; other times, the demand for their proposed product or service may not be strong enough. Other times again, it can be too hard competing against established players.

If you're starting to question the strength of your business idea, don't be afraid to pike out. Stopping at this stage might save thousands of dollars, not to mention months or even years of your time.

If you're unsure whether your business idea is as strong as it could be and whether you should continue, what becomes relevant is measuring up the risks. If starting (or continuing with) this business means little capital outlay and a few lost weekends and holidays, you don't have much to lose. On the other hand, if this business involves your entire retirement savings and/or the threat of a failed relationship if things go wrong, the risk may well be unjustifiable.

Connecting your competitive strategy to your strategic advantage

You may be feeling a little muddled as to how the concepts of strategic advantage, competitor analysis and competitive strategy interrelate.

But interrelate they do, with each concept triggering off one another. As shown in Figure 2-1, the process of identifying your strategic advantage, comparing your-self against competitors and choosing a competitive strategy is a continuous cycle of honing your business idea.

The trick for you is to pick a competitive strategy (focusing on cost, differentiation or a particular niche) that complements both your strategic advantage and any opportunities you've identified in the competitive landscape.

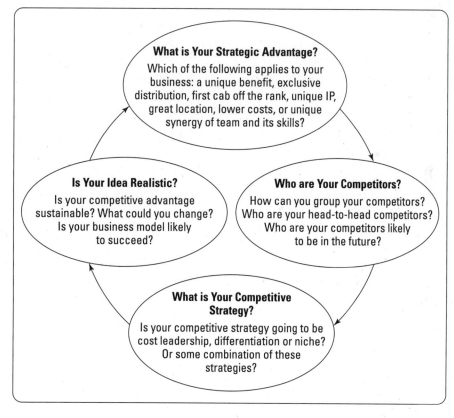

FIGURE 2-1:
Using your strategic advantage, competitor analysis and competitive strategy to continually improve your business idea.

What is Your Strategic Advantage?
Which of the following applies to your business: a unique benefit, exclusive distribution, first cab off the rank, unique IP, great location, lower costs, or unique synergy of team and its skills?

Is Your Idea Realistic?
Is your competitive advantage sustainable? What could you change? Is your business model likely to succeed?

Who are Your Competitors?
How can you group your competitors? Who are your head-to-head competitors? Who are your competitors likely to be in the future?

What is Your Competitive Strategy?
Is your competitive strategy going to be cost leadership, differentiation or niche? Or some combination of these strategies?

REMEMBER

Understanding what your business can do better or differently (including defining your strategic advantage, analysing your competitors and selecting a competitive strategy) is key to business success.

SO WHAT'S SO SPECIAL ABOUT YOU?

Are you ready to take the challenge? Imagine you're stuck in an elevator and someone has just asked you what your business is all about. You reckon you have about 30 seconds to convey what your business concept is, what you do, and what makes you so damned special.

Click the Record button on your computer or smartphone, have a quick look at the clock, and record your reply in 30 seconds or less. Tick, tick, tick . . . stop. How did you go? Listen back and rate yourself out of 10.

Did you remember to include your name, your business name, what you do that helps others, and what makes your business different from others?

This 30-second 'elevator pitch' is surprisingly demanding. In this first stage of getting your business off the ground, keep in mind that practice makes perfect. Say your speech aloud when you get in the shower, turn the ignition of your car, or make yourself a cup of tea. Your family may think you're a little bit potty, but that's a small price to pay.

IN THIS CHAPTER

» Buying your own business — the good, the bad and the ugly

» Doing your research and asking the right questions

» Determining how much a business is worth

» Working through a business purchase checklist

» Understanding the pros and cons of joining a franchise

» Doing your homework before signing the dotted line

Chapter **3**

Starting from Scratch, Buying a Business, or Joining a Franchise

I am often torn when people ask me whether I recommend they buy a business or start one from scratch — or perhaps consider a franchise.

One of the trickiest questions, if considering whether to buy a business, is figuring out how much a business is worth. Occasionally, business owners are prepared to sell their business for a song, especially if they're seeking a quick sale. More often, owners overvalue their businesses, and the unwary buyer can end up paying far too much.

Another challenge is weighing up the risks involved. On the one hand, buying a business involves a greater financial risk in the short term because you have to pay for goodwill. On the other hand, the long-term risk is probably less, because (hopefully!) you're buying a business with a winning formula and long-term security.

One of the alternatives to buying an established business is to join a franchise. When you join a franchise, you're not just buying a business; rather, you're becoming part of a proven system that works. Along with this system, you're also buying a recognised brand name and established reputation. This option is generally the most expensive up-front, but arguably carries the lowest risks.

In this chapter, I provide a summary of the pros and cons of buying a business versus starting from scratch versus joining a franchise. I also help you figure out how much to pay for a business, and provide checklists of the questions you should ask before buying a business or a franchise.

Weighing Up the Good and the Bad of Buying a Business

Just like marriage, having children and getting old, buying a business (as opposed to starting a business from scratch) has its advantages and disadvantages. However, by going into negotiations with your eyes open, you can often minimise the disadvantages and seal a winning deal.

WARNING

Don't get tempted to buy a business just because something is selling for a bargain price. Instead, match your own needs, skills and experience against what's on offer.

Buying an existing business — the upside

So, what's the lowdown on buying a business that's already up and running? The best things are

MONEY STUFF

>> **You can look at the financial records for this business and know roughly what to expect:** Although the financial records of the past are never a cast-iron prediction for the future, they're usually a good indication.

>> **Existing businesses come with established customer and supplier relationships:** Customers are the gold nuggets of any business and so, by buying an existing business, you get your very own pot of gold. Existing

supplier relationships are also a valuable resource that allow you to conduct your business in the most efficient and reliable way.

>> **You're (hopefully) buying something that works:** If the business you're thinking of buying is profitable, chances are the owners have arrived at a formula that works. This formula probably has several ingredients such as good staff, solid management, established premises and (if relevant to the business) stock lines that sell.

>> **You can make money from day one:** If you want instant sales and instant profit, buying a business — as opposed to starting a business from scratch — is the way to go.

>> **You can sometimes score a bargain:** It's true! If a businessperson has had enough of running the business and wants to sell up, occasionally the asking price is very reasonable. You may find a business owner so desperate to get out that they ask for nothing for goodwill and, instead, ask only for the value of the business assets.

Buying an existing business — the downside

So, what are the possible pitfalls of buying an existing business? Consider the following:

>> **You have to pay for goodwill:** Not only does paying for goodwill chew up precious capital but many business owners also overestimate the worth of their business, meaning that you risk paying too much. (Don't worry, I talk about business valuation methods in the section 'Valuing an Existing Business', later in this chapter.)

>> **Goodwill may be linked more to the owner than you realise:** A hairdressing salon is a good example. Sure, the salon may have solid sales and great goodwill, but are customers going to leave in droves because they're attached to the previous owner's way of styling their hair?

>> **Unwanted baggage:** Some businesses come complete with an inherited set of problems such as a particularly difficult staff member or a poor reputation for customer service. Turning around difficult behaviours or a poor culture of customer service can be very challenging.

>> **Your 'dream' can be compromised:** If you inherit someone else's way of running a business, things are going to be a little different from if you start from scratch.

WHY DO THEY WANT OUT?

If this business is so good, why is it for sale? Maybe a legit reason exists such as owner illness, the owner retiring or a marriage break-up.

On the other hand, maybe the reason is more sinister such as a major shopping plaza about to open up next door, a highway about to carve through the town or a lease that isn't likely to be renewed. Maybe the business has never been that successful in the first place.

Ask the owners why they're selling and what they plan to do next. Don't be shy to ask around — does anyone else know the owner? Check out whether any similar businesses in the area are for sale (maybe that proposed highway is going to flatten them all).

Sometimes it takes a wee bit of digging to get to the bottom of why someone is *really* selling, but until you're truly sure of the reason, I recommend you hold back from making an offer to purchase.

Asking the Right Questions

When it comes to buying a business, the law isn't forgiving of idiots. The law expects that if you buy a business, you've done your research and made an informed decision. You're not entitled to a refund simply because you didn't do your homework.

The scope of this book doesn't allow me to tell you everything you need to know before signing a contract to buy a business — that job belongs to your accountant and solicitor. However, I can provide you with a few pointers about what to expect and what to look out for. Read on — with care . . .

Finding out who owns the intellectual property

When you buy a business you're buying not only things such as stock, tools, and fixtures and fittings, but also the *intellectual property*, such as custom computer software, copyright registrations, distribution agreements, domain names, information databases (including customer lists), licences, patents, secret formulas and trademarks.

Check the ownership of any intellectual property that you're buying. For example, when buying a business and its associated domain name (in other words, the name of its website), make sure ownership of the domain name is transferred across to you. With trademarks, make sure a third party doesn't have an interest in the asset or that a loan isn't held over the trademark. Or on the flipside, if trademarks don't exist, ensure that no impediments will emerge for you registering protection for these assets.

Analysing sales trends, profit and break-even

Spend some time considering how robust the business model is. For example, what's the break-even point for sales? If sales drop by 10 per cent (which is quite possible during ownership change), is the business still sustainable?

The second thing to consider is how the gross profit of this business compares with industry trends. If the gross profit margin is higher than average for the industry, this business may be more vulnerable to competition.

Clarifying what the purchase price includes

When you're looking at buying a business, the term *goodwill* is one you'll hear frequently. Specifically, goodwill represents the difference between the purchase price and the combined value of all of the physical assets of the business. The elements that make up goodwill consist of aspects such as the reputation of the business, its loyal customers, its brand identity, its systems, and possibly its staff or any proprietary technology.

The purchase price of a business includes not just goodwill, but also assets such as equipment, furniture, inventory and, in some cases, debtors. In other words, the purchase price of a cafe includes not just the goodwill but the tables, chairs and crockery also, or the purchase of an accounting practice includes not just goodwill but also computers, software, desks and debtors.

When looking at a business that's for sale, ask the seller to break down the purchase price into the individual components and, as soon as this breakdown is in place, home in on the details:

TIP

>> Are you paying for any assets you don't need? If an item is unnecessary or obsolete, don't cough up a cent for it. (Ask for a copy of the depreciation schedule: The written-down value shown on this schedule usually provides a chillingly realistic second opinion on item values.)

>> Does the purchase price include debtors? If so, clarify what will occur if a customer is slow to pay, or does not pay at all.

>> Find out if any of the assets are currently under lease, and consider whether or not you will want to take over these leases.

With this process complete, turn your attention to stock (if that's relevant for this business). Don't agree to pay for *stock at valuation* (otherwise known as *SAV*), without first nutting out how this valuation is going to be made:

WARNING

>> In the contract, place a ceiling value on stock so that you don't end up paying for a whole load of unwanted deliveries.

>> State in the contract that the stock has to be good, usable, current stock. If a stock item is unlikely to sell within six months, based on current sales trends, refuse to pay for it. The last thing you want is a warehouse full of obsolete stock.

>> If a disagreement about the value of stock is a possibility, employ a registered valuer.

>> Agree on a valuation method for stock. This could be the last price paid or the average price paid, and may or may not include the cost of freight.

TIP

>> Ask for supplier invoices to verify the wholesale cost of stock and the date the stock was supplied. (Any stock bought more than a year ago is likely to be obsolete or overpriced.)

TECHNICAL STUFF

GST ON THE PURCHASE PRICE

The sale price of a business doesn't attract GST if the following conditions are met:

- Both you and the seller are registered for GST

- The business is actually for sale and money is changing hands

- The seller carries on the business, right up until the day of sale

- Everything that you need for the continued operation of the business is supplied

- Both parties agree in writing that the business is a going concern

As the buyer, if you're registered for GST, whether GST is charged or not doesn't matter because you can claim the GST back. However, if you're not registered, the seller usually *adds* the value of GST to the purchase price, and you can't claim this GST back. (Most purchase agreements specify that the price is 'plus GST if any'.)

The conclusion? Unless your accountant advises otherwise, register for GST before the sale of the business takes place.

Calculating the 'True' Earnings of a Business

When you buy or sell a business, sooner or later you'll hear the term *EBITDA*, short for Earnings Before Interest and Tax, Depreciation and Amortisation. (People sometimes talk about *EBIT* instead, a simpler version that means Earnings Before Interest and Tax.)

You may even hear people say things like: 'Did you hear that Sam got five times EBITDA when he sold his business?' What they mean is that when Sam sold his business, he received five times his average annual profit, after adjusting this profit for amortisation, depreciation, interest and tax.

Although calculating EBITDA or EBIT is kind of technical, you don't need a degree in commerce. Here's how the whole deal runs:

1. **Ask the owners for copies of Profit & Loss statements for the last three to five years.**

   Five years is ideal, three years is often all you get. Make sure these Profit & Loss statements are final statements certified by an accountant, and not print-outs generated by the owners themselves.

2. **Go through each Profit & Loss report and summarise key totals, finishing with the final net profit (or even loss) before income tax.**

   I recommend you use a spreadsheet, as I do in Figure 3-1. I like to include sales, cost of sales, gross profit and key expenses. If you're working with company financials, remember to write down the net profit *before* income tax, not after income tax.

REMEMBER

3. **Add any amortisation, depreciation or interest back into the profit.**

   The amount of interest paid depends on how much equity the owner has in the business. You're best to ignore interest when calculating average net profit, so add any interest expense back onto the bottom line to increase the profit.

   Amortisation is a bit of an obscure one, and refers to writing off goodwill or borrowing expenses. If you can't see this item on the Profit & Loss report, don't worry — it probably doesn't exist.

4. **Add back any expenses that seem downright excessive.**

   You know, things such as the single owner-operator who puts three cars through his business (one for him, one for his partner and one for the teenage child) or puts all the expenses for the latest, most expensive four-wheel drive through the business. Other likely culprits include voluntary superannuation contributions, overseas holidays or unrealistically high wages paid to relatives.

Refer to Figure 3-1 for how this whole deal works.

5. **If the business is a sole trader or partnership, deduct a reasonable amount for the time the owners spent working in the business.**

If the business is a sole trader or partnership, the Profit & Loss doesn't include wages for the owners. Find out how many hours the owners work in the business, multiply these hours by a reasonable hourly rate (either for you or for employees), and then deduct the total from the profit.

TRUE STORY

One of my clients wanted to purchase a milk bar. The figures looked good, with hefty profit year after year. Then my client figured that the owner, her husband and her son all worked in the milk bar — up to 150 hours a week combined. My client was single and didn't want to work any more than 50 hours a week. This difference meant she had to factor in 100 hours additional employee labour every week. After she made this adjustment, the calculations for the goodwill of the milk bar came up as worthless.

6. **If the business is a company, look at the wages paid to the directors and, if necessary, adjust the profit for what you think are reasonable wages for the time spent.**

If you think the directors' wages were too high, add the amount of the excess to your profit figure. If you think the directors' wages were too low, deduct the shortfall from your profit figure.

7. **Deduct any additional expenses that you know you're likely to have.**

One of the things that often happens when a business is for sale is that everything is a bit run-down and hasn't been properly maintained. In the example in Figure 3-1, I add an extra $4,000 a year for the amount I think *should* have been paid to keep everything in reasonable condition.

8. **Adjust the profit for any irregular or unusual income and expense items.**

Trawl through the financials. You're looking for irregular income such as large insurance claims or capital gains, and you're also searching for unusual expense items such as moving expenses, compensation claims or capital losses.

9. **Calculate the average profit for the period you're analysing.**

You know the deal. If you have three years' worth of figures, add the final profit for each year together, and divide this total by three.

10. **Note down the final value: You've now calculated the average Adjusted EBITDA.**

Now that you've calculated EBITDA, you're ready to make an estimate of what the business is actually worth. Read on to find out more . . .

Figures from Owner's Financials:	2021	2020	2019
Sales	332,000	301,020	270,000
Less: Purchases	57,000	65,180	48,500
Gross Profit	275,000	235,840	221,500
Amortisation	2,500	2,500	2,000
Depreciation	11,200	15,000	22,000
Interest Expenses	3,500	3,800	4,500
Motor Vehicle Expenses	12,500	11,000	9,000
All Other Expenses	165,200	150,200	145,000
Total Expenses	194,900	182,500	182,500
Net Income Before Taxes	**80,100**	**53,340**	**39,000**
Calculation of EBITDA:			
Net Income Before Taxes	80,100	53,340	39,000
Add: Amortisation	2,500	2,500	2,000
Add: Depreciation	11,200	15,000	22,000
Add: Interest	3,500	3,800	4,500
EBITDA	**97,300**	**74,640**	**67,500**
Add back expenses that you would not incur:			
Voluntary super over 9.5% minimum	4,000	3,900	3,500
Donations	800	700	700
Motor Vehicle (excess)	8,000	7,000	7,000
Total addbacks	**12,800**	**11,600**	**11,200**
Deduct additional expenses::			
Reasonable wages for owner hours contributed	45,000	44,000	43,000
Necessary equipment upgrades	4,000	4,000	4,000
	49,000	48,000	47,000
Adjusted EBITDA	**61,100**	**38,240**	**31,700**
Total EBITDA for last three years	**131,040**		
Average EBITDA for last three years	**43,680**		

FIGURE 3-1: Calculating average profit (also known as EBIT).

Valuing an Existing Business

So, how much *is* a business worth? At the end of the day, a business is only worth what a buyer pays for it. Until this value is known, figuring out the real worth of a business is an odd mix of accounting, gut-feeling and the weighing up of probabilities, with a hotchpotch of possible valuation methods all offering different takes on the subject. Experienced valuers often prefer to value a business using a couple of different methods, arriving at an average of the results as their final opinion.

WARNING

Businesses are a bit like children. Sellers (like any parent) can run a little short on objectivity. For this reason, do your own sums and arrive at your own opinion about how much a business is worth. However, do note that interpreting financial statements is complex, and you must always seek expert advice from your accountant before making any kind of offer to purchase a business.

The times earnings method

When you know what the Adjusted EBITDA of a potential business is (refer to the previous section to refresh your memory on how to calculate EBITDA), you're ready to calculate how much moolah this business opportunity is really worth.

The *times earnings method* is based on the idea that you multiply the Adjusted EBITDA by a *times earnings multiplier* to arrive at an overall valuation of goodwill. (If a business has debtors, equipment, furnishings or inventory, you add the agreed value of these assets to this goodwill figure.) Typical multipliers can range from two to six times Adjusted EBITDA. For example, if a business had an Adjusted EBITDA of $100,000 and your accountant recommends a multiplier of four, the total value of goodwill for the business would be $400,000. So, the price for the business would be $400,000, plus the value attributed to debtors, equipment, furnishings or inventory.

TIP

Although I can't advise you as to what multiplier is typical to your industry, here are some rough-and-ready guidelines for EBIT multipliers:

>> Listed companies typically sell for a higher multiplier than private companies, and can even sell for up to ten times EBIT.

>> If a business is suffering downwards sales trends, selling in a rush or operating without a secure lease, it may sell for as low as one or two times EBIT.

>> An asking price anywhere between two and six times EBIT is reasonable for a private business.

>> A service business that relies heavily on an owner's specialist skills may receive a lower EBIT, due to the fact that the owner's skills are hard to replicate.

>> If the profitability of a business is growing, and the owner can prove sustained growth trends, the owner may well ask for a higher EBIT.

TIP

If your accountant lacks experience in valuing businesses, I suggest you seek the services of a business valuation expert.

The capitalised earnings method

This approach to valuing a business provides another way to skin the same cat, and is called the *capitalised earnings* method. This method is more commonly used by the buyer rather than the seller, because the final valuation is so reliant on the rate of return that the buyer requires.

Here's how it goes:

1. Work out the EBITDA.

Sounds like I'm rapping. But no, I'm actually talking about Earnings Before Interest and Tax, Depreciation and Amortisation. I explain this calculation in the section 'Calculating the 'True' Earnings of a Business', earlier in this chapter.

MONEY STUFF

2. Decide what you want as your rate of return.

This figure is usually how much you'd get from the current bank deposit rate plus an allowance for the risk you're taking. For example, if the deposit rate is 2 per cent, you may want to add another 8 per cent for the risk you're taking, and so decide to aim for 10 per cent as your rate of return. (My example here reflects the rates at time of writing, which are historically low. Of course, deposit rates may have changed by the time you're reading this.)

3. Divide the EBITDA by your desired rate of return.

The result of this calculation is called *capitalised earnings*. For example, if the average EBITDA of a business is $50,000 and you want a return of 10 per cent, capitalised earnings would be $500,000. Or, if you want a return of 15 per cent because your perceived risk is higher, capitalised earnings would be $333,333. This capitalised earnings figure represents how much the business is worth in your eyes, given the rate of return that you're seeking. As the examples show, the business valuation goes down as the risk (and so required rate of return) goes up.

REMEMBER

I mention wages earlier in this chapter, but don't forget to adjust the EBITDA to allow for the time owners spend working on the business. This adjustment is particularly important when looking to buy a sole trader or partnership business, because the financials will not include wages paid to owners. For example, a business may look great on paper, showing average profits of $100,000 per year, but if this business is run by a couple who each work 60 hours per week, these profits are not really profits at all.

The strategic advantage method

Sometimes a business sells for way more than it would be worth if it were valued by traditional methods, because it possesses some kind of *strategic advantage* that the buyer can leverage to great success. For example, a major player in a particular market may be happy to pay big bucks for one of the smaller fish in the pond because they want to get their hands on a particular advantage such as a unique business model, a great domain name or a smart bit of software.

Dotting Your I's, Crossing Your T's

Here's a summary checklist to work through when you're thinking of buying a business. Of course, I'm assuming that you already have a lawyer on the case (if you don't, get one now!), and your accountant has checked the financials.

MONEY STUFF

>> *A is for accountant:* Involve your accountant from early on. Ask your accountant to help you put a value on the goodwill and to look through financial statements with a fine-toothed comb.

>> *B is for Balance Sheet:* Pay particular attention to the book value of assets and liabilities.

>> *C is for creditors:* Make sure the contract includes a statement that any money owed to creditors is the previous owner's responsibility, not yours. If the business receives deposits from customers in advance, remember to include details about who owns the liability of security deposits in the contract.

>> *D is for debtors:* Clarify whether any money owed to the business from customers is owed to you, or to the previous owner. If the money is owed to you, detail the total value in the contract, and make an allowance for bad debts. In addition, ask for an *aged debtors listing* (that is, a listing of outstanding customer debts, grouped according to how old each debt is). The longer an invoice has been outstanding, the less willing you should be to take it on.

>> *E is for employees:* Determine whether existing staff are going to stick around (ideally, you want to have flexibility over the decision whether they do or don't). You also need a list of all employees, including relevant awards, hours worked and hourly rates, holiday, personal leave and long service leave due, and superannuation, and ensure the purchase price is adjusted downwards for all employee leave liabilities. Find out when these employees last had a pay rise, and whether another pay increase is likely.

>> *F* **is for family:** Beware the family business where the extended family all pitches in, sometimes for minimal pay. When deciding how much you're prepared to pay for a business, adjust the value to incorporate enough wages to cover all of these hours.

>> *G* **is for guarantee:** Try to include a clause saying that the contract can be revoked if any of the information included in the contract, or supplied with the contract, isn't right. Some contracts even require 10 per cent of the sale price to be held in trust for a period of six months or so, and only released if all conditions are met.

>> *H* **is for help!** Consider whether you want the seller to work alongside you for an initial period so you can learn how everything works. If you do, detail for how long and under what conditions.

>> *I* **is for inventory:** Agree on the method of valuing stock and clarify what stock items you're willing to pay for (refer to the section 'Clarifying what the purchase price includes', earlier in this chapter, for details).

>> *J* **is for job description:** Do existing employees already have job descriptions? If so, ask for copies.

>> *K* **is for knowledge:** The knowledge held within a business often represents a significant intangible asset. Ensure the previous owner provides you with written procedures for core business activities. If these procedures don't exist, negotiate to have them written.

REMEMBER

>> *L* **is for legals and leases:** Chances are buying a business is one of the most significant financial decisions you're ever likely to make, and quality legal advice forms a vital part of your protection. Oh yes, *L* is also for leases: Identify any current leases for fixed assets or for rental premises, and when these leases expire. For retail businesses, ask yourself if the lease weren't renewed, would you still have a viable business?

>> *M* **is for maintenance:** Is the equipment well-maintained or has it been run down?

>> *N* **is for names:** Make sure the business name (as well as any associated domain names, patents, permits, registrations or trademarks) is signed over to you.

>> *O* **is for ownership:** Make sure that nobody other than the owner has legal rights to the assets. This ownership status is particularly important in regard to any intellectual property or leased items.

TIP

>> *P* **is for profitability:** Make sure you obtain Profit & Loss statements for a minimum of the last three years, certified by a public accountant. Examine all expenses and ask whether they're reasonable. Do you think expenses are going to increase or decrease under your reign?

- **Q is for QuickBooks:** Or MYOB or Xero for that matter. If the owner already subscribes to accounting software, ask if they can export all of the lists (the accounts list, the customer list, the supplier list and the employee list) into an Excel spreadsheet. You can then import this information into your own accounting software, thereby saving hours, days or even weeks of typing.

- **R is for restrictions:** Consider whether you want to add a restriction clause preventing the seller from starting up a similar business in the area and for what period the restriction applies.

- **S is for sales:** How many customers made up the bulk of previous sales? If a substantial proportion of sales come from only one or two customers, can you be sure these customers are going to remain loyal to you? Examine trends both for total sales and for profitability. Scrutinise sales figures on a month-to-month basis and make sure you understand the reason behind any inconsistencies, seasonal variations or trends. Downward trends are almost always of significant concern.

- **T is for technology:** Is the business likely to continue its success? Be aware of the impact that technology may have on this enterprise. For example, an appliance repairs business may experience dwindling demand as decreasing costs mean that replacing appliances, rather than repairing them, becomes the trend.

- **U is for utilities:** Organise to get electricity, gas and water transferred to your name, and clarify what happens with these bills at handover time.

- **V is for vendor:** Make sure you know who you're dealing with. Conduct a name search on the vendor. (I recommend you check them out both on Google and Facebook, and ask your solicitor to conduct a full credit check also.)

- **W is for workers compensation:** Are any workers comp claims outstanding? What is the safety record for this business?

- **X is for X-ray vision:** Something you're going to wish your solicitor has.

- **Y is for why:** Yes, I know I'm pushing the envelope here as far as the alphabet is concerned. Never mind. Why is the business *really* for sale?

- **Z is for Zebra, Zebedee and Zulu:** Yeah, right.

See Chapter 7 for more about signing contracts and legal decisions.

Buying a Franchise

Even if you're not entirely sure what franchising is all about, chances are that *you*, as a consumer, do business with a franchise most days of the week. International franchises include names such as The Body Shop, Century 21 and Pizza Hut. Aussie upstarts include Bakers Delight, Boost Juice, Poolwerx and VIP Home Services.

The idea is that an established business (the *franchisor*) licenses its business name and its operating systems to another person (the *franchisee*). In return for an upfront fee and an ongoing royalty, the franchisor agrees to provide the franchisee with the product or the service, as well as the business concept itself. This concept includes marketing strategy, operational standards, software systems, training and guidance.

A win–win relationship lies at the heart of franchising. Franchisors win because they can grow their business much faster because you (the franchisee) provide capital and ongoing revenue. And you, the franchisee, win because you gain a business with a proven formula and a substantially reduced risk.

Before you get stuck into checking out individual franchises, I suggest you take a step back and consider what's good about franchising, and what isn't.

Considering the positives

I like to start with the good things in life. You know, the red wine *before* the cooking begins, and the wild adventures overseas *before* settling in to a sensible university degree. And so, before considering the downside, here are a few reasons that explain why franchising is so popular:

>> **You benefit from an established brand name and reputation:** Assuming that the franchise has a well-established brand with a good reputation, your business is likely to have an intrinsic goodwill before you even open your doors for trading. Customers are going to recognise your business name and associate it with a consistent level of quality products or services.

>> **You're working with a proven formula:** Working within a franchise model is like making a chocolate cake with a tried-and-trusted recipe — as opposed to concocting a creation from whatever's sitting in the back of the cupboard. A company that already has successful franchisees has done the hard yards, proving the demand for its products or services and figuring out a system that works.

>> **You're off to a flying start:** The decisions you make in the first few months of business are often the most crucial. As a franchisee, you receive expert

guidance regarding trading location, shop layout, stock levels, product mix, software systems, signage and much more.

>> **Your risk is reduced:** One key benefit of a franchise is that you don't waste your precious capital repeating someone else's mistakes. Hopefully, the franchisor has ironed out the bugs and found solutions to the most common problems.

>> **You get training to fill the gaps in your knowledge:** A good franchisor is keen for you to succeed. Your initial training can help you to identify your weak points, shore up your knowledge and start your business in a much stronger position. However, if you're really green to business, don't expect that belonging to a franchise is going to completely compensate for a lack of experience.

>> **You're part of a group:** When you're part of a franchise, you get to share ideas and knowledge within your group and, hopefully, you have the positive experience of being part of a dynamic team.

MONEY STUFF

>> **You can increase profitability through economies of scale such as coordinated group advertising and bulk purchasing power:** For example, if you have a Bakers Delight franchise, chances are the head office buys flour at the best possible price and quality, with its high-volume purchases providing leverage when negotiating with suppliers.

>> **You can compare your performance with others in the same franchise in key areas such as wastage, margins and average spend:** This 'benchmarking' helps you identify areas where you can improve.

Weighing up the negatives

You're smart to weigh up the negatives of franchising before you consider signing on that dotted line. Franchising may not be your cup of tea for any of the following reasons:

>> **You're paying for goodwill, rather than exploiting your own creative genius:** The significance of this downside depends on how much of a creative genius you really are.

>> **You may be committing to something you hate:** Like a blind date, you have no time for a slow build-up. What if you bought a shoe franchise and developed a pathological aversion to the smell of feet? Or you bought a lawn-care franchise and discovered your inner loathing of lawnmowers?

>> **You have to abide by other people's rules and decisions:** Even if the franchisor's decisions seem ludicrous, you have to stick by them. You may have to pay for advertising campaigns that seem like total duds, wear a

uniform in a colour scheme you despise or sell a new product that you don't believe in.

>> **You have less control over your long-term future:** No matter how well you run your business, you run the risk that other franchisees may not be so conscientious, acting in ways that damage the reputation of the brand. For example, if one cafe in a franchise chain has poor hygiene standards, disappointed customers are unlikely to patronise other cafes in the same chain when they're travelling around.

>> **You're committed to ongoing costs:** Almost all franchisees pay ongoing royalties in addition to the upfront fees. If these royalties are set too high, you can be left with only marginal profitability.

REMEMBER

>> **You face restrictions if you want to sell:** All franchise contracts (called *franchise agreements*) contain some restrictions regarding the sale or transfer of the franchise, mostly with the intent of ensuring the quality of your successor. While the restrictions are understandable, you may find you can't sell your franchise as readily as you would an independent business. (This limitation is partly outweighed by the fact that a franchised brand is often worth more.)

>> **You face limitations regarding growth:** If your franchise contract defines a specific territory, you can't expand beyond this territory unless you purchase another franchise. Similarly, you may not be able to expand into selling online to customers outside your territory.

>> **You may encounter a conflict of interest with your franchisor:** Any franchisor–franchisee relationship is susceptible to conflicts of interest. For example, a franchisor may feel a franchisee is failing to exploit a territory adequately, thereby underperforming and leaving gaps for a competitor to establish itself. The franchisee, on the other hand, may be quite satisfied with the extent to which it is exploiting its territory.

Exercising Due Diligence

Despite my many positive experiences with franchises, I've also encountered a couple of situations where individual franchisees have failed, and either gone broke or sold their franchise for much less than they purchased it for. For this reason, it pays to spend time doing some research.

Wising up

Your first port of call is the Franchising Code of Conduct, administered through the Australian Competition & Consumer Commission (ACCC). I suggest you check out this code at www.accc.gov.au. The ACCC also publish an excellent document called the *Franchisee Manual*, which serves as a great introduction for understanding your rights and responsibilities as a franchisee.

Other useful references include:

>> **Inside Franchise Business** (www.franchisebusiness.com.au): An organisation dedicated to providing information for potential franchisees about the franchising sector.

>> **Franchise Council of Australia** (www.franchise.org.au): The official website of the body representing franchisors and franchisees in Australia.

>> **Pre-entry franchise education program** (www.franchise-ed.org.au): Funded by the ACCC, this free online program gives prospective franchisees a realistic understanding of franchising.

Putting a franchise through the griller

If you're serious about going into franchising, you're not going to take long to narrow your options to a handful of franchises. At this point, take care not to set your heart on any one franchise but, rather, research each one carefully. In particular, don't automatically choose the franchise with the cheapest initial fee. This fee, when considered in isolation, is a poor indicator of the value of a franchise, and of the total ongoing costs (for more about fees, skip to the section 'Doing your sums', next in this chapter).

Here are some of the questions I suggest you ask about each potential franchise business:

>> **Does the franchise pass the test of time?** How many years has the group been established? When did the first franchise come in?

>> **Are you a test bunny?** How many franchisees are currently in operation? Ask for a list of existing franchise outlets, including names and addresses. If the franchise is newly imported from overseas, has it been market tested locally by careful and thorough pilot testing?

>> **How does the franchise bear up to competition?** What makes the business offering of this franchise different from others? How competitive is the market for the particular products or service?

MONEY
STUFF

>> **How are other franchises performing?** Ask salient questions regarding profitability, turnover and growth. If the franchisor is reticent, find out if any of the existing franchises are for sale. If so, arrange to visit the franchise as an interested buyer, and ask to look at the books.

>> **Who hasn't continued and why?** The Franchising Code requires franchisors to provide details of all franchises terminated in the previous three years. Information about terminated franchises is helpful, but what you also want to ask is how many franchises have been sold, cancelled, not renewed or ceased operating. (***Note:*** Be careful how you phrase this question in order to cover all possible scenarios!) Ask for the last-known contact details for these franchisees and find out why they didn't continue. Then ask the franchisor, too — every story has two sides.

>> **What are the fees?** See 'Doing your sums' next in this chapter for details.

REMEMBER

>> **How much does getting started cost?** Ask for assistance to work through a detailed budget, including legals, set-up costs, shop-fitting, signage, stock on hand and working capital.

>> **How will the site be selected?** For retail franchises, physical location is everything, and you need to have control over this element.

>> **What are the restrictions?** Are you restricted to certain areas, products or even suppliers? What are the competition clauses? In regards to your territory, are you guaranteed exclusive rights?

>> **Are all brand names and intellectual property protected?** Ask your solicitor for assistance with this research.

>> **What is the term of the franchise, and what are the options on renewal? If a lease is involved, does the lease coincide with the franchise term? What conditions/fees will apply when you decide to sell the franchise?** Both leases and franchises run out. You don't want to be stuck with a franchise but without a lease, nor do you want to be saddled with a lease and no franchise agreement.

>> **What training and support will be included?** Don't forget to check whether any fees will be charged for this training.

>> **Is the franchisor technology-savvy?** You're looking for an excellent corporate website, online access to product manuals and sales guides, online inventory management, point-of-sale systems, email marketing software and up-to-date computer systems, and possible additional services such as online scheduling or accounting.

Above all, don't be shy when asking questions — you have a right to know! Any reputable franchisor understands that making sure you're properly informed serves their long-term best interests. If you can, spend a couple of weeks working in one of the franchises to get a proper insight into how everything works.

REMEMBER

If you do decide to go ahead with purchasing a franchise, ensure that the elements listed in this section are adequately covered in your contact, and seek out a lawyer with specific experience in franchising.

IS THE BRAND STRONG ENOUGH?

Over the years, I've come across a few franchisees who feel they paid too much for the initial purchase of their franchise. In every instance, these franchises were for small service-based businesses (such as bookkeeping and lawn mowing), where the nature of the business itself isn't too tricky, and where word of mouth often plays a big part in building the business. These franchisees questioned whether the 'system' was really worth that much, and felt that the brand of their franchise didn't warrant the initial price paid or the ongoing fees.

Before buying any franchise, find out what the initial fee pays for, and ask yourself whether you think this fee is worth it. Also, find out what the ongoing fees are and what they pay for. (Even lawn mowing franchises often provide web-based technology that helps with booking, scheduling, invoicing, credit control and so on, all aimed at maximising franchisees' money-making time.)

How many people around you recognise the brand? Do you think the brand is essential to the success of the franchise? Do existing franchisees think the fees are worth it? If the brand isn't well known, your money may be better spent researching your own business plan, finding out what successful competitors are doing and creating your own marketing materials and campaigns.

Doing your sums

The cost of buying into a franchise isn't just the upfront purchase price. Almost all franchises also involve ongoing fees such as royalties on sales, marketing levies or fees for IT services. You also have to factor in all the regular start-up costs that any business start-up involves, such as legals, working capital and opening stock. Consider the following:

>> **What's included in the initial fee?** Fees can vary from $0 to $700,000, not including shop fit-out or equipment, depending on the franchise. Find out whether this initial fee includes training, sample products, initial marketing materials and so on.

>> **If not included in the quoted figure, how much are the additional start-up costs?** Don't underestimate how much starting up a new business costs, especially if you're planning a retail franchise. Figure 3-2 shows an initial budget for a simple bookkeeping franchise — you can see how the costs for even a simple business such as this mount up. Retail franchises incur costs for additional big-ticket items such as specialist equipment, premises fit-out, vehicles and working capital.

MONEY STUFF

» **How are ongoing royalties calculated?** Find out whether royalty payments are fixed or variable. On the one hand, fixed royalties have the advantage that you know what you're up for; on the other hand, variable royalties are easier going if business gets tough. If the rate is variable but substantial, ask yourself how sustainable this franchise model is likely to be in the long term.

» **How do marketing levies work?** Almost two-thirds of franchisors charge ongoing marketing levies. The Franchising Code of Conduct requires that these levies are kept in a separate account and that franchisors provide audited statements to franchisees as to how this money is spent.

» **What other ongoing fees should you expect?** Many franchisors charge ongoing fees for IT services, and some franchisors even charge ongoing fees for training. You need to factor any ongoing fees into your business plan and profitability models.

» **What about early termination fees?** If things go belly-up, what are the consequences?

REMEMBER

The franchisor has to supply you with a full disclosure document, a copy of the Franchising Code of Conduct *and* a copy of the final franchise agreement *at least* 14 days before you make any payment that isn't refundable.

FIGURE 3-2:
Your total start-up costs involve much more than the initial purchase price of the franchise.

Franchise Startup Costs Budget (Simple Service Business)		
Franchise fees		
Initial fee	$	30,000
Annual marketing levies, paid in advance	$	2,500
Brochures and marketing materials	$	500
Costs of attending initial training	$	950
Legal fees	$	3,200
Uniforms	$	450
Website customisation	$	950
	$	**38,550**
Business setup costs		
Accounting & professional advice	$	1,800
Adding logos to motor vehicle	$	850
Borrowing expenses	$	1,800
Business insurance	$	1,450
Business software	$	620
Computers & accessories	$	2,500
Home office fitout	$	2,500
Registration of company & biz name	$	1,350
Registration of professional membership	$	600
	$	**13,470**
Grand Total	**$**	**52,020**

2

Finding Your Entrepreneurial Spirit

Build a business that can stand on its own two feet.

Understand your business environment and where the risks and opportunities lie.

Maximise your chances of success with a proper business plan.

Pick a legal structure, find out about trademarks, and learn about contracts.

IN THIS CHAPTER

» Working out where you're headed: Cottage industry or multimillion-dollar enterprise?

» Playing with the different roles needed to make a business work

» Creating a business that's independent from you

» Understanding that some businesses are harder to grow than others

Chapter **4**

Separating Yourself from Your Business

Many years ago, I did some consulting work for a guy who'd started his own industrial welding business. The reporting systems for this business were a complete nightmare. As I trawled through the accounts, trying to make sense of it all, my client looked across the room at me and announced, in a somewhat apologetic tone, 'You know something? I'm a really good welder.'

For me, this brief interchange summarises the dilemma many business owners face. People start out in their business doing what they're good at, and what they love to do (whether this is welding, performing music or face-painting at kids' parties). But before long, they find they spend more and more time doing stuff they're not naturally good at, such as bookkeeping, looking through contracts, hiring employees or managing websites. Sometimes this extra work becomes such a burden that the joy of being in business is lost. Or sometimes the business owner rises to the challenge, thriving on these extra demands and enjoying the reprieve from day-to-day tasks.

In this chapter, I explore the questions that get to the heart of what *you* want to achieve with your business. Do you plan to take on employees and grow your business? Do you have a unique concept that means you could potentially sell your business for a substantial profit in five or ten years' time? Or are you happy tinkering away in your home office, earning a modest income with little stress and few demands?

No answer is right, no answer is wrong. However, this chapter provides an opportunity for you to pause and choose the direction that's best for you.

Deciding What Path You Want to Take

Generally, business books assume that you want to grow your business, take on employees, maybe even develop a franchise or expand internationally. However, in the first part of this chapter, I want to spend a bit of time exploring whether you feel this desire for expansion. Maybe you're quite content pursuing a small home-based part-time business, or maybe you don't want the stress of taking on employees.

Taking a step back and thinking of all the self-employed people I know or have worked with, I can see that most people follow one of three different paths (or occasionally all three paths, but one after the other):

>> A simple owner-operated business with no employees

>> A business where the owner focuses on providing the service but employs others to help run administrative functions of the business

>> A business built by the owner that then has a life of its own, where employees provide the services or manufacture products and the owner is in a management role. Ultimately, the owner may even seek to create a franchise.

Which path do you want to take? Even though most business books imply that if you're serious about being in business, the third path is the only way forward, this isn't necessarily true. Small owner-operated businesses may have less opportunity for profit, but profit is only one of the many motivators for being in business.

Doing the thing you love to do

As I touch on in Chapter 1, a starting point for many small businesses is that a person starts a business doing the thing that he or she has experience doing, or possibly the thing that they have just completed studying. So, the person who was working as a high-school teacher starts a business tutoring high-school students, the physiotherapist who was working at her local hospital opens her own practice, or the newly qualified chef opens a restaurant.

The upside of running a business in this way is that you get to do what you love to do, and usually what you're good at. You also have the perks of self-employment (choosing your own hours, possibly charging more for your services and being your own boss).

REMEMBER

The downside of being a solo owner-operator is often long hours, with no income when you're on holidays or if you're sick. The experience of being cleaner, shop assistant, bookkeeper, marketing manager and finance manager all within the course of a single day can be relentless, and you may end up feeling that you're a jack of all trades but a master of none. Your business is utterly dependent on you; if you don't turn up, you don't get paid. In addition, the amount of money you can make from your business is always limited by the number of hours you're able to work.

Some people would argue that the kind of work involved with an owner-operator business, where it's just you and you do your own thing, defeats the purpose of going into business. They would argue that unless you want to conceive of a business that has a life of its own beyond yourself, you're better just to keep working for someone else. Otherwise, you're not really creating a business; rather, you're creating a job with a pile of overheads.

I disagree. Although I acknowledge that this small-scale kind of operation has its drawbacks, I've lived in a regional area and been self-employed for too long to be that naïve. Sometimes no jobs are available and the only option is to be self-employed. Sometimes you may have such substantial family commitments that your business becomes a relatively peripheral part of your life, and the income it generates is just a bonus, not the core. Sometimes the way you generate income is so personal, so idiosyncratic (maybe you're an artist, a faith healer or an inventor) that you can't conceive of a way that this business can be grown beyond yourself. All of these reasons are perfectly valid reasons for being in business, yet staying small.

AHEAD OF THE PACK

Even though you may have perfectly valid reasons for staying small, if you're currently self-employed and you have no employees — or you're planning to start a new business with this structure — do pause to consider what your options might be. Conceiving a way to run your business so that it can operate without you can be challenging, but is the only way forward if you want to generate profits that aren't directly dependent on the hours that you work.

Getting help and delegating what you can

If you're not content to be an owner-operator doing everything yourself, the first and most natural stage of expansion is usually to employ some assistance. Maybe you hire a bookkeeper, employ a casual labourer, or get assistance with marketing or website design.

Many experts and professionals end up with this kind of model. For example, our local orthodontist hires several employees (two receptionists, a dental hygienist and an office manager) but she is the only person doing the actual work (you know, the multi-colour braces and general teenage torture). Sure, she could probably hire another orthodontist to work for her, but she has a great deal invested in her reputation and, for whatever reason, feels she can't trust another person to provide the same quality of service.

In a way, the part of my business income that I generate writing books is similar. I employ a bookkeeper and office admin person, and occasionally get help researching topics, but at the end of day (and I confess that it's truly the end of the day as I write this), the only ones left standing are me and my cute little silver laptop.

This way of working is what many people choose. You get to do the thing you love and you can choose your own hours, be your own boss and usually make a decent living. And, unlike single owner-operators who do everything themselves, you can hire others to help with day-to-day business operations, so that you can focus on doing the thing that you're good at.

The downside, of course, is that you're still 'it' as far as the business is concerned. You are your business, and your business is you. Your income is always limited by the number of hours you're able to work and, if you're on holiday or sick, the business doesn't generate income. You also carry the risk of being responsible not just for your own livelihood, but the livelihood of your employees also.

If your business has this kind of structure, you may find it hard to imagine how you can expand your business so that employees could provide the same services as you currently do. However, nobody is indispensable, and no matter how smart or talented you are, chances are someone's out there who can do all the things you do.

AHEAD OF THE PACK

One of the tricks to making the leap to hiring others to provide the services you currently provide is to imagine a little person is sitting on your shoulder, watching everything you do and documenting your activities in a 'how-to manual'. This is the first step towards separating yourself from your business, so that you can describe to others the attitudes, skills and standards that you expect. (For more on this topic, see the section 'Documenting and building systems', later in this chapter.)

Building a business that's separate from you

The third path that you can take (refer to the preceding sections for an outline of the other two paths) is to create a business where employees are the ones providing your service or manufacturing your products. If you look around you, most medium-sized businesses fall into this category. For example:

>> Our local plumbing company has a team of plumbers, each with their own van and apprentice, providing plumbing services. The owner occasionally helps out on tricky jobs, but mostly focuses on management and marketing.

>> The place where my son used to learn piano is a music school, with lots of different tutors teaching different instruments. The owners teach sometimes, but other teachers run most of the classes.

>> My neighbour runs a small chain of three cafes. He rarely cooks or serves tables any more, but focuses on the finances and management.

>> A girlfriend of mine has a business selling baby sleeping bags. She still does the design and marketing, but she has moved production offshore and uses a distributor for sales.

Can you see that for each of these examples, the business owners have made a leap in how they think of their businesses? The plumber is now the manager of a plumbing services company; the music tutors started their own music school; the barista opened a chain of cafes; the seamstress runs a manufacturing company. In all of these examples, the owner no longer unblocks pipes, teaches violin, serves coffee or stitches fabric. In return, the potential for each of these businesses is that the owners can have more freedom and earn more money than they otherwise would have done.

For me, this transition from owner to entrepreneur is really exciting. Freedom from the shackles of the daily grind provides an opportunity to do the other things in life that have only been dreams up until now.

If you haven't made this transition, and your business is still dependent on you for pretty much every cent of income, my question to you is this: Have you ever consciously made the decision *not* to be entrepreneurial? Or have you never really let yourself imagine how you could do things differently?

If not, do try to give the visionary in you some room to breathe. Spend time thinking about how you can grow your business and create something that has a life of its own.

AHEAD OF THE PACK

In Chapter 9, I make a distinction between budgets and Profit & Loss Projection reports, explaining that a budget sets sales goals and spending limits that you must try to stick to, whereas a Profit & Loss Projection answers the 'what if?' questions, and enables you to model different scenarios. Even if you're just starting out in business, I suggest you spend some time experimenting with what your Profit & Loss Projection might look like in a few years' time, when you have a team of employees and possibly multiple locations or a much increased product range.

Creating a way of doing business

The queen diva of all business models is, of course, the franchise. A franchise is where you figure out such a neat and unique way of doing business that this concept itself becomes something you can sell. A franchise embodies the whole way you do business, including buying policies, logos, marketing techniques, pricing, uniforms and more. Table 4-1 outlines various business models, and how specific owner-operator businesses could move into the franchise or international model.

Note: I'm not talking about you purchasing a franchise here — you can refer to Chapter 3 for more information on that. Rather, I'm talking about you building such a successful way of doing business that you create your own franchise.

TABLE 4-1   **Moving from a Small Business to a Big Business**

Owner-Operator	Business with Employees	Franchise/International Model
Yoga teacher	Yoga school	Patented method of teaching and streaming online yoga classes
Plumber	Plumbing business with a team of ten employees	National plumbing franchise
eBay book sales	eBay business with three employees	eBay model for buying and selling books
A farmer selling homemade chilli sauce and pickles	A chilli sauce company with a recognised brand and national distribution	A method of manufacturing and distributing sauces/pickles that can be replicated worldwide
A corner cafe in the local town	A couple of cafes with several employees	A franchise restaurant chain
A fashion blogger selling clothes online	An online clothing store with 50 brands and national distribution	An innovative system (including software) for selling clothes online that can be replicated in other countries

Creating your own franchise takes the requirement that you separate yourself from your business to a whole new level. To use the example of the plumbing company I refer to in the preceding section, when the owners employed a team of plumbers to do the plumbing work, they entrusted others to provide the core service of the business on their behalf and, to do this, they had to provide a certain level of supervision and training. However, what if this plumbing company does really well and the owners decide to create a franchise? At this point, the owners need to analyse what it is that makes their business different. They need to quantify these differences and create systems so that others can copy these differences.

The upside of expanding to become a franchise is the opportunity to make very healthy profits. In many ways, a franchise is the ultimate realisation of the entrepreneur's dream.

Wearing Different Hats

Have you heard of a book called *The E-Myth* or *The E-Myth Revisited* (written by Michael Gerber and published by HarperCollins)? This book has sold over 3 million copies, and the terminology that Gerber uses to describe the roles owners play in their businesses has become almost standard in some circles.

Gerber likes to describe the roles of a business owner as being technician, manager or entrepreneur. I may not describe these roles here exactly as Gerber might, but here's the general idea:

» **Technician:** These are people who work in their business, not on their business. The plumber who unblocks drains, the cafe owner who serves coffee, or the freelance consultant who goes out to meet clients.

» **Manager:** A manager is someone who organises the day-to-day running of a business, ordering stock, looking at profit margins, paying the bills and replying to customers.

» **Entrepreneur:** An entrepreneur is the visionary, the person who's thinking of the business as a thing that's separate to the service it provides or the product it sells, and who is looking for ways to build the business and expand.

I really like this way of thinking of the roles in a business, because it goes a long way to explaining that feeling I've felt so often as a business owner — of having all these balls in the air that I have to juggle. The idea is that if it's just you in your business (which it is for most people when they start out), you need to balance out these roles. The idea sounds simple, but is tricky to do.

These roles correspond to some degree with what I talk about earlier in this chapter. Someone who is happiest being a 'technician' often ends up not expanding their business, and instead typically provides services or makes products themselves (refer to 'Doing the thing you love to do' earlier in this chapter). A person whose 'manager' side wins out typically ends up organising others. This person is content to get employees to assist in running the business and is good at monitoring costs and ensuring efficient operations (refer to 'Getting help and delegating what you can'). The 'entrepreneur' personality is the one who's always looking for the winning idea, and is keenest to create a business with a life of its own (refer to 'Building a business that's separate from you' or 'Creating a way of doing business').

WARNING

If your business is still pretty small, letting any one of the three roles of technician, manager or entrepreneur dominate at the expense of the others can be a problem. The technician will probably fail to grow the business, the manager may well fail to look to the future and plan for change, and the entrepreneur, if left to their own devices, may burn through a whole load of money very fast pursuing one idea after another.

What I think is so clever about the way Gerber identifies these roles is that you can apply this thinking to yourself and your own business. For example:

>> Most people find that the technician role (doing the thing that they're good at, such as fixing pipes, teaching music or making a mean espresso coffee) feels comfortable and safe.

>> The role of manager fits well with some people but not with others. (Many businesspeople hate having to think about money, tax, legals, schedules and so on, but others are relatively okay with this role.)

>> The role of entrepreneur is the role that comes hardest to most people. If you're inherently a bit conservative (as I confess to being myself), whenever the entrepreneur voice pipes up with a good idea, the conservative manager voice calls out, 'Oh no, that's way too scary'. The entrepreneur and manager are so busy tussling away that the only person left to do anything is the technician, who continues to get on with the job. And then nothing changes.

The way to move on from this situation, and give all three roles a part to play, is to build a business that has a life of its own. Which just happens to be the next topic in this chapter . . .

Building a Business with a Life of its Own

In the preceding sections in this chapter, I talk about why creating a business with a life of its own is generally the best way to gain more freedom and flexibility, and hopefully more profits to boot. I also talk about the different roles or 'hats' people typically wear in business, and how important it is to balance these roles, especially when you're just getting started and you have only you in the business.

However, the transition to creating a business with its own identity, separate from you, isn't always easy. In the following sections, I provide some guidelines as to how you may be able to make this happen.

Defining your difference

The first step in giving your business some of its own life force is to be clear about what it is that makes you different. I spend a heap of time deliberating on this very topic back in Chapter 2, so I won't repeat myself here. Suffice to say that you must identify what makes your business different, and this difference must relate to the identity of your business, and not you personally.

Some examples may help to set this in context:

>> A dry-cleaning company uses alternative chemical processing, arguably better for the environment and for those with sensitive skin.

>> An online clothes store offers multiple views and videos of each item of clothing, and provides recommendations as to the body types each garment is best suited for.

>> A mechanic workshop offers a free home drop-off and pick-up service, and routinely details all vehicles as part of any service or repair work.

None of the preceding ideas is particularly revolutionary but, if executed well and combined with a cohesive marketing strategy and company commitment, they have the potential to make these businesses stand apart from others.

I find that business owners can be very vague regarding what it is that makes their business successful, especially with smaller businesses where the owner is still very much hands-on. To use the mechanic workshop example from the preceding list, this mechanic may offer free home drop-offs and detailing, but is this really the reason for the workshop's success? Or is it that the head mechanic is so skilled and capable that customers instantly warm to him? Or that this workshop is the only repair service within a 10-kilometre radius?

Without an understanding of what makes this business successful, the owner is vulnerable. If the drawcard is the head mechanic, what might happen to the business if he leaves? If the lack of competition in a 10-kilometre radius is the reason for steady business, what might happen if another mechanic opens up shop nearby?

You can try to deduce the reasons for your success using a few techniques:

» If your business operates in more than one location, experiment by trialling specific services or marketing techniques in one location but not the other, and see what happens.

» Return to the competitive analysis you completed in Chapter 2 (or if you haven't already done it, do it now). This objective comparative process is a good way to get a sense of why your customers come to you.

» Ask your customers why they love you! You can ask customers face to face, set up online surveys, put up quick questions on Facebook, or do whatever fits your customer base best.

» Try opening a new location and trying to replicate your success from the first location. If the new location performs differently, try to get to the bottom of why.

» If you think that part of your success is due to something relatively simple (I think of my local butcher who, after each interaction, looks at me with a smile and says, 'Can I get you anything else today?' — even if a queue of people is waiting behind me), then try measuring sales when you employ this technique or strategy for a week, and compare sales to another week where you don't do this.

TIP

If you can figure out why you're successful, and measure how much difference this strategy, product or technique makes to your business, you're well on the way to being able to replicate your success and grow your business.

Documenting and building systems

One of things that a franchise offers, in contrast to other businesses of a similar type, is consistency. As my husband likes to say in a satisfied voice regarding the coffee he buys from a certain fast-food chain, 'This bunch make the best worst coffee in the world'. In other words, he knows the coffee is going to be average, he knows it won't be that hot, but still it hits the spot and it's the same every time, wherever we are in the country.

This consistency is one of the secrets to expanding a business beyond one location, building a brand or even preparing your business to become a franchise in its own right. Take the example of my aunt, who ran a guesthouse in the wilds of northern Scotland for 30 years or more. She was a wonderful hostess, but occasionally she'd be away for the weekend or even for a week or two. How could she guarantee that her guests would get exactly the same quality of experience when she was away as when she was there?

REMEMBER

A happy customer may share the love with one or two people, but unhappy customers share their disgruntlement with ten. If you can get rid of the hit-and-miss element that plagues so many businesses, positive word-of-mouth recommendations may be almost all the marketing you need.

So, how do you guarantee consistency, particularly as your business grows and you're not around to serve each customer or supervise each employee? The answer is in procedures and documentation. First, you figure out what it is that your business does well (which I refer to in the preceding section); next, you articulate this difference in words in a way that employees can follow.

Here are some examples of how to provide a consistent experience for customers:

>> **Checklists:** For any complex activities, where employees need to fulfil several tasks in a specific sequence, create a checklist. For example, if your business is such that a customer order can be quite complex (maybe you need to check quantities, availability, delivery dates, payment methods and more), a checklist ensures nothing gets forgotten.

REMEMBER

>> **Complaints procedures:** Do you know that one of the ways to make customers happiest is to do everything you can to fix something when they complain? However, the gentle art of responding well to a grumpy customer isn't something that comes naturally to most people, and so procedures for dealing with complaints are essential.

>> **Customer service procedures:** Ideally, you need a procedure for any customer interaction that happens on a regular basis, whether this is a customer enquiry, order or sale.

>> **Manufacturing procedures:** If you're a manufacturer, even if you're operating on a relatively small scale making things to sell locally or at markets, the quality of your product needs to be the same each time. Sounds simple, but imagine you're making homemade jams, and the quality of produce available varies according to the time of year. In this scenario, you may need to limit production to certain times of year in order to guarantee consistency.

Similarly, if you've been manufacturing products yourself and you're now ready to delegate this process, you need to document exactly what you do, using precise quantities, times, production methods and so on.

>> **Phone scripts and email templates:** I can feel you wincing a little here, as you wonder if you're really so dictatorial that you can bear writing out scripts for employees to follow when they answer the phone, or templates for when they reply to emails. Remember two things, however: Firstly, what you're trying to achieve is consistency for the customer; secondly, if you have spent time figuring out the ingredients that have made your business successful and you know that how you answer the phone or reply to emails is part of this success, then, of course, you want to be able to repeat this formula, time and time again.

>> **Presentation:** As someone who hates uniform in almost any shape or form, I squirm a little as I write this. But businesses love uniforms for the reason that they provide consistency for the customer and reinforce the company's image. Even something as simple as a polo shirt with your company logo monogrammed on the front can make a difference to how customers perceive you.

>> **Rates and pricing:** Standardised rates and pricing are a must. So, if you tend to quote on a somewhat intuitive basis for jobs, you need to spend time figuring out a method for pricing and stick to that instead.

AHEAD OF THE PACK

If you're still small and you're thinking about how to expand your business, one great source of inspiration (if available) is to look at franchises that offer a similar service or product to your own. For example, if you're starting a lawn mowing business, take a look at how the lawn mowing franchises approach their branding, marketing and customer service. If you're starting a bookkeeping business, look at the bookkeeping franchises and how they organise their pricing and services. I'm not suggesting you steal intellectual property here or that you try to copy the systems of a franchise without paying to belong — more that you take a look at the general approach of this franchise and use this as inspiration.

Setting goals for you and your business

I've worked as a business consultant for over 20 years now, and I've noticed a certain quality in the handful of very successful businesspeople I've encountered during this time. Each of these people has had a very specific goal in mind, and they've been possessed by an inner drive to meet this goal.

Interestingly enough, these goals have been ultimately personal, rather than business-orientated — such as the desire to be able to retire by the age of 50 on a guaranteed income for life, or the dream to be able to buy a house for each one of the children, or to be able to work only 20 hours a week and still be financially secure.

If you're trying to create a business that grows and is ultimately independent of you, ask yourself what you want to achieve from this growth. Do you have a specific financial goal or a certain time frame? If not, spend some time thinking what this goal might be, and then building your business plan around this goal.

WARNING

While setting goals is an important part of business success, just wanting to be a millionaire isn't enough. You need to ensure that your business has some kind of competitive edge or winning strategy (refer to Chapter 2 for more on this topic) and you need to understand how to build on this strategy with good systems. Unless you have these elements in place, ambitious plans to open a new shop every six months or become an internationally recognised brand are just pie-in-the-sky.

Planning for a graceful exit

One of the best ways to get yourself into the mindset of thinking of your business as independent from you is to imagine selling it.

Always try to have an exit plan simmering away, even if you don't plan to sell any time in the immediate future. Ask yourself the following questions: If I were to sell this business today, what could I get for it? Can this business run independently of me? What assets or business systems do I have to sell? How can I maximise the price I can get for this business?

Appreciating the Limitations of Your Business

In this chapter's preceding sections, I talk about the idea of creating a business that has a life of its own, separate from you. I also mention early in this chapter that not everyone wants to go down this path, and I talk about the pros and cons of operating your business in different ways.

When thinking on these topics, you also have to keep in mind that some businesses are much harder than others to expand. Here are some of the kinds of businesses that can be hard to grow, along with why:

>> **Businesses limited by physical constraints or high set-up costs that require substantial capital:** An obvious example here is a farmer, limited by the amount of land they have, and lacking capital to expand. Other examples could be a professional truck driver limited by the high capital cost of

additional trucks, or the capacity of a guesthouse owner to expand due to the high cost of purchasing real estate.

>> **Businesses based on the artistic skills of the owner:** Examples include a classical pianist performing around the country, a stand-up comedian or a theatre producer. Sure, you could team up with other artists in a similar field, but the actual core of what you do (such as playing virtuosic piano) is almost impossible to delegate.

>> **Businesses making products that require very specific skills, particularly those of an artistic nature:** For example, glass blowing, fine-art painting and pottery. Custom manufacturing of one-off goods also falls into this category, where the craftsperson (such as a cabinet-maker) builds a reputation that is very much linked to that person as an individual, rather than to the business.

>> **Businesses with expert services where the service provided is very much associated with the individual providing the service:** Think specialist medical professionals (acupuncturist, paediatrician, orthodontist) or specialist consultants (business mentors, human resources consultants).

>> **Businesses servicing a rural location where the owner provides the services and expansion involves too much travel:** Our local horse dentist (yes, such a thing as a horse dentist does exist!) springs to mind.

If you have more of an entrepreneurial personality, you may have read the preceding list thinking that I'm lacking imagination, and that the businesses in the list could be expanded in plenty of ways. The artist could commercialise her images as cushions, postcards or wallpaper; the horse dentist could set up an online consultancy; the cabinet-maker could spend oodles on high-end marketing and build up an international reputation. In my defence, I'm not saying that these businesses are impossible to grow — I'm just saying they're harder to grow than others. (And besides, the artist may not want to design wallpaper, and online horse dentistry may prove impractical.)

AHEAD OF THE PACK

If your business falls into one of the categories outlined in the preceding list and you're having problems imagining how you separate yourself from your business, hop onto the internet and search worldwide for the product you sell or the service you provide. Look for examples of others similar to you and how they have grown their business to be something bigger.

REMEMBER

Although businesses with expert services can be hard to expand, for those who manage to do so and build a network of professionals who provide a high consistency of service, the rewards can be substantial.

WARNING

KEEP HOLD OF THOSE REINS

One of the things that you may experience when you hire your first employees is a feeling of relief so strong that you declare, 'Here you are. I trust you. Please feel free to organise me, my business and my life.'

Don't kid yourself that this letting go is you being a hands-off manager or a good delegator. Handing over the reins to someone else in this way is bound to end in tears: If an employee takes over and does everything well, you'll be left with a huge hole when that employee leaves and your business will suffer; if the employee fails to perform, you've just given that employee the chance to do a great deal of damage.

Instead, your responsibility is to delegate, but delegate using clear instructions and good systems. (I talk about creating systems in 'Building a Business with a Life of its Own', earlier in this chapter.) You never want an employee to become indispensable because, at that point, you have built a business that may not be dependent on you, but sure as anything is dependent on someone else.

IN THIS CHAPTER

» Reflecting on your industry and where it's heading

» Doing an honest no-holds-barred assessment of your abilities

» Spotting possible opportunities and threats

» Matching your strengths to opportunities, and guarding weaknesses from threats

» Building a winning action plan

Chapter **5**

Staying One Step Ahead

As I write this chapter, Melbourne is still in lockdown, almost all Australian state borders are closed, four out of five of my adult children are unemployed due to COVID, and pretty much every businessperson I know is reeling from the chaos of the last six months. Across Australia, and indeed the globe, 2020 has been a year of unprecedented change.

Being responsive in the face of change has always been essential to the success of any business, but I feel confident in asserting that this ability is now more important than ever. Even if we don't face another pandemic in our lifetimes, fast-paced change is a reality for pretty much every business, whether this be new competitors, shifts in government regulation, the impact of a changing climate or fluctuating economy, or the arrival of new technology.

If your business is still relatively small, you may find it challenging to think about how change might affect you. However, anticipating change, and responding quickly, is key to capitalising on new opportunities. And if COVID has shown us anything, it's how quickly we can deal with change. I think with admiration of the craft beer companies who, in recent months, teamed up with distilleries to make hand sanitiser, or the thousands of restaurants that shifted almost overnight to takeaway services.

In this chapter, I provide a few simple tools to help you analyse what's happening in your industry. I also explain how to do a simple SWOT (strengths-weaknesses-opportunities-threats) analysis, and how you can position your business for the best possible chance of success.

Taking an Eagle-Eye View

To be strategic in business, you need an understanding of how the industry in which you're operating is faring, and what outside factors may affect this industry in the near future.

Imagine you were the owner of a video and DVD rental business 20 years or so ago when this industry was thriving. Maybe your business was very profitable (you had great taste in movies, your shop was in a central location and you had no competitors). Despite all these advantages, chances are, unless you were able to pivot not only quickly but also extremely dramatically, you would have ceased trading by now.

Looking at what's happening in your industry

If you've been working in an industry for a while already, you probably have a feeling for general industry trends on an intuitive level. However, I recommend you take time to think more analytically about all outside factors that influence your business, such as the economy, the demographics of your target market, and the average profitability and trends of this industry.

This analysis is known as a *PESTEL analysis*, standing for political, economic, social, technological, environmental and legal. The primary purpose of analysing the environment in this way is to identify the drivers of change affecting future industry growth.

Here's what you should focus on:

AHEAD OF THE PACK

>> **Political:** What political forces could affect the industry? For example, think about how solar rebate policies have affected solar panel retailers, or how federal legislation has affected financial planning businesses.

>> **Economic:** How do recessions, interest rates and exchange rates affect this industry? Exporters and importers, for example, are particularly vulnerable to exchange rate fluctuations.

>> **Social:** Consider the interaction between the industry and demographic trends. For example, businesses in the aged care industry are benefiting from the ageing population.

>> **Technological:** How is this industry affected by technological change? Think of how online portals have created enormous challenges for many kinds of retailers, including bookshops, music stores and travel agencies.

>> **Environmental:** Increasing environmental awareness may present opportunities for an industry — for example, organic foods — or challenges — for example, chemical garden fertilisers.

>> **Legal:** Increasing government regulations can often serve to polarise an industry, especially if compliance is very expensive, making an industry more profitable for the larger players but tougher for the small fry.

Table 5-1 provides a much summarised analysis I did for an established regional accounting firm — you can see that even for a business as stable as this, many forces can shape future success.

TABLE 5-1   **Industry Analysis — Regional Accounting Firm**

	Industry Change	Likely Consequence
Political	Superannuation reforms	Possible decline in demand for self-managed super funds
Economic	Increasing downwards fee pressure	Growth in larger firms able to implement cost-saving processes
Social	Demographic changes as baby boomers move into retirement	Growth in demand for retirement planning
	Different expectations from Gen Y clients	Pressure to be more interactive and technologically adept
Technological	New technology that enables clients to perform their own tax returns	Decline in routine compliance work
	Video conferencing and email replacing face-to-face contact	Erosion of niche markets based on location
Environmental	Demand for accountants to report on non-financial performance	Growth in demand for sustainability reporting
Legal	Increased regulation of self-managed super funds	Growth in specialist firms providing super services only

As part of researching these outside influences, I recommend you hunt for 'state of the industry' reports wherever possible. These reports are often published by industry associations and available for free download from their websites. In addition, see if you can find financial benchmarks for your industry. Such profiles often include handy info about employment, average income and average operating profit before tax.

AHEAD OF THE PACK

HA, HA. YOU CAN'T CATCH ME!

One of the points you may want to consider as part of your industry analysis is barriers to entry. Barriers to entry are very high set-up costs that make it hard for other competitors to enter the fray.

Obvious examples are new airlines, car manufacturers or supermarket chains. (Although I guess it's unlikely that anyone reading this book would really be planning to start a new airline.) At a more everyday level, barriers to entry can be expensive tools or specialist equipment, many years of study, big infrastructure costs such as software systems or warehousing, complex distribution networks or expensive real estate.

If you plan to start a new business within an industry where significant barriers to entry exist, you may find growth is impossible because you don't have enough capital or time to invest. If this is the case, you need to be open to the idea of changing your business model.

On the other hand, changes in technology have caused entry barriers in many industries to crumble, opening up a gamut of opportunities. For example, owners of small businesses who formerly couldn't compete because they didn't have enough capital to fit out an expensive retail outlet can now sell direct to the consumer using online channels; real estate agents who couldn't afford a shopfront can now operate from their home office; authors who couldn't secure distribution without going through a publisher can now self-publish their own ebooks; niche consultants with formerly high travel costs can now deliver services via online conferencing.

If you are a small player, see if you can identify any new technologies that present opportunities in markets where, up until now, the big players have dominated the field. Not only are barriers to entry crumbling at an ever-increasing pace, but large companies can also be very slow to change.

Being realistic about industry decline

The idea behind completing an industry analysis is to gain a sense of what's happening overall in the industry. Of course, an industry that's in decline is going to be a whole load tougher (if not impossible) to succeed in than an industry that's growing very quickly.

TRUE STORY

I mention the decline of video and DVD rental stores earlier in this chapter, and when I did so, I thought of the video store that used to be in my village. Doug's business was a solid one, and his store (as one of the only places open after 6 pm) was always social and lively. In hindsight, I can look back and think, *Doug should have changed to more DVDs and fewer videos earlier; Doug could have downsized and halved his rent; Doug could have explored a niche market and developed an online presence*. Pish tosh. For Doug's particular business, there was no hope. The best thing Doug could have done was close his business while he was still ahead.

WARNING

If your industry is in severe decline, your best bet is probably to try to sell your business now, close your business if it is already unprofitable or, if you're still at the planning stage, walk away from the idea of starting a new business. Closing a business can be particularly scary, because you may have significant funds invested that you'll never recoup. However, if you're already trading at a loss, selling your business in the context of a declining industry may be impossible. The longer you trade unprofitably, the more you stand to lose financially.

Riding the wave of opportunity

What about other scenarios than those I cover in the preceding section, such as enormous industry growth? Generally, industry growth is a great thing for anyone involved and, if you're in the right place at the right time, you can make handsome profits.

For start-up businesses, if you can find a niche that works, I believe the opportunities are greater than ever. I've been thinking about this the last few days and each time I look around, I spot another ingenious business idea that seems to be thriving — whether this is a queer gym, an online business helping Chinese parents choose 'Western' baby names, or a restaurant in Amsterdam installing a dozen greenhouses in its forecourt to manage social distancing.

The flipside of jumping on the bandwagon for any industry experiencing rapid change can be higher risks, because the direction of change and new technology can be hard to predict.

Part of the secret to mitigating this risk lies in matching the internal strengths of your business against the potential opportunities of the industry. And guess what? That's what the next section of this chapter is all about . . .

Rating Your Capabilities

I'm sure you don't have to pause for very long to think of someone who always seems to choose the more difficult paths in life. Maybe you have a friend who's dyslexic but has chosen to be a linguist as a career, or you know someone in a wheelchair who travels the world.

Chasing one's dreams and persisting in the face of adversity is undoubtedly character building and often deeply rewarding. However, in the world of business, you will find that it usually pays to be more strategic about where you channel your energies. You want to identify the possible opportunities and see if you can match these opportunities against your natural skills and abilities.

Putting yourself through the griller

I have a morbid fascination for those personality quizzes you see in magazines in doctors' waiting rooms — the ones where you get to answer inane multiple-choice questions and then read a chilling verdict at the end.

With these guilty pleasures in mind, Figure 5-1 provides you with your very own quiz, with the added benefit of not having to get stuck in a waiting room in order to enjoy it. (In the example shown in Figure 5-1, I've also included sample responses.)

REMEMBER

When you answer the questions in Figure 5-1, respond from the perspective of your business, rather than from you as an individual. Think of the collective skills that you, your employees, any family members, business mentors or outside consultants bring to the party. Also, keep your competition in mind when you rate your business on things such as customer service or marketing. (For example, you may be aware of small areas where you can improve your customer service but if you know that you beat all of your competition hands down, you can probably award yourself a rating of 'awesome'.)

WARNING

When rating how important each function is for your business (sales, finance, people and so on), I suggest you put a tick in the 'Yes' column for all aspects of financial management. Even if your business chugs along just fine and you're a shoebox-receipts kind of person, poor financial management is almost always a limiter to business success and growth.

	STRENGTH			WEAKNESS		Is This Important to Your Business?		
	Awesome	Pretty good	Average	Not great	Terrible	Yes	Sometimes	Not Really
Sales and marketing. How does your business rate in regards to . . .								
Cold calling, direct sales, or telesales?	✓						✓	
Negotiating skills?		✓					✓	
Skills in social media?	✓					✓		
The ability to organise and run strong advertising campaigns?		✓						✓
The ability to write a good press release?		✓						✓
Finance. How does your business rate in regards to . . .								
Keeping a good set of up-to-date books?					✓	✓		
Invoicing customers and making sure you get paid on time?					✓	✓		
Financial reporting, particularly regular Profit & Loss reports?				✓		✓		
Cashflow management and tax planning?				✓		✓		
Availability of capital and ability to pay bills on time?						✓		
Management ability. How does your business rate in regards to . . .								
Depth (number of years) of experience?		✓				✓		
People-management skills?				✓			✓	
Range of experience in different business situations?				✓			✓	
People. How does your business rate in regards to . . .								
The balance and synergy of skills in the team?		✓					✓	
The vibe and morale in the workplace?		✓					✓	
Physical resources. How does your business rate in regards to?								
Physical location?	✓					✓		
Up-to-date tools and equipment?					✓			✓
Customer service. How does your business rate in regards to?								
Ability to fulfill orders or respond to enquiries quickly?	✓					✓		
Ability to communicate well with customers?	✓					✓		
Responsiveness to customer requests?	✓	✓						
Computer systems. How does your business rate in regards to?								
Good reporting systems and sales management?			✓				✓	
Ability to manage websites, custom software or any other IT requirements?		✓				✓		
Product or service. How does your business rate in regards to?								
Range of products on offer?			✓			✓		
Technical expertise and ability?				✓		✓		

FIGURE 5-1:
Rating your business on key areas of performance.

Prioritising where you need to do better

If I'm a psychologist running a counselling business, chances are cold calling or direct marketing skills aren't going to be that big a deal. On the other hand, if I'm selling a new product that few people have ever heard of, being able to sell anything to anyone is going to be an essential skill.

In Figure 5-1, can you see how I've highlighted some of the ticks in the strengths and weaknesses columns? I've highlighted all business functions where the capability rating is 'not great' or 'terrible' but the function itself is rated as being important.

TIP

The combination of something being both important to your business but a weakness in your capabilities is an unhappy one. Can you identify any business functions in which you're really weak, but which are crucial for your business?

Identifying Opportunities and Threats

Industry trends aren't the only things that can greatly affect your business but over which you have little control. What about changes in the economy, or the arrival of new competitors on the scene? For you to stay one step ahead, the name of the game is to try to anticipate the impact these outside factors may have on your business.

AHEAD OF
THE PACK

For each of the following categories, ask yourself what opportunities and what threats lie in store. Remember that any change can be an opportunity or a threat (or even both), depending on where you stand in the scheme of things. Organise these opportunities and threats in two columns, similar to Table 5-2. (Although bear in mind that Table 5-2 is a somewhat simplified example — your list will almost certainly have a bit more detail.)

Consider the following:

>> **New competition:** How likely is it that new competitors could affect your business? Do you have special skills or a strategic advantage that safeguards you from competition? (I talk more about strategic advantage in Chapter 2.) Or is the thing that makes your business so successful easy to copy? What if the competitor has more capital, a better location or superior marketing abilities?

» **Emerging technologies:** How is technological change going to affect your business? Could new technology end up putting you out of business (think of the video store example at the beginning of this chapter)? Or are you skilled in the direction that new technology is heading, and could this be an opportunity?

» **Changes in demographics:** Demographic change is a long-term thing, but so (hopefully) is your business. If your business serves a local population (as opposed to having national distribution or being online), it pays to watch the trends in population patterns. (Running a children's toy store in a suburb with a rapidly growing retiree population and a declining birth rate may not be the most brilliant strategy. Although marketing quality products to cashed-up and indulgent grandparents could turn this into an opportunity.)

» **Changes in government regulations:** If your business is dependent in some way on government regulations (maybe you're a taxi driver, you work in health, or your business relies on government grants in some form or other), you're particularly vulnerable to changes in the political landscape. Ask yourself what impact changing regulations could have on your business, and how you could respond.

» **Changes in the economy:** Is your business very dependent on the ebb and flow of the economy? Some businesses (for example, a business selling staple food products) are relatively stable regardless of what's happening in the economy; other businesses (such as those selling high-end luxury goods or even tourism) tend to move in tandem with booms and busts.

» **Changes in your domestic affairs:** You won't find personal stuff listed in other business-planning books, but if you're a small business, I know (from experience!) the impact that changes in your home life can have. A divorce can split business assets in two and turn a viable business into a struggling one, or the need for your family to move to another town for your spouse's job can dramatically affect your business. So, if you think that a change of this nature is possible, don't be shy to include this in your plan.

When you're thinking about opportunities and threats for your business, you may also want to refer to the industry analysis process earlier in this chapter ('Taking an Eagle–Eye View'). However, keep in mind that opportunities and threats in this context have a different scope than just one particular industry. For example, a global recession or a change in government isn't industry–specific. Or at the other end of the scale, the arrival of a new competitor may be a reflection of a growing population in one geographic region rather than an indication of general industry trends.

TABLE 5-2   **Summarising Opportunities and Threats**

Opportunities	Threats
Analysis for iPhone app development company	
Steady growth in demand	Growth in number of competitors
Opening up of labour market means possibility to hire overseas programmers at lower rates	Offshore labour market means new competition often at very low prices
Some clients willing to sign up for profit-share arrangements in lieu of lower charges	Changes in programming languages mean hard to keep up, especially with small employee base and high cost of training
Lots of government contracts available as government bodies seek to create new apps for community info	Strong trend towards android phones, and expectation from clients for apps to be available for androids as well as iPhones
Analysis for solar panel installation company	
Huge growth in demand	Some serious new competitors with major muscle
Depending on changes in government, potential additional subsidies for consumers	Exclusive distribution licence ends in two years
Schools and government bodies recommended by their own policy to stick with local suppliers	Rapid growth requires high borrowings and puts pressure on cashflow
	If new government, all subsidies could finish

AHEAD OF THE PACK

Keep your mind open to the fact that some things don't fit neatly into boxes as an opportunity or as a threat. Be willing to get creative. Although your analysis of threats and opportunities usually reflects your current position, stay open to new possibilities.

IT'S COOL TO BE GREEN

One overriding long-term global trend that's unlikely to change any time soon is the growth of environmental awareness, and the resultant demand for ecological products and services. Couple this with the growing impacts of climate change, and you end up with a perfect example of something that is both a business opportunity and a business threat.

For those in the 'green' industry (ecological products, alternative energy, environmental consulting and so on) this long-term trend presents an opportunity. For those in industries with high energy demands, particularly those dependent on fossil fuels, this trend is a threat.

Doing a SWOT Analysis

If you've read any other business books or worked in larger organisations, you've probably already heard of a SWOT analysis (**s**trengths, **w**eaknesses, **o**pportunities and **t**hreats). As a model, the SWOT analysis sticks around while other business concepts come and go, simply because this way of looking at things is both easy to understand and surprisingly powerful.

Putting theory into practice

The idea of a SWOT analysis is simple:

>> Aim to build on your strengths but minimise your weaknesses.

>> Endeavour to seize opportunities and counteract threats.

Are you ready to try your own SWOT analysis? Then here goes:

1. **Make a list of the strengths and weaknesses of your business.**

   I explain how to do this earlier in this chapter in 'Putting yourself through the griller'.

2. **Make a list of possible opportunities and threats.**

   Refer to 'Identifying Opportunities and Threats' to find out how.

3. **Draw a grid similar to Figure 5-2.**

4. **Divide your strengths into two categories: Strengths that can help you take advantage of opportunities, and strengths that can help you deal with threats.**

5. **Write down these strengths in the first row of your SWOT grid, along with the related opportunities or threats.**

   Strengths that help realise opportunities go in the top-left. Strengths that could help counteract threats go in the top-right.

6. **In the same manner, divide your weaknesses into two categories: weakness that may hinder you taking advantage of opportunities, and weaknesses that may make threats even more of a threat.**

7. **Write down these weaknesses, as well as the threats, in the second row of your SWOT grid.**

   Weaknesses that hinder opportunities go in the bottom-left; weaknesses that exacerbate threats go in the bottom-right.

Business SWOT Analysis		
	OPPORTUNITIES	**THREATS**
STRENGTHS	*Write strengths that assist with opportunities here, along with a description of the opportunity*	*Write strengths that help counteract threats here, along with a description of the threat*
WEAKNESSES	*Write weaknesses that may hinder you from exploiting opportunities here, along with a description of the opportunity*	*Write weaknesses that may compound threats here, along with a description of the threat*

FIGURE 5-2:
The principles of a SWOT analysis.

Translating your SWOT analysis into action

After you've completed your SWOT analysis (refer to preceding section), what next? Put simply, this grid encapsulates four different business strategies:

>> Aim to exploit any areas where your business is strong and is a good fit for an opportunity.

>> Keep a watchful eye on any areas where your business is strong, but a threat may be looming.

>> Try to improve on any areas where your business is weak but opportunities exist. (For example, you could consider getting extra training, hiring employees with different skills, or employing consultants.)

>> Take pre-emptive action and attempt to get rid of any areas in which your business is weak but a threat is looming.

Figure 5-3 shows a SWOT grid in action, matching the strengths and weaknesses of the iPhone app company in Figure 5-1 with the opportunities and threats identified in Table 5-2.

>> **Top-left corner (where a strength meets an opportunity):** Strong marketing skills (as per Figure 5-1) balance perfectly with strong growth in customer demand, just as the use of domestic employees (rather than offshore employees) make a good fit for growth in government contracts. The business should aim to exploit these strengths.

>> **Top-right corner (where a strength meets a threat):** Strong marketing skills also serve to mitigate the threat of rapidly increasing competition. The business needs to keep a watchful eye on both marketing strategy and new competitors.

>> **Bottom-left corner (where a weakness meets an opportunity):** A significant weakness (identified against technical expertise in Figure 5-1) is that the business only develops apps for the iPhone platform, and not for androids. The business should aim to improve this area of their business, particularly as the android market is a clear opportunity.

>> **Bottom-right corner (where a weakness meets a threat):** The weaknesses in financial management may create problems as downwards pressure in pricing is likely, given growth of overseas developers. This weakness and threat create an unhappy synergy, indicating an area in which the business needs to take action.

Business SWOT Analysis		
	OPPORTUNITIES	**THREATS**
STRENGTHS	*Strong sales and marketing skills, which are perfect for capitalising on huge growth in demand. Use of local (rather than overseas) labour mean we're well placed to secure work from government organisations*	*Strong marketing skills will assist in meeting the challenges of many new competitors*
WEAKNESSES	*Programming skill in only one platform may limit potential, particularly if android phones continue to take market share from iPhones*	*Weaknesses in financial management may leave us exposed as cheap overseas labour puts downward pressure on pricing*

FIGURE 5-3: Plotting business strategy using a SWOT analysis.

Creating a Plan for Change

In some ways, creating a business plan can be very 'bitty'. You've got missions and visions and financials and marketing plans, then industry analysis and more. (I talk about creating a business plan in much more detail in the next chapter.)

Each one feels like a separate topic in its own right, and addressing each area may even require you to use a different mindset or different skills. However, as you delve deeper and deeper into the process, you hopefully find that everything starts connecting.

Right at the beginning of this book, in Chapter 2, I talk about identifying your strategic advantage and analysing how your business compares to the competition. In many ways, the industry analysis and SWOT analysis in this chapter follow a similar process, but provide another layer of clarity regarding what areas in your business to exploit, as well as the weaknesses to guard against.

In your business plan, try to include the following:

>> The issues or problems you face

>> The opportunities that lie ahead

>> A plan of action that outlines how you intend to mitigate your problems and exploit these opportunities

When drawing up a plan of action, try to express this plan in clear goals that are very specific and which have a timeframe. For example, 'A weakness in our business is our limited experience in creating android apps. We will attempt to hire a new employee with these skills within the next three months.' Or another example: 'A clear weakness in my business is the lack of financial skills and also the general lack of attention to my finances. I plan to focus on financial management with an aim to being able to produce and review my own Profit & Loss every month. If this proves too difficult, I will employ a casual bookkeeper.'

REMEMBER

Are you a half-full glass person or a half-empty? Sure, threats may be on the horizon, but do opportunities lie within these threats? As Winston Churchill is widely (although incorrectly) attributed to have said, 'A pessimist sees the difficulty in every opportunity; an optimist sees the opportunity in every difficulty'.

IN THIS CHAPTER

» Finding tools to help you build your business plan

» Examining the world outside and checking out your competitors

» Figuring out your strategies and how you can get the winning edge

» Describing what your business is all about

» Keeping your feet on the ground with financial projections

Chapter **6**

Creating a Business Plan

Deciding where this chapter should appear in this book was tricky. I didn't want this chapter to appear too late in the piece, because creating a business plan should never be an afterthought; rather, it should be a process that you start early on. Nor did I want this chapter to appear too early — if you're browsing this book sequentially, I wanted you to dwell on the bigger strategic questions from Chapters 2 to 5 before getting drawn into the fine details of a written plan.

So, in this chapter, I connect the many interrelated threads from Chapters 2 to 5, recapping how important it is to have a good understanding of your industry and competition. I reiterate the need to define how your business will be different from others and return to asking what kind of future you imagine for your business. These big questions are so important to resolve early on.

This chapter also foreshadows topics that I talk about in later chapters, such as developing marketing plans and creating financial projections. You'll almost certainly need to skip ahead to these chapters before you return here, ready to complete your business plan.

No matter how complicated this sounds, please don't skip this chapter, or close this book with a sigh. It's time to make a plan, and there's no time like the present . . .

Getting Started with Your Plan

In this chapter, I take the following approach to structuring a business plan:

>> **Business description:** Under this main heading, I include subheadings for your mission statement, business profile, and goals and objectives. I cover these elements first in this chapter, in the section 'Charting a True Course'.

>> **Business environment:** Under this main heading, I include subheadings for analysing outside factors and trends, testing the demand for your services, and competitor analysis.

>> **Business strategy:** Under this main heading, I include subheadings for strengths and weaknesses, competitive advantage, choice of strategy, and overviews of marketing plans and people plans.

>> **Marketing plan:** This is where you articulate your marketing plan in greater detail, describe your customers and explain your online strategy.

>> **Your team:** To grow a business, you can't be an island. In this section of your business plan, you get to describe how you'll work with others to achieve success.

>> **Financials:** The headings that I suggest in this section depend on whether your business is up and running or already well established. See 'Presenting Financials', later in this chapter, for more details.

TIP

I suggest you make things easy for yourself by using one of the Word templates available free off the internet, and build your plan from there (see the following section for details). Alternatively, if you're an established business wanting to develop a more complex plan, purchasing business planning software may be the way to go (see the sidebar 'Getting help online' for more details).

REMEMBER

Whatever template you choose, the headings are likely to vary a bit from those I suggest in this chapter. However, in the final wash-up, what's vital is that you tailor your business plan so it reflects the nature and size of your business, and that you incorporate lots of strategy, plenty of marketing and some sensible money stuff. Quite *how* you present this information isn't of paramount importance.

GETTING HELP ONLINE

TIP

One swift way to create your first business plan is to use one of the many tools or templates available online:

- Head to www.business.gov.au for excellent business planning templates, guides and videos. Under Business Information, click Planning and then Business Plans.

- Business Victoria also offers business plan templates, available for free download from its website (www.business.vic.gov.au). To find the template, go to the website and search for 'business plan template'.

- Many of Australia's banks also offer business planning templates. Although these templates may lack sophistication, if you're applying for a loan with a particular bank, using their format may be a good tactic.

- For highly developed industry-specific templates customised for Australia, visit www.maus.com.au and check out their MAUS MasterPlan product.

- International company Bplans, found at www.bplans.com, offers a range of business planning solutions, most of which are payable via a monthly subscription fee. (Bear in mind that this software is pitched exclusively at the American market, and doesn't cater well for things such as GST.)

Because I'm only devoting one chapter to business planning in this book, by necessity I take a fairly simple approach. However, for more detail about the marketing element of your business plan, skip ahead to Chapter 11.

Charting a True Course

In the first section of a business plan, you need to describe your business, along with a mission statement and a brief outline of goals and objectives.

TIP

Sounds easy, but if you're starting a new business, you may prefer to leave this section until you've completed your industry analysis, SWOT analysis and business strategy choice. (See 'Assessing the Environment' and 'Declaring Your Battle Plan', later in this chapter.) Then, you can return to the beginning of your plan and complete this section.

Setting off on your mission

Your business plan needs to start with a simple sentence, or couple of sentences, telling readers what your business is really about. The trick is to encapsulate your *raison d'être* in a few well-chosen words while keeping the bigger picture in mind, kind of like the mission statement shown in Figure 6-1.

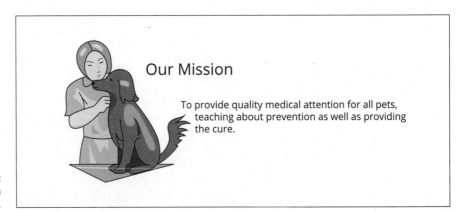

Our Mission

To provide quality medical attention for all pets, teaching about prevention as well as providing the cure.

FIGURE 6-1: A mission statement.

No-one but you can come up with a mission statement that truly fits your business. You may have to sweat over it for some days, discuss options with colleagues and business partners, or mull over possibilities for hours while lying on the beach (someone's got to do it — I recommend Fraser Island in Queensland). Don't be tempted to write too much — if your mission statement is more than two sentences long, ditch it and begin again. And try to create a mission with the potential to inspire and motivate others (unlike my brother's first stab at his mission statement, which read 'Make heaps of money in the shortest possible time').

If you run short on ideas, try checking out the missions of other businesses similar to your own. Go to your favourite search engine and type the words **mission statement** plus a word to cover whatever line of business you're in (for example, type: **mission statement plumbers**).

REMEMBER

After you complete your mission statement, don't hesitate to use it to inspire you, your staff and your customers — all at once. Include your mission statement on the home page of your website and incorporate it into your advertising and other business documents.

Some business planning consultants talk about creating *vision statements* as well as mission statements. In this context, a vision statement encapsulates longer-term goals and aspirations, along with the ideals that a business is striving for. A mission statement is more about stating what you do, why you do it and who you do it for. I find that the boundaries between these two kinds of statements get blurred. If you're just starting out in business, a simple mission statement does just fine.

Saying what you're about

After writing your mission statement, map out your business profile: The bit that describes who you are and what you do. Although this description need only be three or four paragraphs long, it should include information such as

>> **How long your business has been running:** If your business has been running for some considerable time, say so. Be proud of your accomplishment.

>> **The kind of services your business provides:** Be specific here. If you're a physiotherapist, say what your area of speciality is and who your customers are. If you're a consultant hydro-geologist, explain what it is you do and what this activity involves.

>> **The kind of industry your business belongs to:** Talk about your particular industry, what the trends are and what factors are peculiar to it.

>> **Your key strengths:** Refer to Chapter 5 for ideas on this topic.

>> **Your business strategy:** I'm hoping that you've already chosen a business strategy of some kind — if not, refer to 'Choosing a strategy' later in this chapter, for more details.

Matching goals to your mission

The next section of your business plan lists your business goals and objectives, and aims to back up your mission statement and business profile.

If you find the distinction between a goal and an objective is a little fuzzy, think of a *goal* as the overarching aim of the game and the corresponding *objective* as the means by which you get there. The main thing is to remember that the best goals are always SMART: **s**pecific, **m**easurable, **a**chievable, **r**ealistic and **t**ime-specific.

REMEMBER

Goals and objectives are quite different from dreams and hopes. A good example of this distinction is a business plan I came across that proposed to open a gift shop in a country town. The plan was fine, except that one of the owner's proposed objectives was then to open an additional outlet every six months until a chain of 50 stores was established. Dream on.

Here are some ideas about objectives and how to keep 'em real:

MONEY STUFF

>> **Profit objectives:** Decide how much you want to make, and by when. Your objective might be to make $4,000 net profit every month, increasing to $5,000 a month by the end of the next financial year.

>> **Sales objectives:** Say how much you want sales to grow by. For example: 'We aim to increase sales by 20 per cent on last financial year.' Don't forget to add how you hope to achieve this result and why — logically — you think this growth is possible.

>> **Service objectives:** Express customer service in a way you can measure. You may aim 'to answer all email enquiries or phone messages within two hours', or 'to provide a same-day pick-up and delivery service, six days a week'.

>> **Product objectives:** Define product objectives in terms of price, supply, range or availability. A product objective might be 'to source cheaper prices for at least 10 per cent of products' or 'to expand the range of products available, adding one new stock line every three months'.

>> **Marketing objectives:** Say what kind of customers you want to reach and how many — for example, 'to expand our customer listing from 150 to 200 by the end of June'. Remember to include how you plan to achieve this outcome.

Assessing the Environment

After the 'Business Description' section of your business plan, the next section is where you justify — either to yourself, to prospective lenders or prospective investors — why your proposed business is such a great idea. Or, if your business is already up and running, you explain why your existing business is such a winner and, hopefully, why external trends make it a sure bet in the long term. I like to put this section under the heading of 'Business Environment' in my business plans.

If you haven't started your business yet, you may find that this stage of the business planning process makes you change tack. This change could involve deciding to focus more on web sales, or to open up in a more mainstream location, to change pricing structures or even to ditch the idea completely. Don't be perturbed if this change means returning to the beginning of your plan and starting again. This willingness to be open to objective feedback is part of what the business planning process is all about.

Analysing outside influences

I talk lots about analysing outside influences in Chapter 5, where I explain how to do a PESTEL analysis for your industry, and how to analyse opportunities and threats.

Head back to Chapter 5 to see an example (albeit a very simple one) of how this analysis might look. You don't need to go overboard here, but I reckon it's great if you can dedicate one full A4 page to this analysis process. Remember that you want to foreshadow not only industry trends that could impact your business, but also the likely consequences of these.

Checking out the competition

In Chapter 2, I explain how to conduct a competitor analysis. This forms an essential part of any business plan. Again, one full page of competitor analysis is usually enough for a business plan, and you're best to summarise this in a simple table format.

Remember to include not only current competitors but competitors who could appear in the near future also, particularly in response to changes in technology. Rate yourself against these competitors and clarify why your business is going to have a competitive edge.

Justifying market demand

The next part of the Business Environment section of your business plan needs to include some kind of market analysis. If you're starting a new business, you need to think about who your customers are going to be. If yours is an existing business, you must define who your customers are. Are the numbers of potential customers growing or declining? (Customers wanting home-delivered meals are an example of a growing market; those wanting home-delivered newspapers are a declining market.)

If you're just getting started, a good way of presenting this part of your business plan is to (if possible) test your business idea on a small scale first. This approach lets you get a feeling for the demand for the products or services that you plan to sell. After all, without customer demand, your business doesn't stand a chance.

TRUE STORY

A friend of mine had an idea to start a business selling alternative cleaning products. She decided to test this idea by running a stall once a week outside the local health food store. The response seemed good at first, but she soon found that people were reluctant to pay the extra dollars for her products, and that the low sales generated were barely enough to pay for her time, let alone the costs of renting the stall. The result was that she decided not to pursue this business idea, but to explore other ways of making money instead.

In Chapter 3, I talk about the pros and cons of buying a business versus starting a business from scratch. Certainly, one benefit of buying an established business is that demand for the product or service is already established.

Declaring Your Battle Plan

The third section of your business plan goes under the heading 'Business Strategy' and goes into detail about what it is that *your* business has to offer. What are your strengths and capabilities, what are your weaknesses? What advantages do you have over your competitors, and how do you plan to capitalise on these? How can you match your strengths against industry opportunities, and how should you guard against industry threats, especially in areas where you have weaknesses?

Building your SWOT analysis

I explain how to analyse strengths, weaknesses, opportunities and threats in Chapter 5, along with the importance of considering these elements in your plan. You can present this information by using a simple table with Opportunities and Threats listed in columns, and matched against the row headings of Strengths and Opportunities.

Don't just list these elements, but use your plan to outline what actions you intend to take. Chapter 5 explains the importance of capitalising on opportunities in areas in which you have strengths, and minimising threats in areas where you are weak. For example, if a threat exists in an area where you have weaknesses (maybe you're often exposed to currency rate fluctuations and you're terrible with figures), use your plan to explain how you will act to eliminate this threat (for example, by hiring an external consultant to help in this area).

Choosing a strategy

In Chapter 2, I explain that any business, including yours, is faced with three possible competitive strategies: You can aim to be the cheapest, you can develop a clear point of difference that capitalises on your skills, or you can focus on a specific niche or market segment. I warn against trying to be all things to all people:

You don't want to get 'stuck in the middle', where neither you nor your customers are quite sure what your business is all about.

Your chosen strategy needs to make sense when considered alongside your SWOT analysis. For example, if you have unique skills in marketing and you can also identify a particular niche that's likely to grow quickly, choosing a strategy of focusing on this narrow segment makes good sense.

Expressing your competitive advantage

Competitors again? Yes, I know that I suggest that the previous section of your business plan includes an analysis of your competitors, but in this section you want to explain how you're going to fight your way into the mob.

To do this, you need to define your competitive advantage. What do you have over the competition? Where does this advantage stem from? Why should customers choose your business when other competitors in the industry offer similar stuff? In particular, think of capabilities within your business that are hard for others to copy. These capabilities tend to be a unique blend of assets, knowledge, people networks, skills or technology.

I explain competitive advantage in much more detail in Chapter 2.

Outlining Your Marketing Plan

Marketing plans do tend to vary substantially depending on the size and nature of your business. However, when you write a marketing plan with the intent that it form just one part of an overall business plan, you want to stick to the big picture. Usually a couple of pages is sufficient.

Developing your marketing plan

Key headings for your marketing plan include branding strategy, marketing objectives, and marketing strategies. I talk more about all of these elements in Chapter 11.

REMEMBER

Don't be put off by how corporate the words 'branding strategy' sound. The very process of creating a brand for your business is the glue that unites all your business plan elements. Creating your logo, colour scheme and marketing taglines requires you to be super clear and articulate about your point of difference, competitive strategies and the kind of customers you're after.

Once you've outlined your branding strategy, proceed to your marketing objectives and strategies. Remember to be super specific about how you will achieve market growth, and the cost of doing so, and stick to a timeframe of the next 12 months. Marketing objectives are the same as any other business goals and objectives and again need to be SMART (refer to the section 'Matching goals to your mission', earlier in this chapter).

MONEY STUFF

Mention how your pricing fits into the big picture of your marketing strategy and, if you plan to modify pricing in any way, say how you intend to do it.

Defining your customers

Any marketing plan needs to include some form of customer analysis. As I explain in Chapter 11, you can analyse customers and define target markets in many ways. However, one thing that often works well in a business plan is a high-level analysis where you describe your target market according to age, sex, occupation, interests and so on. For each of these demographics, you then describe what benefits the business offers. (*Remember:* Think of benefits from the perspective of the customer, not from your perspective!)

Table 6-1 shows a simple customer analysis for a business offering personal training services. This analysis focuses on the 'average' customer, but a more detailed analysis would identify other key customer segments, and what benefits are offered to them.

TABLE 6-1   **Customer Analysis — Fit and Fun Personal Training**

Description	Analysis	Benefits Offered
Age	Primarily 25–40	Sense of belonging (trainers belong to same age group as clients)
Gender	Female	Emphasis on building trust and friendships
Occupation	Mostly professionals	Flexible hours, combination of online and in-person services
Income	Varied	Range of rates to match needs, from one-on-one sessions to group sessions
Location	City	In the CBD, with access to both gym and park spaces
Attitude	Fun and light-hearted	Humour and offering a place to laugh is an essential part of the brand

Articulating your online business strategy

Your online presence needs to be an integral part of your business and an essential part of your brand. If your business is exclusively online, you may not need a separate heading within your marketing plan that addresses online strategies. However, if your plan is for a 'bricks and mortar' business, or a business that delivers services to local clients, then you almost certainly want to devote some of your plan to articulating your online strategy.

How can you use your online presence to develop unique markets on behalf of your business, or become an income stream in its own right? Imagine a local electrician just setting out in business. You may find it hard to think how an electrician could justify creating an online business strategy. However, imagine that the electrician decides to specialise in solar installations, and builds a website with this in mind. His site includes lots of information about choosing solar panels, installation costs, government rebates and feed-in tariffs. He runs a question-and-answer service via his blog and offers online quotes using Google Earth to view the rooflines of prospective customers' homes. His website is integral to his business model and, before long, he's the locally acknowledged expert in this area.

Similarly, imagine a dentist who wants to focus on families and young people. She uses her Facebook page to include lots of information about dental hygiene and preventive care, adding links to simple games and dental health quizzes aimed specifically at children. She also offers an appointment calendar on her website so that busy parents can browse availability and pick the most suitable appointment times.

REMEMBER

Your business plan needs to specify what part your online presence is going to play in your overall business strategy. Your online presence can take many forms, such as a traditional website, a Facebook page or a virtual shopfront on eBay. For more information, skip to Chapter 11, which explores developing a marketing plan in detail.

Describing Your Dream Team

In Chapter 4, I suggest you explore the vision you have for your business. Perhaps you hope to make your first million within five years, or perhaps you're content to run a modest business from home that helps maintain your work/life balance. Of course, either of these paths, as well as everything in between, is just fine. However, if you plan to scale up your business to be anything other than a small home-based enterprise, the key to your plan is the question of how you will build your team.

When considering this aspect of your plan, make sure to include the following:

>> **Desirable skills:** Consider where your existing skill set may be lacking —
particularly relevant if you're a one- or two-person operation — and how you
intend to compensate for this gap (for example, with extra training or by using
subcontractors or consultants).

>> **Existing skills:** Describe the existing skills of yourself and your employees.

>> **Recruitment policies:** Consider your recruitment policies — state the basis
on which you intend to select your staff, and what you can do to make sure
the selection process is as successful as possible.

>> **Roles and responsibilities:** Describe the roles, responsibilities and skills of
existing staff and key subcontractors.

Presenting Financials

The presentation of this part of your plan depends on whether you're just starting
a new business or whether your business is already up and running.

Balancing dreams against reality

So, you're starting up a new business? Your job is to balance dreams against reality, keeping your feet firmly on the ground. As a minimum, I recommend that
your business plan includes the following:

**MONEY
STUFF**

>> **A breakdown of start-up expenses:** Skip to Chapter 15 for a checklist of
start-up expenses to make sure you have everything covered.

>> **Projections for sales for first 12 months:** Try to provide as much detail as
you can with these projections, demonstrating the logic you use to arrive at
the totals. I talk more about sales projections in Chapter 9.

>> **Calculation of break-even point:** Skip to Chapter 10 for more details about
how to calculate break-even.

>> **Projected expenses for next 12 months:** Remember, things always cost far
more than you expect! Use one of the templates I refer to earlier in this
chapter (in the section 'Getting Started with Your Plan') to present this
information.

>> **Projected profitability:** Combine projected sales and expenses to arrive at a
month-by-month projection for net profit for the next 12 months.

>> **Finance details:** Include details about how you intend to finance the set-up expenses for this business. If you anticipate making a loss in the first 12 months, indicate how you intend to finance this loss.

REMEMBER

Although I like to keep business and personal expenses separate, you still need some kind of plan about how you're going to survive while the business is getting established. For this reason, I suggest you also create a personal budget. (Of course, you may choose to keep this budget for your information only, and not share it with any prospective investors.)

Building on history to create a picture of the future

If your business is already up and running, the financial information within your business plan needs to include a combination of historical financial information as well as projections for the years to come. Here's what I recommend you include:

MONEY STUFF

>> **Profit & Loss reports for the last three years:** Or, if you haven't been in business that long, include the Profit & Loss reports for as far back as you can.

>> **Your most recent Balance Sheet:** Chapter 17 looks at the ongoing importance of your Balance Sheet report in terms of what you own and what you owe.

>> **A graph of sales trends:** I'm assuming here that your trends are positive. If they aren't, and you're using this plan to go for a bank loan, you may want to skip this bit!

>> **Calculation of break-even point:** Skip to Chapter 8 for more details about how to calculate break-even.

>> **A budget of income and expenses for the next 12 months:** Skip to Chapter 17 for more about creating budgets.

>> **A cashflow projection if you have substantial stock holdings, debtors or creditors:** For example, if you import goods from overseas and pay for them several months later, your cash position is going to vary significantly from your budget position. Skip to Chapter 17 for more about cash flows.

MONEY STUFF

If you intend to use this business plan in order to apply for a loan, get your accountant to look through your financials before you present them to the bank.

Staying real with benchmarks

In order to stay honest with financial projections, especially if you haven't started your business yet, a good strategy is to find out how similar businesses are faring. For example, if you want to start a cafe, find out what an average cafe spends on wages as a percentage of turnover, or how much average profit it makes each year.

You can find out how other businesses in your industry are faring by using something called *business benchmarking*. Here are some ways to look for this info:

TIP

» The ATO supplies many core business benchmark ratios for free. Go to `www.ato.gov.au/Business/Small-business-benchmarks` and search for your industry. (And now for a bonus tip: These benchmarks are what the ATO use to identify businesses as audit targets, so if the financial results of your existing business fall far outside of these benchmarks, beware!)

» Ask your accountant whether they subscribe to a benchmark service.

» Visit `www.benchmarking.com.au`. This service isn't cheap, but the benchmark reports are very useful and highly detailed.

TRUE STORY

A client of mine had been struggling for many years with his general store, eking out a living and working long, hard hours. At my suggestion, he purchased a set of 'Corner Store/Mixed Business' benchmarks and he realised that his gross profit was far too low when compared to successful general stores, and his wages were too high. He installed a point-of-sale system, revamped his pricing and restructured wages (legally), and soon his business was looking much, much healthier.

IN THIS CHAPTER

» Choosing a legal structure to fit your business

» Naming your 'baby'

» Protecting your name and your brand

» Complying with all the rules and regulations

» Understanding and negotiating contracts

» Signing up for a lease that's fair

Chapter **7**

Getting the Legals Right

D eep down, I'm a bit of an anarchist. Sometimes I wish you could start a new business just by putting up a sign and pocketing the cash each day. Employment law? A daily rate that's agreed upon with a simple handshake. Health and hygiene? A good mop of the floor at the end of each day.

However, when I stop being so cantankerous, I acknowledge that the law has a vital role to play. The law influences lots of decisions when you first start up a business, such as the best legal structure to choose, what name to trade under, how to build and protect your brand, what taxes you're liable for and much more.

Although these legalities may seem onerous and time-consuming, I suggest you don a different mindset and think of them as your armour, providing you with the vital protection you need before setting off into battle.

Picking a Business Structure

Choosing a legal structure that best serves your business is a complex but very important decision. Depending on the nature and size of your business, choosing one structure over another may minimise legal liability, save significant tax dollars, provide flexibility in the event of ownership changes, and even maximise the eventual sale price of your business.

The three main structures to choose from are sole trader, partnership or private company. (Other less common structures include cooperatives, limited partnerships and trusts.)

As you can see from Table 7-1, every business structure has both advantages and disadvantages. While this table provides initial guidance, you're best to talk to your accountant or solicitor about what structure is going to work best for you.

TABLE 7-1   **Summary of Different Business Structures**

	Sole Trader	Partnership	Private Company
Description	A single person who controls and owns the business.	Two people or more, sharing profits in agreed proportions.	A legal entity in its own right. The owners are the shareholders (often husband and wife teams).
Advantages	Simple and quick to set up or to close down.	Benefits from combining your skills and capital with that of others. With care, tax can be minimised, especially with family partnerships.	Directors aren't normally liable for debts unless they've given a personal guarantee or have acted negligently. Flexible in managing tax (the company pays tax on profits and the shareholders then receive dividends on surplus profit). Tax losses can (generally) be carried forward.
Disadvantages	Owner is personally liable for all debts. Few options to minimise tax.	When they don't work out, partnerships can become very acrimonious. All partners are personally liable for all debts, regardless of their partnership equity, and regardless of who incurred the debt.	Higher ongoing compliance costs and more complex reporting obligations.

	Sole Trader	Partnership	Private Company
Establishment costs	Minimal.	Varies; the biggest cost is usually legal fees incurred in drawing up a partnership agreement.	Depends on complexity of the venture; ask your accountant for an estimate.
Ongoing costs	Normal accounting fees plus periodic renewal of business name.	Normal accounting fees plus periodic renewal of business name.	Higher accounting fees plus annual review fee.

Independent and single

The simplest business structure is that of *sole trader*. When you're a sole trader, the business becomes an extension of yourself. You can register a business name if you want to; otherwise, you can keep everything simple and simply trade under your own name.

The cool thing about being a sole trader, especially if you're operating from home and not employing anyone, is that complying with government requirements is mercifully easy. The only essential step before you start operating as a sole trader is to register for an *ABN* (short for *Australian Business Number*) — a unique identifying number that you use when dealing with other businesses. Of course, you may need to register for other taxes or permits as well, depending on the nature and size of your business.

REMEMBER

If you want to trade under a business name other than your own, you have some homework to do first. Skip to 'Making sure you're not on someone else's patch', later in this chapter, to find out more.

Tea for two

Another possible structure for your business is to become a *partnership*. You can form a partnership with anyone you like, whether your spouse, de facto, best friend, mother, business colleague or second cousin twice removed. You can even go into partnership with more than one person. Large legal firms may have 20 or 30 partners, all working together.

Partnerships work well as a legal structure for many thousands of Australian businesses. However, I suggest that you note the following comments about partnerships before moving on:

>> A partnership is a legal structure in its own right and requires its own Tax File Number and ABN.

>> Partnership agreements are essential, even if the partnership consists of you and your one and only true love. (I know you may feel that true love lasts forever, but statistics cast cruel light on this presumption.) A standard partnership agreement covers lots of vital issues such as how the profit is divvied up, the roles and responsibilities of each partner, how disputes should be resolved, and what happens if one of the partners wants to leave or dies.

MONEY STUFF

>> When it comes to business partnerships between married or de facto couples, be aware that how you split the profits should be an accurate reflection of who has done the work. For example, if you're slaving away on the farm most days while your partner swans around on a boat in Tahiti, you can't minimise your tax by allocating 50 per cent of the profit to your partner.

WARNING

>> If you're already having communication difficulties with a prospective business partner, I suggest you hesitate before going into partnership together. Business partnerships tend to magnify any residual conflicts or personality clashes that exist between people, and when a partnership fails, the fallout can make an acrimonious divorce look like a picnic.

We've got company

The *private company* is one of the most common business structures. When I talk about private companies, I mean those where individuals have their own company with their own shareholders and directors, instead of being listed on the stock exchange.

Probably the most significant benefit of a company is that it has *limited liability*. For example, if you own a building company and a customer sues your company for damages because a wall collapsed in one of the houses that you built, only the company is liable, not you. The only exception to this limited liability arises if you give a personal guarantee on anything (banks often ask for personal guarantees from directors on loans), if it can be clearly proven that you were personally negligent in your actions, that you were otherwise in breach of the law, or if you trade while knowingly insolvent.

TECHNICAL STUFF

Whether a company structure can help you minimise tax depends on current company tax rates, personal tax rates, whether the business is likely to have losses that might be carried forward to future years, and how much money you earn. You're best to ask your accountant about the effect a company structure may have on your tax bill.

Be aware that the legal structure of a company is more complex than a partnership or sole trader structure, and is almost always more expensive in terms of ongoing accounting fees.

Matching the Name to the Game

I remember spending weeks agonising over names for my first son, finally registering his birth on the last possible day. I found our shortlist the other day, written on the back of a hospital sick bag, and laughed aloud at some of the names we considered.

Picking names isn't easy, and the choice of a name no doubt influences the perceptions of others. In the same way, your business name creates its own personality, and is the first point of contact between you and your customers.

Here's the lowdown on the different kinds of business names:

>> **Domain names:** If you want to have your business name as part of a website address, you need to check the availability of and register a *domain name*. For example, if your proposed business name is Red Rubies, a likely domain name is www.redrubies.com.

>> **Business names:** All companies, as well as all sole traders or partnerships not trading under their own name(s), must register their business name with the Australian Securities and Investments Commission (ASIC) (see 'Registering your business name', later in this chapter, for details). For companies, if you intend to trade using a different name from your company name (for example, maybe you want to trade with your company name but without the words 'Pty Ltd' at the end), you also need to register this name as a business name.

>> **Trademarks:** If you want to buy exclusive legal rights to your business name, you must register a *trademark* with IP Australia. Skip to 'Protecting Your Brand', later in this chapter, to find out more.

Using your own name

If you don't want a whiz-bang new business name and you're quite content to trade under your own name — you know, the one your parents gave you — then, as a sole trader, you can do so quite legally. For example, if I decide to start a lawn mowing business and generate invoices that simply say *Veechi Curtis* with my address at the top, I don't need to register 'Veechi Curtis' as a business name. On the other hand, if I want to call my business 'Veechi Curtis Mowing Services', I do have to register the business name.

TIP

The only time you have to register your own name as a business name is if you're going into business with a partner and you're not intending to use both your first name and your surname. For example, if Hamish McTavish and Fergus McSween go into partnership together and want to call their business 'McTavish & McSween', they have to register this name.

Thinking about how others will find you

Before you go too far with choosing a business name, think about how your customers are going to find you and whether you want to reflect key search terms in your business name itself.

TIP

Imagine you have a holiday house in Narooma called 'Beach Daze'. Sure, you could register www.beachdaze.com.au as the domain name. However, how often do people search on the term **beach daze** when looking for holiday accommodation? Likely never. You're much better having a domain name, and probably also a business name, such as www.beachhouse-narooma.com.au or www.narooma-holidays.com.au.

Another example may help. Imagine your name is Rick Dark and you're a dentist in Sydney. Do you think www.rickdark.com.au would be a good domain name? No. Instead, look for domain names such as www.sydney-dentist.com.au or www.dentist.com.au or www.affordable-dentist.com.au. Depending on what domain names are available and what best suits your business, you may consider registering a business name to match.

Researching domain name availability is straightforward: Simply go to the website of a company that offers domain name registrations to see if the name you want is available. (Crazy Domains at www.crazydomains.com.au is a good bet, I find.) Registering a domain name costs peanuts, and if you're not sure which direction your new business is heading, go the whole hog and register a few.

Making sure you're not on someone else's patch

To check the availability of a name, either for a business or for a company, go to www.asic.gov.au and enter your proposed business name in the business names register. (I'm assuming you've already done your homework and you've looked at what domain names are available, so that you can get a business website with a name close to that of your business.) Figure 7-1 shows what comes up if you search on the availability of the business name 'Silk Road Fabrics'. Note that the national business names register no longer differentiates between company names and sole trader names; all business names now have equal status.

Checking for trademarks

So, you reckon the name you're after is available? Your work isn't over yet. The next step is to double-check that this name, or any part of this name, isn't a registered trademark. For example, referring to my proposed business name of 'Silk Road Fabrics' from earlier in this chapter, I can have a look at what trademarks are registered against the words 'Silk Road'.

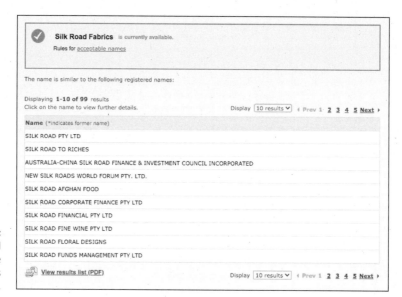

FIGURE 7-1:
Digging around for names in the ASIC business names register.

REMEMBER

Head to IP Australia at www.ipaustralia.gov.au, go to Search Trade Marks under the Trade Marks tab, and search for the words that you're considering as part of your business name. Remember to explore different versions and spellings of the business name you're considering.

Figure 7-2 shows some of my search results for the phrase 'Silk Road'. Fortunately, this phrase having a few registered trademarks against it doesn't necessarily mean I can't use 'Silk Road Fabrics' as a business name. Click on the details of any trademark and you will see that each trademark only applies for a specific class — for example, 'gaming machines', 'frozen and dry meals' and other surprisingly obscure categories. If no trademark is registered against the class in which I propose to trade, I may still be okay to register my proposed business name.

WARNING

While looking up a prospective business name on the IP Australia Trade Mark Search may provide you initial reassurance that your proposed name is available, the only way to guarantee your future ownership of this name is to register a trademark of your own. See 'Protecting Your Brand' later in this chapter.

Registering your business name

If you don't already have an ABN, you can apply for an ABN and register your business name at the same time via the federal government's Business Registration Service at register.business.gov.au. If you already have an ABN and now you wish to register a business name, go to the Australian Securities and Investments Commission (ASIC) website at www.asic.gov.au.

#	Number	Image	Words	Status	Owner	Class
Search criteria:	Silk Road					
1	845722	Silk Road	SILK ROAD	Registered Expired renewal possible	Endeavour Interiors Pty Ltd	18, 20, 25
2	878248		SILK ROAD	Registered Registered/protected	Aristocrat Technologies Australia Pty Ltd	9
3	1144819		SILK ROAD	Registered Registered/protected	Ronald Brown	33
4	1342319		SILK ROAD	Registered Registered/protected	PUNJ INTERNATIONAL PTY LTD as trustee for PUNJ I.P. TRUST	16, 29, 30, 43

FIGURE 7-2:
Check the
Australian Trade
Mark Search for
relevant
trademarks.

WARNING

Registration of a business or company name doesn't provide full ownership of that name — only a trademark can give you that kind of protection. For more details, see the section 'Registering trademarks', later in this chapter.

Avoiding trouble

When you go to register a business name, a few names are no-go areas:

>> **Names that include restricted words:** For example, a business name that includes the word 'ANZAC' is only allowed if you're given special approval.

>> **Names that are too similar to another name:** You're not allowed to register a name that is too similar to another business name. So, if you want to register a business called Dynamic Plumbing Services, and someone else in the same locality is already called Dynamic Plumbing, your application is likely to be rejected.

>> **Names that are offensive:** Four-letter words, rude words, insults, racist names or words that promote drugs aren't cool. So, to call your new restaurant, 'You Eat, You S**t, You Die', probably isn't okay.

Protecting Your Brand

Your brand is likely to be one of the biggest assets in your business, and for this reason, you want to make sure that nobody else can damage, threaten or steal it from you. Remember that your brand is much more than your business name and can also include your logo, tagline, the names of the products or services you sell, the colour scheme or your marketing, and many other things besides.

Registering trademarks

In years gone by, registering trademarks for business names or products was typically the domain of larger businesses. However, the rise of social media and global communications means that trademark protection is increasingly important for smaller businesses, too.

The only sure way to protect the name of your business, your logo, or even the names of the products and services that you sell, is to register trademarks for each one. (*Note:* You can't trademark a product or a process; rather, you can only trademark the name of the product or process. See the section 'Protecting other kinds of intellectual property' for more on protecting products and processes.)

At first, registering a trademark seems like a straightforward process. As I explain earlier in this chapter in 'Checking for trademarks', the IP Australia Trade Mark service is relatively easy to navigate. Friends may even tell you that they managed to register a trademark in a matter of minutes and for nominal expense.

Dig a little deeper, however, and you find that registering trademarks is a process that requires a certain level of experience — whether it's understanding the different classes that a trademark can be registered under, or knowing how to search for different permutations of names or how to navigate the international implications of trademark registration. (Trademarks are typically only registered for one country at a time.) Even the most seasoned corporates can make mistakes with trademark registrations, as the American franchise Burger King famously discovered when they went to expand their chain into Australia and found the name to be already taken. (Thereby explaining the origin of the Hungry Jacks chain.)

In summary, I suggest that if you have a unique business or product name that's central to your brand, seek legal advice about how best to register a trademark.

TRUE
STORY

UGH! AMERICAN BOOTS MADE IN CHINA

One of the more interesting trademark cases in Australia concerns the beloved sheep-skin boot, the ugg boot. Way back in 1971, an Aussie ugg boot manufacturer registered the term 'ugh-boot' as a trademark, and then much later onsold this trademark to an American company. In 2003, this American company started a campaign of legal action against any Australian manufacturers who were using the terms 'ugg boots', 'ugh-boots' or 'ugh boots' to describe their goods. Ironically, this American company's ugh boots were made in China, despite being sold as 'Australian UGGs', and the Australian manu-facturers under threat were selling products that were truly Australian-made.

You can check out the full story online, a chilling example of the importance of protect-ing your brand and your intellectual property.

Protecting other kinds of intellectual property

Words, phrases, sounds, shapes, logos, pictures or a combination of these things can be protected by trademarks. However, these elements aren't the only examples of intellectual property. Intellectual property may also include the following:

>> Circuit layout rights for the 3D configuration of electronic circuits

>> Confidentiality and trade secrets such as the secret recipe for KFC's chicken

>> Copyright for original material in literary, artistic, dramatic or musical works, films, broadcasts, multimedia and computer programs

>> Designs for the shape or appearance of manufactured goods, such as an innovative design of pizza box

>> Patents for new or improved products or processes that are both inventive and useful (registering a patent means you can protect your invention so that only you have the right to make money out of it)

>> Plant breeder rights for new plant varieties

WARNING

In many instances, creating intellectual property doesn't mean you own the rights to it. With the exception of copyright and circuit layout rights, which are auto-matic, in order to own the rights to intellectual property, you have to register it. In addition, you may wish to seek legal advice regarding confidentiality clauses in your staff contracts.

Registering with the Powers That Be

Every business operates within a certain legal environment. The most relevant competition and consumer protection legislation is the Competition and Consumer Act (CCA), which covers unfair market prices, product safety, product labelling and price monitoring. In addition, each state and territory has its own fair trading or consumer laws that provide additional consumer protections, such as the NSW Fair Trading Act or the Australian Consumer Law (Tasmania) Act.

Other legislation specific to small business includes the state Acts relating to business licensing and stamp duties, the *Corporations Act 2001 (Cwth)*, and myriad workplace safety, employment and environmental legislation.

Thankfully, you don't need a law degree in order to go into business. In this section, I explain how to sign up for taxes, verify what licences you need and, if necessary, apply for planning permission.

Getting that baby's number

Every single business has to have its own ABN. Even if your business is relatively small — maybe you offer gardening services, dressmaking or live entertainment — in order to operate as a business, you need an ABN. The only exception to this rule is if you're doing something as a hobby. The easiest way to apply for an ABN is to go to `register.business.gov.au` and follow the prompts to register.

Signing up for taxes (unavoidable, I'm afraid)

Depending on your situation, you may also need to consider a couple of other taxes such as GST and employee withholding tax.

The government makes it really easy to sign up for GST and PAYG (PAYG stands for Pay As You Go and refers to the tax you deduct from employees' wages). All you have to do is tick the boxes for both GST and PAYG when completing your application for an ABN (refer to the previous section for details).

TIP

For most businesses, registering for GST is optional if your turnover is less than $75,000 a year. For more about the pros and cons of registering for GST, skip ahead to Chapter 18.

REMEMBER

Being an employer is a serious business, and doesn't just involve registering as a withholder of PAYG tax. Other considerations include superannuation, workers compensation insurance, industrial awards, and occupational health and safety. For the lowdown on becoming an employer, head to Chapter 13.

Checking out what else you need

Sometimes I feel a pang of envy for those countries where permits and licences are few, and those that do exist can be purchased for a handsome bribe.

Typical business controls include licences, permits, approvals, registrations, codes of practice, standards, guidelines and much more. Some licences are obvious: If you want to start trading as an electrician, you're gonna need a sparky's licence. Some are less so: Did you know that you need a special permit if you start a wedding photography business and want to take photos of the bride and groom in a national park? Or that you will require a Background Music Licence if you plan to play the radio in your cafe?

The best one-stop shop is the Australian Business Licence and Information Service (ABLIS) website at ablis.business.gov.au. After asking a few questions, this website provides a customised list of all the licences, permits and regulations relevant to your business.

REMEMBER

Planning law is another important point to consider. For example, if you take out a retail lease in a shopping precinct, just because a similar shop was there before you doesn't mean you don't need to apply for planning permission. Making contact with the planning department at your local council, and completing whatever forms they require, is vital.

Another common question from people starting out in business is whether they're allowed to run their business from home. The answer to this question depends on the attitude of the local council. Some councils are quite reasonable; others behave as if they're the rulers of a galaxy in a science fiction movie.

Whether or not you're allowed to run a business from home depends on the type of business you're conducting, where your house is within the locality and your council's particular regulations — think *zoning laws*. A business that has heaps of large deliveries coming and going, generates a lot of noise (oh, what a shame about your firework-testing business), or has more than one employee, definitely needs to apply for council permission. However, if all you intend to do is sit at your computer and make the odd phone call, applying to council for permission is probably not required.

Working with Contracts

When you're in business, you probably participate in contracts more often than you realise. A contract doesn't always entail a formal document such as a retail lease or partnership agreement, but can be as simple as a supplier invoice, a straightforward credit application form or a verbal order placed with a supplier for goods.

The essentials to working with contracts include understanding when you're legally bound, dealing with standard form contracts, using contracts wisely to protect yourself against risk, and knowing what to look for in a contract. Guess what? That's what the rest of this chapter is all about.

Understanding when you're legally bound

For an agreement to be regarded as a contract, it must contain four essential ingredients:

>> An offer of some description must be made.

>> Acceptance must be given. (***Note:*** An agreement doesn't have to be in writing in order to be a contract. An agreement can also be verbal or a combination of both written and verbal elements.)

>> The reasonable expectation that if the agreement is breached, legal consequences could eventuate.

>> Some consideration (for example, payment of money) must change hands or be due to change hands as part of the agreement.

In everyday business, you engage in contracts with employees, business partners, suppliers and customers. In order to minimise risk in your business, I recommend you ensure that these agreements are kept up to date. In particular, take care to secure written agreements wherever the possibility of liability, poor performance or even confusion could arise. For example:

>> An adventure company gets its clients to sign a standard form where each of the clients acknowledges they're undertaking a risky activity and that they're not going to hold the adventure company liable should an accident occur (so long as the adventure company takes all reasonable care).

>> A website designer gets all customers to sign off on quotes before proceeding.

>> A hardware store offering credit to customers makes sure it receives an authorised signature every time account customers purchase goods.

>> A retail store sends purchase orders to suppliers with a specific delivery date, saying that if goods aren't delivered by that date, the order is cancelled.

AHEAD OF THE PACK

Think about your business and the kind of contracts you participate in every day. For example:

>> Do you need to review the terms and conditions on the quotes or invoices that you send to customers?

>> Do you charge interest on late payments and, if so, do your conditions comply with the law?

>> Are you aware of the terms and conditions that your suppliers impose when you place orders with them?

>> Do you have confidentiality agreements and appropriate restraint of trade agreements in place with your employees?

>> Does your company have any loans to directors, or loans from directors, or loans from other investors? If so, do you have formal loan agreements in place?

Dealing with standard form contracts

Standard form contracts are pre-prepared contracts where all the terms have already been set, such as standard finance documents, insurance contracts, retail leases or credit application forms. Usually, you have little or no opportunity to negotiate any of the terms in this kind of contract, and all you're left with is a few blank spaces to fill in your name and signature.

REMEMBER

All standard forms are written with the interests of the person for whom the form was written in mind. You're the bottom of the food chain, and usually little scope exists to negotiate the terms. However, you can always choose to walk away from the deal. For example, if you read through the fine print of an insurance contract and discover that although your house is covered for fire, it isn't covered for arson or bushfires, then although you can't negotiate with the insurance company, you can go elsewhere and hunt down a better deal.

Sometimes, however, you may be dealing with a standard form contract between you and another individual, rather than between you and a major financial organisation. A good example is a retail lease. Yes, this is a standard form, and one that's typically hideously in favour of the landlord, but because the landlord is often a real-life, warm-and-breathing person, you often have room to negotiate.

Knowing what to look for in a contract

The essential questions to ask yourself before signing any contract are 'What am I agreeing to do?', 'What charges am I agreeing to pay?' and, most importantly of all, 'What happens if things don't go smoothly?'

I find the question 'What happens if things don't go smoothly?' one of the most challenging. Of course, when you enter into a contract, you're usually entering into the contract in good faith, with some essential trust between you and the other party. Sometimes it runs against the grain to be asking questions such as 'What if it all goes wrong?' or 'What if you do the dirty on me?' However, the essence of a good contract — and, indeed, why contracts are so vital — is to protect both parties should things go awry.

Imagine a situation where an aluminium-window manufacturer enters into a contract with a builder to supply windows for a large project by a certain date. This manufacturer then orders a large shipment of aluminium from its supplier. Imagine that this supplier is late supplying the aluminium. Who do you think bears the consequences (and possibly penalties) for the windows not being supplied to the building project in time? The manufacturer, the supplier, or possibly even the builder?

Other issues you need to consider before signing any kind of contract include

>> **Amendments:** Are any amendments properly documented as part of the contract?

>> **Confidentiality:** Are you or is the other person bound by confidentiality in any way?

>> **Conflict of interest:** Can you identify any potential conflicts of interest, either for yourself or the other party? (For example, a real estate agent is purportedly acting in your interest, but the larger the value of the sale, the more commission the agent receives.)

>> **Delegation:** Can you delegate any of the tasks specified in this contract to others?

>> **Dispute resolution:** How do you go about resolving disputes if they occur?

>> **Effective date:** When is this contract effective from?

- >> **Exchange rate:** If you're making an agreement to export or import goods, in what currency are payments to be made, and are agreements as to exchange rates in place?

- >> **GST:** Does GST apply to any of the amounts referred to in this contract?

- >> **Indemnity:** Do you need to be protected from any claims an outside person may make against you?

- >> **Independent legal advice:** Have both you and the other party sought independent legal advice?

- >> **Intellectual property rights:** Who owns these? What are they?

- >> **Laws:** What laws or regulations apply to this contract?

- >> **Performance:** Is a certain level of performance or quality required by this contract?

- >> **Privacy:** If signing this contract enables the other party to access your private details (for example, to do a credit check), is your privacy guaranteed?

- >> **Termination:** How long does this contract go for, and when does it expire? Can the contract be renewed and, if so, how? Does the contract include a notice period that needs to be complied with?

REMEMBER

Whatever the contract, don't be duped into thinking that trust is enough, and make sure that the contract specifies what happens if things go wrong. Just like marriage, even the best of business relationships can flounder, and a contract is vital to navigating the stormy waters of any dispute.

Signing on the dotted line

A few last do's and don'ts before you sign your life away? Yeah, I know you're ready for it:

WARNING

- >> **Remember that this is serious stuff:** A signed written contract is very difficult to make inoperative. Make sure that what was claimed, either verbally or in writing, and relied upon, is clearly incorporated in the written contract.

- >> **Read all the fine print before you sign:** Contracts are so deadly boring, I start skipping the words after getting through about three paragraphs. If you're impatient like me, try sitting down and reading every section aloud, line by line. If you don't understand something, read it over and over until you do.

>> **Keep a signed copy of the contract, as well as any changes:** If you sign anything, keep a copy. If something changes, keep a signed copy of the changes, too. With contracts that you sign digitally, remember to save the signed contract offline in a format that you can access in the future. (Keeping copies of contracts may sound obvious, but I confess to learning this the hard way. A client once disputed the copyright of some freelance writing work I had done for them many years before. I was horrified to find I had lost the original contract for this work, in which it had clearly stated that the copyright for the work was mine.)

>> **Don't rely on verbal stuff:** Although verbal agreements can be legally binding, they are much harder to prove in court. If someone says to you, 'It's not in the contract, but I promise so-and-so and such-and-such', I suggest you smile sweetly and get your lawyer to amend the contract to include the promise, in writing.

>> **Don't skimp on legal advice:** When working with contracts, don't skimp on legal advice. Despite their reputation — and the temptation here to make a lawyer joke is almost overwhelming — lawyers don't necessarily cost an arm and a leg. If you're about to sign a contract worth tens of thousands of dollars, the associated legal bill is probably going to be chicken feed in comparison.

REMEMBER

A fellow author once said to me that simply accepting the terms of a contract offered to him would be like not answering back when someone asked him a question. He said that negotiation was an important part of building business relationships and, in many situations, the other side expects it. So remember: Look after your own needs and be confident when you negotiate the terms of a contract. Try to think of this negotiation as healthy dialogue rather than conflict. Even a contract agreement that looks set in stone is usually negotiable.

Negotiating Lease Contracts

A commercial lease is often used as an example of the potential inequality of parties, with many of the conditions drafted in favour of the landlord, rather than the tenant. (However, if the lease in question is a retail lease, you have a lot more rights as a tenant.) Instead of being fazed by this current set of conditions, be prepared to haggle on the following in order to arrive at a fairer deal for both parties:

MONEY STUFF

>> **Annual rent increases:** Look carefully at the proposed rent increases. Most leases are linked to the CPI, but some leases request an increase linked to the CPI plus an additional percentage. In most instances, stick to your 'guns' and say you're prepared to pay increases according to the CPI only.

>> **Bond:** The lease needs to specify the value of the bond, where this bond is to be lodged, and whether you're to receive interest when you recoup the bond at the end of your lease.

TIP

>> **Extras:** As soon as you're getting close to agreeing on a price, ask for extras. For example, if you offer $2,400 a month and the landlord says they can only go as low as $2,600, offer $2,500 on the condition that the landlord fixes up the paintwork and lays new flooring (or whatever it is that needs doing).

>> **Interruption of use:** Make sure the lease specifies what happens if the space becomes unusable or your use of the space is interrupted. Similarly, do you have any rights if another retailer of the same type wants to rent in the same shopping centre or precinct?

TRUE STORY

>> **Outgoings:** You're quite within your rights to ask for details of all outgoings that you're expected to pay. Outgoings shouldn't include any capital improvements, substantial repairs or excessive expenditures (such as my experience, where I discovered my landlord was paying his daughter an outrageous hourly fee to clean the outside precinct and expected me to cover the cost). Another tip: Ask the landlord to charge for rent and outgoings separately. That way, even if rent increases by a significant percentage each year, the outgoings probably won't.

>> **Ownership of improvements and new fit-outs:** Establish who is responsible for property improvements and who owns these improvements after they're complete.

>> **Relocation clauses:** Some shopping centre leases include clauses specifying they can demand you to relocate to another position in the shopping centre. This clause can spell death for a business, especially if you're required to pay for a fresh fit-out as part of the compulsory relocation.

REMEMBER

>> **Rent increases when taking up an option to renew:** When you take up an option to renew a lease, the rent normally comes up for review. Make sure your lease includes an option for you to get a market valuation in the event of a dispute about the rent on renewal, and that a reduction in the rent is a possibility, if need be.

>> **Start dates:** If the landlord has promised to make significant improvements to the premises, you may want to enter into a formal agreement *before* you sign a lease, agreeing that the lease is to commence from the date these improvements are complete.

>> **Term of the lease, and options to renew:** Leases are normally either $3 \times 3 \times 3$ or 5×5. This means that at the end of every three or five years, you have the option to renew your lease for another three or five years, and your landlord has to offer you this option. Usually, the rent comes up for negotiation whenever you renew. At the end of nine years (with a $3 \times 3 \times 3$ lease), or at the end of ten years

(with a 5 × 5 lease), the lease agreement terminates. Both you and the landlord have the right to terminate the lease or negotiate an entirely fresh agreement.

>> **Usage of premises:** Make sure the lease is flexible enough in its definition of usage so that you can change the nature of your business, if need be. For example, if you rent premises for your naturopathy business, but have a notion in the back of your mind that you may use the premises to conduct yoga classes, make sure the usage in the lease isn't limited to a naturopathic practice.

REMEMBER

WHEN THINGS GO WRONG

Lots of business owners go into a state of denial if faced with a threat of legal action, behaving like ostriches and not seeking legal advice until the last minute. If the matter is already before a magistrate before you seek help, you're not going to need a lawyer — you're going to need a magician.

So, in the event of a dispute, don't wait too long before seeking advice.

3

Planning for Profit

Understand the psychology (and maths!) behind setting prices for your goods and services.

Build a financial plan for your business to predict sales and expenses.

Calculate profit margins and your break-even point.

Create a marketing plan that sparks from creative genius, relies on common sense and inspires immediate action.

IN THIS CHAPTER

» Looking at different pricing strategies and thinking about what's best for you

» Mixing up price strategies so you can capture as wide a market as possible

» Applying price strategies to your business

» Keeping tabs on your pricing and not letting things slip

» Calculating how much you're likely to sell this week, this month and this year

» Building a sales forecast for the next 12 months

Chapter **8**

Figuring Out Prices and Predicting Sales

I f you're like most people starting out in business, you may be tempted to under-charge for your products or services. Maybe you're unsure about how much customers are willing to pay, or you're anxious that customers won't value your services. Maybe you're worried that you won't secure enough business to cover your expenses.

By undercharging, I'm talking about charging less than your customers are will-ing to pay. Precisely what this amount is can be tricky to judge, especially if you're pricing a service rather than a product. Calculating the value of your skills and expertise through the eyes of a customer is a very subjective process.

In this chapter, I talk about pricing strategies and how best to go about setting a price for your products or services. I also explain how to create your sales forecast for the next 12 months, one of the fundamental building blocks for any business.

Choosing a Pricing Strategy

Business educators use a heap of different terminology for price strategies, but essentially any price strategy boils down to one of three things: *Cost-based pricing, competitor-based pricing* or *value-based pricing.* In the following sections I explore each strategy in turn.

Setting prices based on costs

Cost-based pricing is where you start by figuring out what it costs you to make a product or provide a service, and then you add an additional amount to arrive at the profit that you're after.

For example, imagine I decide to start a business selling sunhats at the local markets. The hats cost $8 each to buy, the stall costs $100 rent for the day and I reckon I can sell 50 hats a day. I want to make $250 profit to cover my time, so this means I decide to charge $15 per hat. (Sales of $15 × $50 = $750; less the $400 for the cost of the hats, less the rent of $100, and I'm left with $250 in my hot, sticky hand.)

This pricing model may sound like perfectly logical, good business practice, but it's not, because this way of working doesn't pause to consider how much customers are actually prepared to pay for these hats. Maybe another stall opposite is selling the self-same hats for only $12. Maybe the hats are a real bargain, and I should be charging $20.

WARNING

From a strategic perspective, cost-based pricing is the weakest of all business models. On the one hand, if the resulting prices are too high in relation to the competition, the business will flounder; on the other hand, if resulting prices are less than people are prepared to pay, you'll miss out on the possibility of above-average profits.

Setting prices based on competitors

Competitor-based pricing is where you look at what your competitors are charging for similar products or services, and then set your prices accordingly. This pricing strategy is the most common strategy used by business.

As I mention in the introduction to this chapter, if you're just starting out in business, you may fall foul of the temptation to be cheaper than everyone else. However, unless everyone else in the industry is driving around in sports cars with money to burn, chances are your competitors' prices are the level they are for a very good reason. Unless you have a competitive advantage that enables you to produce products or provide your services cheaper than your competitors, setting your prices lower than everyone else is likely to lead to poor profitability for you, as well as a risky business model.

Instead of trying to undercut competitors, look at the prices that your competitors are charging and use this analysis as a reflection of what the market is prepared to pay. Then pitch your pricing accordingly.

**AHEAD OF
THE PACK**

Competing on price alone is always a dangerous strategy. Sure, you need to be aware of competitor pricing and factor this information into your pricing decisions. However, how you position and sell your products and services should almost always be based on a combination of many different factors, such as quality of product or quality of service, delivery times, location, availability and ambience, and never just price alone. (For more about identifying your competitive strategy, refer to Chapter 2.)

Setting prices based on perceived value

Value-based pricing is where you reflect on the products or services you provide, look at the customer demand, and then set your price according to how much you think customers will be prepared to pay.

Here are a few examples of value-based pricing:

>> Apple uses value-based pricing for many of their products (sought-after items such as iPads and iPhones), where no direct head-to-head competition exists and customers are prepared to pay premium prices for a brand upon which they place a high value.

>> The stallholders selling umbrellas outside the city train station close to where I live push up the price of umbrellas by $3 or $4 every time it rains. Why? Because customers place a much higher value on staying dry when the rain is bucketing down.

>> I know of a very gifted network engineer who has earned an almost god-like status among local businesses for being able to troubleshoot and solve network issues when everyone else has failed. He charges top dollar — significantly more than his competitors — but people will pay because they place such a high value on having reliable business systems, and getting those systems back up and running.

In many ways, value-based pricing represents the essence of good business sense and marketing. After all, how better to set your prices than by judging the maximum that customers are willing to pay? The only tricky thing about value-based pricing is that any judgement is subjective. For example, I love the design and funky look of Apple's gear and will happily pay premium dollars for a new MacBook Air or latest iPhone. My son Daniel, however, doesn't place much value on Apple's design and prefers generic products. Therefore, the value Daniel places on an iPhone is significantly less than the value I place on the same item.

Building a Hybrid-Pricing Plan

So far in this chapter, I talk about the theory of pricing and different pricing strategies. However, most successful businesses don't employ a single price strategy; instead, they employ a combination of strategies.

An example is a luxury inner-city hotel. Most of the time, they use *competitive-based pricing*, setting rates with the awareness of competitors' pricing very much in mind. However, with their premium rooms, they use *value-based pricing*, often improvising rates on the spot according to demand and what they think customers will be prepared to pay. Finally, for last-minute rates where they have a bunch of empty rooms and they know they won't be able to fill all of them, they use *cost-based pricing*, charging just enough above cost to make it worth their while to fill the room.

Using a combination of pricing strategies is called *hybrid pricing*, and is a key element in any successful business. The next part of this chapter explores ways to introduce hybrid pricing into your business, including premium products, no-frills products, package pricing and differential pricing.

Offering a premium product or service

With hybrid pricing, offering a premium product or service is only part of the picture. The idea is that as well as offering a premium product or service, you also offer a regular product or service. In other words, you target more than one type of customer.

Here are some examples:

>> Amazon offers different pricing for freight, depending on how quickly you want your order delivered.

>> My butcher sells two types of minced beef: Low-fat and not-so-low fat.

>> The guy who mows our lawns offers two services: Regular just-with-a-lawnmower mowing and premium all-grass-edges-trimmed-within-an-inch-of-their-life mowing.

REMEMBER

Offering a premium product doesn't necessarily mean you compromise on the quality of your other products (a strategy that could risk your brand reputation). You can structure premiums in many different ways, such as faster service, guaranteed response time, additional services and complimentary extras.

MONEY STUFF

PRICING GOODS THAT YOU MANUFACTURE YOURSELF

If you're manufacturing goods yourself, you must differentiate between what you charge at wholesale versus what you charge at retail. Even if you currently don't sell your goods at wholesale — maybe you're selling your wares at market stalls or directly to retail outlets — for your business model to be sustainable you almost certainly have to consider wholesale pricing at some point.

Why? Most manufacturers who work on a small scale (and I'm kind of assuming you do, because if you're the general manager of Ford Motors, you're probably not reading this book) don't have enough of a range or a broad enough sales team to service a wide range of retail stores. Range is always an issue for smaller businesses, because most large retailers don't want to bother dealing directly with suppliers who only offer two or three products.

In addition, although you may be able to service retailers in your local area personally, chances are you won't be able to visit retailers interstate or in regional areas. Servicing these retailers almost always involves selling the products you make to some kind of distributor or wholesaler.

The crunch in regards to your pricing will be that your wholesale price ends up being a relatively small percentage of the retail price. For example, a shopkeeper selling an item for $20 probably doesn't want to pay much more than $10 for that item. The wholesaler who receives $10 probably won't want to pay much more than $7. So, out of a possible revenue of $20, you only receive $7, and out of that $7 you need to pay all the costs of production. This is fair, and reflects the reality of doing business and the costs of distribution, but can sometimes put a damper on what you may have been thinking is a great business idea.

Cutting back the frills

The flipside of premium pricing (refer to the preceding section) is *no-frills pricing*. No-frills pricing doesn't necessarily mean inferior quality, but can include things such as off-peak pricing, lower service standards, longer response times or shipping times or limited availability. Here are some examples:

>> Frequent-flyer programs place restrictions on what flights are available for frequent-flyer points.

>> Many gyms offer low-cost membership if you attend outside peak periods.

>> Tourism operators employ no-frills pricing for off-peak periods.

>> Supermarkets offer generic brands with basic product packaging.

TRUE STORY

My husband's recording studio business offers a no-frills product on Mondays and Tuesdays (traditionally the quietest days of the week for bookings). Musicians can visit the studio for a fixed duration of eight hours to record and mix up to four tracks. John doesn't offer any flexibility with this model (you can only book on a Monday or Tuesday, you can't book fewer than eight hours, and you don't get to choose your engineer), but nonetheless, these days are almost always booked out, because there are always musicians looking for a good deal. With this no-frills deal, John manages to attract customers he would normally miss out on with his regular pricing.

Getting creative with packages

Package pricing, where one product or service is bundled with something else, is another example of hybrid pricing. Package pricing can include bundling two or more products or services together, offering bonus products, and extended warranties.

Examples of package pricing include

>> A day spa offering a pedicure, waxing and massage as a package.

>> A tourism operator offering flights, accommodation and meals as a package.

>> A club offering a free giveaway of some kind for every membership renewal.

AHEAD OF THE PACK

If you're just starting up a new business, you may be pushed to think of how you could offer package pricing. Keep thinking creatively. Keep in mind that your business doesn't need to provide all elements of the package and that often the best approach is to team up with another business.

FIXED RATE OR BY THE HOUR?

For many types of services, you get a conflict between customers who want a fixed fee and business owners who want to charge by the hour. For example, a carpenter renovating a house would probably love to work on an agreed hourly rate, because they can be sure that they'll be paid properly for their time and won't risk being out of pocket if they underquote. However, the home owners almost certainly want a fixed quote for this job, because they need to budget and can't afford for the costs to blow out.

For you as a businessperson, no right or wrong answer exists as to whether to charge a fixed fee or charge by the hour. However, be aware that you'll often find a natural tension between what customers prefer and what business owners prefer. If you're in an industry where you feel you're able to offer a specific service for a fixed fee, this can be an excellent marketing edge, especially if your competitors are charging by the hour.

Charging different prices for the same thing

Yet another pricing strategy — and one that sounds kinda dodgy at first — is to charge different prices for the same thing (this is also known as *differential pricing*). Don't worry — I'm not proposing you breach trade practice guidelines. Instead, I'm talking about charging different prices depending on the quantity ordered, the total size of an order, the costs of shipping to customers, how promptly customers pay, how much the customer orders in the course of a year, and so on.

Differential pricing works really well for almost any business because it enables you to maintain your margins for regular sales, but generate extra income by selling to other customers at a discount.

You have so many ways to implement differential pricing that I'm going to spell out a fair few examples:

>> **Pricing based on customer location:** Charging different rates (either for shipping or for on-site service) depending on where the customer is located makes good sense, although you still want to keep your pricing structure pretty simple.

>> **Pricing based on loyalty:** Offering special pricing to customers who are members of your loyalty program or members of an affiliate organisation is a good marketing strategy and rewards customer loyalty.

>> **Pricing based on order size or quantities ordered:** This kind of pricing makes intuitive sense straight off the bat. Almost any business will charge a different price for someone who buys 1,000 units rather than 10. (When you structure pricing according to quantity, this is called *quantity-break pricing*.)

>> **Pricing based on payment terms:** Offering credit terms is expensive, not just in terms of using up working capital but also because of the risk of bad debt. Consider offering higher discounts for payment upfront or payment within 7 days.

>> **Pricing based on total spending:** Providing reward incentives for total spending often features as part of loyalty programs and makes good business sense. For example, if customers spend more than $500 over the course of the year, they get something for free.

>> **Pricing based on customer commitment:** Another clever strategy is to offer discount pricing but make the customer jump through hoops to get it. Money-back coupons where you have to post proof of purchase to the supplier or price-match guarantees are examples of this kind of pricing.

Forming Your Final Plan of Attack

Earlier in this chapter, I talk about a whole load of pricing strategies. Thinking about possible pricing strategies in this way may help spark some new ideas and creative thinking in how you approach pricing your products or services. However, you may also be feeling a little overwhelmed and wondering where to start. So here's my specific recommendation for the process to follow:

1. **Do some research as to what you think customers will be prepared to pay.**

   This research will involve looking at what competitors are charging as well as thinking about how your product or service is different and what value customers are likely to place on this difference.

2. **Think about how you could vary your product or service to provide two or three 'levels' of pricing (no-frills, regular and premium).**

   Not every business can offer multi-level pricing (for example, I don't know that I'd seek out a surgeon offering a no-frills service), but you'd be surprised how many types of businesses can. (Refer to the section 'Building a Hybrid-Pricing Plan', earlier in this chapter, for more on pricing levels.)

3. **Investigate at least two ways to bundle or package your offering with other products or services.**

   'Getting creative with packages', earlier in this chapter, provides a few ideas on this topic.

4. **Find two or three ways to charge your customers different prices for the same things.**

   This pricing strategy (differential pricing) is probably the most crucial of all. Even if you can't figure out how to have more than one level of pricing, or you can't come up with a method to create a package, you should be able to incorporate some form of differential pricing in your strategy. 'Charging different prices for the same thing', earlier in this chapter, provides some pointers as to how you can do this.

TIP

Although the upside of a hybrid pricing strategy is that you maximise the number of customers you can reach, and hopefully make premium profits on at least some of your sales, you can risk confusing customers if you offer too many options. As your business grows and changes, experiment with different pricing combinations to see what works best and gets the best response from your customers.

Monitoring and Changing Your Price

If you've already been in business for a while, you may feel that your price strategies are pretty well settled and working just fine. That's good, but regardless of whether you're just starting out in business or you're running a 50-year-old family legacy, you still want to keep an eye on your pricing.

The biggest indication that your pricing may need to shift is if you have poor financial results. (Of course, poor results can be caused by many factors, not just pricing.) However, if you know that your competitors have just raised their prices, your customers are commenting what good value you are, or you haven't raised your price in more than a year or two, it's probably time to do a price review.

REMEMBER

Changing prices doesn't only mean raising prices. Always be open to new pricing plans, special offers, package pricing and so on. If you do decide to raise prices, try to do so incrementally and avoid big price hikes that may scare your customers. Alternatively, find ways to sneak price rises through the back door, such as only increasing prices on certain low-profile products or services, or getting rid of discounts.

MONEY STUFF

DISCOUNT DRAMAS

If you build discounts into your pricing strategies, be careful that when you offer discounts, your business receives something tangible in return. For example, offering a discount for cash payments rather than credit card payments makes sense because you normally pay merchant fees on credit card transactions. Similarly, offering a discount for prompt payment probably makes sense (depending on how much discount you offer) if you're currently in debt to the bank and paying interest.

Another example is if you discount overstocked or end-of-season items. This makes sense because these slow-moving items are taking up valuable shop or warehouse space that could be better used for product that actually sells.

However, if you routinely offer discounts without receiving something that benefits your business in return, you risk eroding your profitability model. In addition, regular customers may get used to these discounts and come to expect them.

Building Your Sales Forecast

Once you have figured out your pricing strategy (what you intend to charge per hour, per unit or per service rendered), the next step in building financial projections is to create a sales forecast for the next 12 months (or, if your business hasn't started yet, create a sales forecast for the first 12 months of operation).

Creating sales forecasts prompts all kinds of questions. If you're charging by the hour, what's a reasonable number of hours to bill for each week? If you're selling items, how do you know how many you'll sell? What if you sell lots of different items, at different prices? In the following sections, I talk about the details behind creating these kinds of projection.

Calculating hours in a working week

If your business charges by the hour (maybe you're a bookkeeper, consultant, electrician, gardener, music tutor, maths tutor, plumber or some similar business), one of the first questions to answer is how many hours can you reasonably charge for per week, per month or per year.

Imagine a recent music graduate (I'll call her Maddie) wants to set up a business as a music tutor. Maddie reckons she can teach about 48 students a week (and if each lesson is 30 minutes, that's 24 hours of teaching), and that she's going to charge $60 per hour. With this in mind, she reckons that she'll earn $74,880 per year. (That's 24 multiplied by 52 weeks multiplied by $60.)

Is Maddie correct in her estimate of income for the next 12 months? I'm going to test her calculations using the following step–by–step method, which you can use as well:

1. **Estimate how many days you're going to work each week, and how many hours you can realistically charge for each day to arrive at your average number of billable hours per week.**

   When doing this calculation, remember to include billable hours only. Don't include travel time between locations, non-billable time due to administration/paperwork, or time spent running your business (bookkeeping, customer phone calls, marketing and so on).

2. **Estimate how much holiday you're going to take (or be forced to take) each year.**

   Here, don't only think in terms of lying on the beach watching the surf, but include both holidays where you go away and breaks where you may be available to work, but you can't. (For example, a school tutor probably won't get much work in school holidays, a gardener may find it hard to work in heavy rain or snow, or a business consultant may find that work grinds to a halt the month before and after Christmas.)

   In Table 8-1, I've included 12 weeks against the holiday time Maddie will take annually, because that's the number of weeks of school holidays each year.

3. **Make an allowance for public holidays.**

   Most people don't work public holidays. If you don't plan to (or maybe you can't because your customers will be unavailable), you have to allow for public holidays as well. Public holidays of ten days a year equate to an equivalent of two weeks per year. In Maddie's case, many public holidays also coincide with school holidays, so I've only allowed for one week's worth of public holidays per year.

4. **Think of what will happen if you get sick.**

   My observation is that being a freelancer (or sole trader) is one of the best possible ways of ensuring good health. Knowing that you won't get paid if you don't show up is a real incentive to getting out the door, however you're feeling. However, most people do get sick from time to time, and it's realistic to make an allowance for this. For Maddie, I've allowed another one week's worth of sick days per year.

5. **Calculate how many weeks per year you will be able to charge for.**

   In Maddie's case (see Table 8-1), after taking out holidays, public holidays and sick days, she can likely work a full week (that's 24 billable hours) for only 38 weeks of the year. (Most businesses that aren't dependent on school terms can probably work more weeks per year than this, however.)

6. **Multiply the number of working weeks per year by the number of weekly billable hours, to arrive at your maximum billable hours per year.**

   As shown in Table 8-1, for Maddie this equals 38 weeks per year multiplied by 24 hours per week, making a total of 912 hours.

7. **Multiply your maximum billable hours per year by your hourly rate.**

   The result for Melody is $54,720 per year, quite different from her initial estimate of $74,880.

Note: The method shown in Table 8-1 only gives you the maximum billable hours per year. If you're still getting your business established, it may be some time before you can build your business up to this point.

TABLE 8-1

Calculating Maximum Billable Hours per Year

Number of days per week	5
Average number of billable hours per day	4.8
Total billable hours per week	*24*
Number of holiday weeks per year	12
Number of public holidays per year, expressed in weeks	1
Number of sick days per year, expressed in weeks	1
Total working weeks per year	38
Maximum possible billable hours per year	**912**
Hourly rate	$60
Maximum possible income per year	*$54,720*

Increasing sales with extra labour

If your business is primarily labour-based, don't forget to think beyond your own labour, how many hours you can pack into a week, and what you can charge for your time. Instead, expand your thinking to include delegating some of the work involved to employees or subcontractors.

Building a plan that involves employees servicing your customers (rather than just you servicing customers) is a vital part of any entrepreneurial conception. For example, don't just think of how many lawns you can mow, kids you can tutor or companies you can consult to. Instead, picture a team of people mowing lawns, a whole school of tutors or an entire posse of consultants.

AHEAD OF THE PACK

If your business is labour-based, leveraging your expertise in this way is the only possible method by which you can hope to earn more than the industry average. For example, if you start up a business as a gardener, a music tutor or a physio-therapist, you can only work so many hours in the week. However, with a team of employees working for you, all delivering this service, you may be able to make a decent profit.

Refer to Chapter 4 for more on working out what path you want to take with growing your business.

Predicting sales for a new business

If a business is still getting established, making an estimate of your first 12 months' sales can be really hard. Maybe people are going to flood through the door, maybe you're going to be a ten-week wonder, or maybe your business will grow steadily and organically over time. However, in order to forecast sales for your business, you're going to have to make some kind of estimate.

TIP

To ensure your sales forecast is as realistic as possible, the more detail the better. Try to slice up sales targets by *market segment*, *product* or *region*:

>> **Market segment targets:** *Market segment* is a fancy word that really means type of customer or type of work. For example, a building contractor may split his market into new houses and renovations, a musician may split her market into weddings, private functions and pub gigs, and a handyman may split his market into private clients and real estate agents.

>> **Product-based targets:** Product-based targets work best if you sell products rather than services. You can set sales targets according to units sold, or dollars sold, of each product. For example, a car yard could aim to sell at least 20 cars a month, a real estate agent could try to sell five houses every month, and a lawn mowing business could set sales targets of 80 lawns per month.

>> **Regional targets:** With regions, you set sales targets according to geographic regions. This works best for slightly larger businesses that typically have a dedicated salesperson or sales team in each region.

If you take on board any of the pricing strategy stuff I talk about earlier in this chapter (refer to the section 'Building a Hybrid-Pricing Plan' for more), chances are you're going to have a few different prices or packages on the go. This makes your sales forecast even more complicated. However, in Table 8-2, you can see how a few different businesses make a stab at constructing their initial estimates.

The idea behind any detailed sales forecast is that you start by itemising the different items that you sell or the different prices that you charge, and you try to make an estimate of weekly sales against each of these items.

TIP

Try to incorporate a decent level of detail into initial sales estimates, including all items you sell or services you provide.

Predicting sales for an established business

If you've been running your business for a while, one of the most accurate ways of predicting sales is to analyse what sales have been for the last 12 months, and then build from there. Sure, you may have changed things — maybe you've switched to a new location, introduced new products or increased your pricing — but, nonetheless, your historical sales results are always going to provide you with the best indicator for future sales.

REMEMBER

When basing sales forecasts on historical data, consider the following:

>> When looking at sales figures for previous months, check whether these figures are shown including or excluding GST. (Most salespeople think in terms of the final value of each sale, but when working with financial projections and budgets, you should look at sales figures excluding GST.)

>> Does your business have significant seasonal variations? If so, have you factored this into your monthly forecasts?

>> If you examine the trends, is the business growing or declining? Ideally, you should analyse trends over two or more years to truly get a sense of what's happening.

>> Have any changes to pricing or product range occurred between last year and this year?

TIP

When looking at sales forecasts, also factor in personalities. Salespeople are often very buoyant with their predictions (this optimism tends to be part of the job), while accountants are typically gloom and doom. Hopefully, your financial projections can arrive at a happy medium.

TABLE 8-2   **Examples of Sales Estimates for Different Business Types**

	Unit Price	Units Sold	Sales per Week
Cakes to Cafes Business			
Friands	$2.00	100	$200.00
Muffins — regular	$1.50	100	$150.00
Muffins — wholesale	$1.30	50	$65.00
Chocolate brownies	$2.20	130	$286.00
Teacakes	$7.00	60	$420.00
Total			**$1,121.00**
Hairdresser			
Women's cuts	$80.00	20	$1,600.00
Men's cuts	$50.00	10	$500.00
Colour — short hair	$85.00	10	$850.00
Colour — long hair	$110.00	5	$550.00
Cut and colour package	$160.00	12	$1,920.00
Foils — half head	$120.00	8	$960.00
Foils — full head	$150.00	5	$750.00
Total			**$7,130.00**
Naturopath			
Short consultation	$65.00	20	$1,300.00
Long consultation	$130.00	5	$650.00
Consult + massage	$200.00	2	$400.00
Herbs	$45.00	15	$675.00
Phone consultation	$50.00	3	$150.00
Total			**$3,175.00**
Retail fashion			
Clothing $11 to $20	$15.00	88	$1,320.00
Clothing $21 to $30	$25.00	32	$800.00
Clothing $31 to 40	$35.00	48	$1,680.00

(continued)

TABLE 8-2 *(continued)*

	Unit Price	Units Sold	Sales per Week
Clothing $41 to 50	$45.00	30	$1,350.00
Clothing $51 to $60	$55.00	18	$990.00
Clothing $61 to $70	$65.00	6	$390.00
Total			**$6,530.00**

Creating Your Month-by-Month Forecast

At the simplest level, creating a forecast of sales for the next 12 months can be as simple as listing the names of the months in one big row across a sheet of paper and writing an estimate underneath each one. However, this method is somewhat unsophisticated, to put it mildly.

Figures 8-1 and 8-2 show a couple of different possible formats. In Figure 8-1, I use the example of a kids' party business that offers three kinds of packages at different prices. This level of detail helps keep forecasts realistic — for example, the business owner in this example can see just how many parties they have to do during the month in order to meet expected sales. In Figure 8-2, I look at a business selling cakes to cafes. The sales projection provides a healthy dose of realism (this business has to sell a hell of a lot of friands and muffins to make even the most scant of incomes at these prices).

FIGURE 8-1:
Building a
12-month sales
forecast in Excel
for a service
business.

	A	B	C	D	E	F	G	H	I	J	K	L	M
1		Price											
2	1 hour 30 Package	$ 170.00											
3	2 hour Package	$ 190.00											
4	2 hour Plus Package	$ 210.00											
5													
6		Jul	Aug	Sep	Oct	Nov	Dec	Jan	Feb	Mar	Apr	May	Jun
7	**Parties with owner's labour**												
8	1 hour 30 Package	12	12	12	12	12	12	12	12	12	12	12	12
9	2 hour Package	4	4	4	4	4	4	4	4	4	4	4	4
10	2 hour Plus Package	1	1	1	1	1	1	-	1	1	1	1	1
11													
12	**Parties with subcontract labour**												
13	1 hour 30 Package	8	12	13	8	12	80	4	5	12	13	18	22
14	2 hour Package	7	6	8	10	12	18	2	10	14	16	18	20
15	2 hour Plus Package	1	3	4	4	5	8	-	4	4	6	6	6
16													
17	**Income Generated**												
18	1 hour 30 Package	$ 3,400	$ 4,080	$ 4,250	$ 3,400	$ 4,080	$ 15,640	$ 2,720	$ 2,890	$ 4,080	$ 4,250	$ 5,100	$ 5,780
19	2 hour Package	$ 2,090	$ 1,900	$ 2,280	$ 2,660	$ 3,040	$ 4,180	$ 1,140	$ 2,660	$ 3,420	$ 3,800	$ 4,180	$ 4,560
20	2 hour Plus Package	$ 420	$ 840	$ 1,050	$ 1,050	$ 1,260	$ 1,890	$ -	$ 1,050	$ 1,050	$ 1,470	$ 1,470	$ 1,470
21	Total Sales	$ 5,910	$ 6,820	$ 7,580	$ 7,110	$ 8,380	$ 21,710	$ 3,860	$ 6,600	$ 8,550	$ 9,520	$ 10,750	$ 11,810

	A / B	C	Jul	Aug	Sep	Oct	Nov	Dec	Jan	Feb	Mar	Apr	May	Jun	Annual Totals
1	Friends	$ 2.00													
2	Regular Muffins	$ 1.50													
3	Wholesale Muffins	$ 1.30													
4	Chocolate Brownies	$ 2.20													
5	Teacakes	$ 7.00													
10							Sales Forecast for July to June for Cakes to Cafes								
11			Jul	Aug	Sep	Oct	Nov	Dec	Jan	Feb	Mar	Apr	May	Jun	Annual Totals
12	Friends		400	400	420	440	460	480	500	500	500	500	500	500	5600
13	TOTAL		$ 800	$ 800	$ 840	$ 880	$ 920	$ 960	$ 1,000	$ 1,000	$ 1,000	$ 1,000	$ 1,000	$ 1,000	11,200
15	Regular Muffins		400	400	400	400	400	400	400	400	400	400	400	400	4800
16	TOTAL		$ 600	$ 600	$ 600	$ 600	$ 600	$ 600	$ 600	$ 600	$ 600	$ 600	$ 600	600	7,200
18	Wholesale Muffins		200	200	200	300	300	300	400	400	400	400	400	400	3900
19	TOTAL		$ 260	$ 260	$ 260	$ 390	$ 390	$ 390	$ 520	$ 520	$ 520	$ 520	$ 520	520	5,070
21	Chocolate Brownies		520	520	520	520	520	520	520	520	520	520	520	520	6240
22	TOTAL		$ 1,144	$ 1,144	$ 1,144	$ 1,144	$ 1,144	$ 1,144	$ 1,144	$ 1,144	$ 1,144	$ 1,144	$ 1,144	1,144	13,728
24	Teacakes		250	250	250	250	250	250	250	250	250	250	250	250	3000
25	TOTAL		$ 1,750	$ 1,750	$ 1,750	$ 1,750	$ 1,750	$ 1,750	$ 1,750	$ 1,750	$ 1,750	$ 1,750	$ 1,750	1,750	21,000
27	GRAND TOTAL		$ 4,554	$ 4,554	$ 4,594	$ 4,764	$ 4,804	$ 4,844	$ 5,014	$ 5,014	$ 5,014	$ 5,014	$ 5,014	$ 5,014	$ 58,198

FIGURE 8-2:
Building a 12-month sales forecast in Excel for a business selling products.

Consider the following when preparing monthly sales forecasts for your business:

>> If you've been thinking about your sales in terms of weeks, keep in mind that some months have four weeks and others have five.

>> You need to factor in holidays and other seasonal aspects. Unless you run a Santa Claus for hire business, Christmas and early January are quiet months for most businesses.

>> Show your sales net of GST.

AHEAD OF THE PACK

Can you see how in Figure 8-1, I separate services that the owner plans to provide herself, and services that she plans to use employee or subcontract labour for? I do this because the costs of labour are so different. For example, the owner of the party business does the entertainment at many of the kids' parties herself, and for each of these parties she earns at least $170. However, if she pays for someone else to go to the party, she only earns $50. Separating out services in this way, analysing what services you'll provide and what services you plan to use subcontractors for, makes good sense when you get to predicting costs in the next stage of building detailed financial projections for your business (a topic I cover in the next chapter).

REMEMBER

ARE YOU DREAMING?

I have a friend who trained as a naturopath, spending years of study with the expectation that this is how she would make her living in the years to come. However, after she graduated and started out on her own, she found it very difficult to make much money out of her practice. After a year or two, she started attending monthly network meetings with fellow naturopaths. Through these meetings she learnt that it wasn't just her who was having a hard time building up her practice, and that the pickings naturopaths typically survive upon are scant indeed.

If you're starting off on a brand new business, how can you ensure your sales forecasts are realistic? If your business is something that has been done before, I suggest you do some research first. Research industry benchmarks, talk to your accountant, chat to people already working in the industry, or go to industry conferences and network meetings. So long as the quality of your product or service is up to scratch and you have decent marketing materials, you can probably expect to achieve similar results to those already working in the industry.

Things are trickier if you've invented a new product or you're launching a specialist service of some kind. In this situation, it's very hard to measure customer acceptance or interest in your product without first testing the market in some way. Ways of testing the market may include selling at markets, launching your service or product on a small scale locally or possibly (depending on the product) launching your product online.

IN THIS CHAPTER

» Working out the costs for every sale you make

» Creating a 12-month forecast for business expenses

» Pulling it all together to reveal your bottom line

» Understanding the nature of the beast

» Keeping the hungry wolf at bay

Chapter **9**

Building Profit Projections

A recent summer stretched into weeks of long, sunny days. The next-door kids, Callum and Rhys, hatched a plot to make homemade lemonade and sell it to thirsty passers-by. Most days I'd stop and buy a glass, and the kids would happily announce how much profit they'd made so far. The holidays were almost at a close the afternoon I bumped into their mother in the supermarket. She had a trolley piled high with lemons. 'This profit the boys are making is costing me a fortune,' she laughed.

Chances are that such halcyon days belong only to childhood and that, in your business, you're going to have to be seriously realistic about what everything costs. No more lemons for free.

Any small business needs financial projections to map the way forward. If you're starting a new venture, financial projections help calculate how much capital you require, and assess the profitability of your proposed business model. If you're an established business, financial projections guide decisions about growth and change.

This chapter helps build your financial literacy, explaining how to bring the elements of income, costs and expenses together in order to predict profitability one, three or even five years ahead. Also, for new businesses, this chapter talks about the importance of managing your personal expenses. After all, in the absence of benevolent fairy godmothers or inheritances from wealthy great-aunties, starting a business that requires your full-time input but doesn't generate enough profits for you to survive is never going to fly.

Understanding the Cost of Your Sales

In order to manage the financials of your small business effectively, you first need to grasp the difference between variable costs and fixed expenses. *Variable costs* (also sometimes called *direct costs* or *cost of goods sold*) are the costs that go up and down in direct relation to your sales.

Keep the following in mind when considering variable versus direct costs:

>> If you're a service business, you may not have any variable costs, but possible variable costs include sales commissions, booking fees, equipment rental, guest consumables or employee/subcontract labour.

>> If you're a retailer, your main variable cost is the costs of the goods you buy to resell to customers. Other variable costs, particularly for online retailers, may include packaging and postage.

>> If you're a manufacturer, variable costs are the materials you use in order to make things, such as raw materials and production labour. (For the boys next door making lemonade, their variable costs were lemons and sugar.)

Fixed expenses (also sometimes called *indirect costs* or *overheads*) are expenses that stay constant, regardless of whether your sales go up and down. Typical fixed expenses for your business may include accounting fees, bank fees, electricity, insurance, motor vehicles, rental, software subscriptions and wages. I talk more about fixed expenses later in this chapter, in 'Forecasting business expenses'.

Costing your service

I mention in the preceding list that if you're providing a service, you may not have any variable costs associated with your business. However, you may well have some minor costs associated with providing your service and, as soon as your business grows, you will have the cost of hiring employees or contractors to provide the service on behalf of your business.

Table 9-1 shows some examples where variable costs apply for service businesses.

TABLE 9-1

Variable Costs Examples for Service Businesses

Type of Business	Likely Variable Costs
Contract cleaning	Cleaning staff wages, cleaning materials
Holiday house	Guest consumables, booking commissions
Massage therapist	Daily room hire
Home maintenance business	Building materials, cost of subcontractors
Medical practitioner	Medical supplies, pathology

TIP

If you're unsure whether something is a variable cost or a fixed expense, ask yourself this: Do you spend more on this item as sales increase? If your answer is yes, chances are this item is a variable cost.

Costing items that you buy and sell

When calculating costs for items that you buy and then sell, you have two types of costs to consider:

>> **Incoming costs:** These are the costs involved in getting the goods to your door. Incoming costs usually include freight and, for importers, may also include customs charges, duties and tax. Incoming costs may also vary significantly depending on the quantity you order.

>> **Outgoing costs:** These are the costs involved in making the sale and getting the goods to your customer. Outgoing costs include sales commissions, discounts, outwards freight, packaging and storage.

If you decide to import goods from overseas, doing your product costings carefully is particularly important. Even if current exchange rates make your prices look cheap as chips, this rosy picture may soon fade when you add the costs of freight, customs, distribution and taxes, which can easily add a further 40 to 50 per cent to the cost of a product.

TIP

If you're restricted to buying and selling in different currencies — maybe you buy in US dollars but sell in Euros — take the time to generate multiple pricing models, and make sure you can still be profitable even if the exchange rate changes substantially.

WARNING

THE DANGERS OF CUSTOM MANUFACTURE

Over the years, I've observed that almost any business doing custom manufacture struggles to make a profit. Why? The very nature of creating one-off pieces — whether these are original sculptures, handmade furniture, custom spiral staircases or hand-built guitars — means that you are engaging with the unknown.

The unknown factor may be materials that cost more than you expect, a customer who isn't happy with the first prototype, underestimating the cost of labour, or many other factors. The time taken up discussing a job with a customer, drawing up designs, communicating changes and working out how to do something is almost always more than you expect.

When you create one-off items, you don't have the same ability to control your costs in the way that you do when you make the same item over and over again.

Am I warning you never to engage in this kind of business? No, not quite. After all, without custom manufacturers our society would be without potters and artists, sculptures and artisans, furniture makers and craftspeople. However, if you're planning this kind of business and you want to make a profit, you will need to be particularly brutal about quotations and costings, and you need to be prepared to reject jobs where the margins are too slight.

Costing items that you make

If you manufacture products, one of the most crucial steps in building financial projections is to create an accurate costing worksheet for each product that you sell. This process can be pretty tedious, but without knowing exactly what everything costs, you can't move forward and plan.

Table 9-2 shows a possible product costing and the kind of information to include.

TIP

Can you see how the example in Table 9-2 puts a value on labour? You may think this doesn't apply to you, because chances are if you're just starting out in business, you're contributing your own labour for free. However, when creating a product costing, you're best to include a realistic allowance for how much the labour would cost if you were to pay for someone else to create the product. This way, you can see the 'true' profitability of each product, and you get a better sense of the long-term potential of your enterprise.

TABLE 9-2 **Cost of Producing One Bottle of Pickle**

Item	$	Notes
100 g fresh tomato	$0.80	Based on seasonal average
30 g onion	$0.05	
20 g sugar	$0.03	Based on buying in bulk 50kg bags
5 g salt	$0.01	Based on buying in bulk 10kg bags
Cost of labour	$0.88	Average 400 bottles per day, with labour $350 per day
Kitchen rental	$0.38	Average 400 bottles per day, with rental $150 per day
Bottle plus lid	$0.45	
Label	$0.35	
Packaging	$0.40	$3.20 per custom box, 8 bottles per box
Total	**$3.34**	

MONEY STUFF

CALCULATING GROSS PROFIT

You've almost certainly heard of the terms *gross profit* or *gross profit margins* but are you entirely clear what these terms mean?

Put simply, gross profit is equal to sales less variable costs and . . .

- Gross profit is always more than net profit.
- The more you sell, the more gross profit you make.

With this under your belt, how do you calculate *gross profit margins*? As follows:

Gross profit margin = gross profit divided by sales multiplied by 100.

A few examples may help bring this concept to life:

- A fashion retailer buys a skirt from the wholesaler for $20 and sells it for $50. Her gross profit is $30, and her gross profit margin is therefore, 60 per cent.
- A massage therapist charges $80 per massage but the therapy centre takes $25 as a booking and room fee. His gross profit is $55 and his gross profit margin is 71 per cent.
- A carpenter charges $800 for fixing a veranda. Materials cost $200 and labour for her apprentice costs $100. Her gross profit is $500 and her gross profit margin is 63 per cent.

The other interesting thing to consider is volume discounts. For example, in the product shown in Table 9-2, the cost of sugar is based on buying 50 kilograms at a time. However, how much would this business save if the owner was able to buy 100 kilograms at a time? (Even if your business can't afford to buy in large quantities yet, just knowing that your costs may reduce dramatically as your business grows is an important part of understanding your profit-making potential.)

Forecasting Expenses

When planning for business expenses, always separate *start-up expenses* from *operating expenses*:

>> *Start-up expenses* are one-off expenses that you encounter when you first start a business, such as new equipment, company formation expenses, legal expenses and signage. I talk lots about start-up expenses in Chapter 15.

>> *Operating expenses* are the kind of expenses that occur year in and year out, and which form a regular part of everyday trading. Operating expenses are the focus of the next part of this chapter.

Forecasting monthly expenses

If you've been running your business for a while, you already have a good idea of what your expenses are going to be. However, if you're just getting started with your business, thinking of the types of expenses you may encounter can be tricky. Are you going to take out insurance? What about accounting fees? Will you need to pay any professional memberships? What expenses could you face that you have not even thought of yet?

Figure 9-1 shows a Business Expenses worksheet that lists expenses in the first column, how often they occur in the second column, an estimate of the amount in the third, and a calculated monthly total in the fourth.

Here are some tips for how you might create a similar worksheet to forecast expenses for your own business:

>> Most business forecasts are calculated on a monthly basis and, for this reason, be careful when converting weekly expenses into monthly expenses. To calculate a monthly budget for something you pay weekly, you need to first multiply the weekly amount by 52, and then divide it by 12 (rather than simply multiplying the weekly amount by 4). In this example, $300 a week rent multiplied by 52 equals $15,600. Divide this by 12 and you get $1,300 a month (not $1,200).

	A	B	C	D
1	**Type of Expense**	**Frequency**	**Estimate**	**Monthly total**
2	Accounting Fees	Annually	$1,500	$125
3	Advertising	Monthly	$1,200	$1,200
4	Bank Charges	Monthly	$100	$100
5	Cleaning Expenses	Weekly	$50	$217
6	Computer Consumables	Monthly	$150	$150
7	Consultant Expenses	Monthly	$300	$300
8	Couriers	Monthly	$80	$80
9	Customer Consumables	Monthly	$60	$60
10	Electricity	Quaterly	$500	$167
11	Equipment Rental	Monthly	$200	$200
12	Freight Fees	Monthly	$300	$300
13	Gas	Quaterly	$300	$100
14	Hire Purchase Payments	Monthly	$650	$650
15	Insurance	Annually	$3,000	$250
16	Interest Expense	Monthly	$520	$520
17	Internet Fees	Monthly	$150	$150
18	Lease Expenses	Monthly	$800	$800
19	License Fees	Annually	$1,200	$100
20	Merchant Fees	Monthly	$320	$320
21	Motor Vehicle rego & insurance	Annually	$1,500	$125
22	Motor Vehicle Fuel	Weekly	$80	$347
23	Motor Vehicle Repairs & Maint	Annually	$2,000	$167
24	Motor Vehicle Tolls	Weekly	$70	$303
25	Office Supplies	Monthly	$150	$150
26	Parking	Weekly	$35	$152
27	Professional Memberships	Annually	$1,800	$150
28	Rates	Quaterly	$400	$133
29	Rental Expense	Fortnightly	$1,500	$3,250
30	Repairs and Maintenance	Annually	$6,000	$500
31	Replacements	Annually	$3,000	$250
32	Security Expenses	Monthly	$120	$120
33	Staff Amenities	Monthly	$300	$300
34	Storage Expenses	Monthly	$150	$150
35	Subcontractor Expenses	Monthly	$520	$520
36	Subscription and Dues	Annually	$2,200	$183
37	Telephone (inc mobile)	Monthly	$550	$550
38	Travel Domestic	Monthly	$350	$350
39	Travel Overseas	Annually	$3,500	$292
40	Wages and Salaries	Weekly	$3,500	$15,167
41	Wages oncosts	Weekly	$350	$1,517
42	Website expenses	Monthly	$850	$850
43	**Total Expenses**			**$29,672**

FIGURE 9-1:
Start by estimating an amount for each expense, along with how often it occurs.

» If your business is already trading, the best way to make estimates is to look at what you've spent in the past. Old supplier invoices, accounting software transaction journals and monthly Profit & Loss Statements are all good sources for this information.

>> Always keep variable costs (costs of purchasing goods for resale, or costs of production) separate from expenses. (Later in this chapter, see how to create financial projections, and where the different elements of income, variable costs and expenses belong.)

One more thing. If you're registered for GST, don't include GST in the budgets for any of your expenses. Instead, show the value of each expense before GST is applied. (Why? Because GST applies only to the final sale to the consumer — as a business, you're entitled to claim back any GST that you pay.)

Forecasting expenses for the year ahead

In Figure 9-2, I show an example of a 12-month expense projection for a relatively small business. I've used a spreadsheet, but the principle is pretty much the same whatever tool you use. You can see the months running along the top, the names of the expenses down the first column, and an estimate of how much each expense will be along each row.

Type of Expense	Freqency	Estimate	Monthly total	Jan	Feb	Mar	Apr	May	Jun
Accounting Fees	Annually	$1,500	$125						
Advertising	Monthly	$1,200	$1,200	$1,200	$1,200	$1,200	$1,200	$1,200	$1,200
Bank Charges	Monthly	$100	$100	$100	$100	$100	$100	$100	$100
Computer Consumables	Monthly	$150	$150	$150	$150	$150	$150	$150	$150
Consultant Expenses	Monthly	$300	$300	$300	$300	$300	$300	$300	$300
Customer Consumables	Monthly	$60	$60	$60	$60	$60	$60	$60	$60
Electricity	Quarterly	$500	$167	$500	$0	$0	-$500	$0	$0
Freight Fees	Monthly	$300	$300	$300	$300	$300	$300	$300	$300
Gas	Quarterly	$300	$100	$0	$300	$0	$0	$300	$0
Hire Purchase Payments	Monthly	$650	$650	$650	$650	$650	$650	$650	$650
Insurance	Annually	$3,000	$250	$0	$0	$0	$0	$3,000	$0
Interest Expense	Monthly	$520	$520	$520	$520	$520	$520	$520	$520
Internet Fees	Monthly	$150	$150	$0	$0	$150	$0	$0	0
Lease Expenses	Monthly	$800	$800	$800	$800	$800	$800	$800	$800
License Fees	Annually	$1,200	$100	$700	$0	$0	$0	$0	$0
Merchant Fees	Monthly	$320	$320	$320	$320	$320	$320	$320	$320
Motor Vehicle rego & insurance	Annually	$1,500	$125	$0	$1,500	$0	$0	$0	$0
Motor Vehicle Fuel	Weekly	$80	$347	$347	$347	$347	$347	$347	$347
Motor Vehicle Repairs & Maint	Annually	$2,000	$167	$167	$167	$167	$167	$167	$167
Motor Vehicle Tolls	Weekly	$70	$303	$303	$303	$303	$303	$303	$303
Office Supplies	Monthly	$150	$150	$150	$150	$150	$150	$150	$150
Professional Memberships	Annually	$1,800	$150	$0	$1,800	$0	$0	$0	$0
Rental Expense	Fortnightly	$1,500	$3,250	$3,250	$3,250	$3,250	$3,250	$3,250	$3,250
Repairs and Maintenance	Annually	$6,000	$500	$500	$500	$500	$500	$500	$500
Replacements	Annually	$3,000	$250	$250	$250	$250	$250	$250	$250
Staff Amenities	Monthly	$300	$300	$300	$300	$300	$300	$300	$300
Subcontractor Expenses	Monthly	$520	$520	$520	$520	$520	$520	$520	$520
Subscription and Dues	Annually	$2,200	$183	$200	$0	$500	$0	$0	$0
Telephone (inc mobile)	Monthly	$550	$550	$550	$550	$550	$550	$550	$550
Travel Domestic	Monthly	$350	$350	$350	$350	$350	$350	$350	$350
Travel Overseas	Annually	$3,500	$292	$0	$3,500	$0	$0	$0	$0
Wages and Salaries	Weekly	$850	$3,683	$3,683	$3,683	$3,683	$3,683	$3,683	$3,683
Wages oncosts	Weekly	$85	$368	$368	$368	$368	$368	$368	$368
Website expenses	Monthly	$850	$850	$850	$850	$850	$850	$850	$850
Total Expenses			$16,205	$16,088	$21,788	$15,338	$15,188	$17,988	$14,688

FIGURE 9-2: Forecasting expenses for the months ahead.

If you've created an estimate of monthly expenses already (refer to the previous section), you have a head start for building a projection for 12 months ahead. However, here are some tips to help you along the way:

WARNING

AHEAD OF THE PACK

>> **Beware five-week wages months:** If you pay wages every week, bear in mind that every third month you'll get a month with five paydays, not four.

>> **Show expenses in the month they occur:** You'll find some expenses occur only once a quarter or once a year (such as accounting fees or membership dues). For these expenses, you can simply enter the whole budget for the year in the month(s) when payment is going to fall due.

>> **Split large expenses into more detail:** If your expenses forecast includes any one expense that's more than 10 per cent of total expenses, see if you can split this expense up in more detail.

>> **Think about seasonal variations.** Depending on your business, expenses can increase or decrease dramatically at different times of year.

>> **Think about when you may take holidays:** Owner-operated businesses may need to increase wages expense during this time.

>> **Use formulas to calculate related expenses:** If you're using a spreadsheet, set up formulas for any expense categories that are directly related. For example, if you know that wages oncosts average 10 per cent of wages, create a formula so that if you change the figure for wages in your spreadsheet, the figure for wages oncosts changes automatically, too.

Allowing for loan repayments and interest

If your business has borrowed money and you're paying off a business loan, deciding how to show loan repayments in your expenses budget can be quite tricky.

Imagine that you have a bank loan and your repayments are $1,000 per week. You've almost paid off this loan, and you currently only have $15,000 left to repay. The interest on this loan only equals about $15 per week.

Any accountant will gladly explain that in terms of the profit of your business, the only expense that you can claim is the interest. However, when you're doing financial projections, this kind of analysis is too simplistic. The interest may be inconsequential, but budgeting $1,000 a week in repayments is not.

The best way to show loan repayments in your financial projections depends on the circumstances:

>> If you decide to include both a Profit & Loss Projection and a Cashflow Projection in your workings, you should show the value of the interest expense in your Profit & Loss Projection, and the value of the loan repayment in your Cashflow Projection.

>> If you're only doing a Profit & Loss Projection at this point, stay on the side of caution, and show the full value of the loan repayment in your expenses worksheet. This way, the final net profit that you arrive at in your projections will be as close as possible to your likely surplus in cash.

Allowing for personal and company tax

One of the questions people often ask is whether to include personal or company tax in the worksheet. The answer depends on whether your business is structured as a sole trader, partnership or company.

A BUDGET, PROJECTION OR CASHFLOW?

People tend to use the words 'budget', 'projection' and 'cashflow' synonymously, but there are subtle differences. A *budget* is about setting sales targets and expense limits. In larger businesses, for example, part of the responsibility for each manager is to meet agreed sales budgets, and ensure spending doesn't exceed allocated expense budgets.

On the other hand, a *projection* often looks further into the future than a budget. Rather than being a document that sets out expectations and responsibilities, a projection is more a statement of what might be possible. I often use projections to experiment with 'what-if?' scenarios, looking at what would happen to my profits if sales were to slump by 10 per cent, or expenses increase by a similar amount. (In this chapter, when I talk about building an expenses worksheet, I'm still really at the projection stage. Later on, if I'm confident that my business model is viable, I can take these projections and use them to create budgets.)

A *cashflow* is a different report again, and looks at the actual cash flowing in and out of a business. For example, if you receive a $20,000 loan from the bank, this appears on your cashflow projection report but doesn't show on your budget or your profit and loss projection. For more about cashflow reports, see Chapter 17.

If your business operates as a sole trader or partnership, you're responsible for paying tax on any profit that the business makes. The amount of tax you pay depends on many factors, including whether you have any sources of income other than the business. Generally, I don't include personal income tax as an expense on any business plan.

If your business has a company structure, you do need to include company tax expense on your expenses worksheet. Typically, the best approach is to add two extra lines below the row showing Net Profit. The first line is Company Tax Expense, and the second line is Net Profit After Company Tax.

Building Profit Projections

So far in this chapter, I've explained how to calculate the cost of your sales and how to create a 12-month forecast for expenses. If you've been reading this book consecutively, you know that in Chapter 8, I explain how to set prices and create a 12-month forecast for sales. In the next few pages of this chapter, I join the pieces of the puzzle together to show you how to build a 12-month profit projection.

The examples in this chapter use a spreadsheet for creating financial projections and, for me, spreadsheets tend to be my preferred poison. However, you may choose to use a business planning app to arrive at the same point, and that's fine too.

Step one: Starting with sales

In Chapter 8, I explain how to create a 12-month sales forecast. The idea is that you list the names of the months along the top and then, starting from the current month or the month that you intend to start trading, you list your predicted sales in each column.

If possible, try to split sales into different categories, such as type of product, service provided, customer type, location or distribution method, with a final row that shows Total Sales for each month. In general, I find the extra level of detail helps keep sales predictions more realistic.

Step two: Adding variable costs

Earlier in this chapter, in 'Understanding the Cost of Your Sales', I talk about calculating the cost of your sales. The next step in building your profit projection is to make a prediction about how much your sales will cost each month, based on the sales projections you've already made.

Quite how you do this depends on the type of business.

If you have a service business with no employees and no variable costs

This type of business has the simplest of financial forecasts. Simply enter the heading 'Variable Costs' and leave the figures in this row blank. (However, note that if you forecast substantial growth for your business, you may not be able to do all the work yourself, and you may need to hire subcontractors or use employee labour — creating variable costs.)

If you have a service business and you use employee or subcontract labour

Examples of this kind of business could be a plumber who subcontracts out some work, a party business that pays employees a casual rate to go to parties, a builder who uses labourers or a consultant bookkeeping service that hires lots of bookkeepers.

To show the cost of labour accurately, ensure that your sales projections for the next 12 months separate out sales where you're going to do the work, and sales where you'll get employees or subcontractors to do the work. Show your variable costs below your sales, similar to Figure 9-3. (For ease of display, I only show six months in this example, but I'm sure you get the general idea!) In this example, I know that for jobs that I don't do myself, I'll spend 60 cents in every dollar earned on labour, and I use a formula to calculate these costs. That way, every time I alter my sales forecasts, my labour costs change automatically.

Don't forget to add other variable costs here as separate rows also, such as commissions, consumables, materials or room hire.

If you buy and sell products

Sometimes, the idea with variable costs is that they are a stable percentage of income. For example, if you're a retailer, the cost of the goods you buy is probably a similar percentage of sales each time you make a sale.

FIGURE 9-3:
Building a gross
profit projection
for a service with
employees or
subcontractors.

	A	B	C	D	E	F	G
1		Jul	Aug	Sep	Oct	Nov	Dec
2	Sales - Owner Delivering Service	5000	5100	5200	5300	5410	4900
3	Sales - Subcontractor Delivering Service	1000	1000	1000	1100	1600	1500
4	**Total Sales**	6000	6100	6200	6400	7010	6400
5							
6	**Cost of Sales**						
7	Subcontractors Expense	600	600	600	660	960	900
8	Materials @ 15% of Sales	900	915	930	960	1052	960
9	Tool Hire	300	300	300	300	300	300
10	**Total Cost of Sales**	1800	1815	1830	1920	2312	2160
11							
12	**Gross Profit**	4200	4285	4370	4480	4698	4240
13							

If your variable costs are always a pretty stable percentage of sales, the trick is to set up your gross profit projection so that your variable costs calculate automatically. In other words, set up your worksheet so that if you increase sales, variable costs automatically increase as well.

For example, in Figure 9-4, the online bookseller knows that for every $100 of full-price books they sell, it costs them $60 to buy the books. In other words, their variable costs represent 60 per cent of sales. Similarly, they know that postage costs them, on average, 15 per cent of the sale value.

FIGURE 9-4:
Building a gross
profit projection
for a business
selling products,
calculating costs
on a percentage
basis.

	A	B	C	D	E	F	G	H
1			Cost as a % of sales					
2	Full-price books		60%					
3	Postage & Packaging		15%					
4								
5								
6			Jul	Aug	Sep	Oct	Nov	Dec
7								
8	**Sales**		12,000	12,500	12,300	13,000	13,100	13,800
9								
10	*Less: Variable Expenses*							
11	Cost of Books for Resale		7,200	7,500	7,380	7,800	7,860	8,280
12	Postage & Packaging		1,800	1,875	1,845	1,950	1,965	2,070
13	Total Variable Expenses		9,000	9,375	9,225	9,750	9,825	10,350
14								
15	**Gross Profit**		3,000	3,125	3,075	3,250	3,275	3,450
16								
17								

In this scenario, start by completing your sales projections for the next 12 months. (I show only six months in my example, for space reasons.) Below these sales, insert rows that show the cost of making these sales. If you're using a spreadsheet, you can use formulas so that these costs update automatically whenever you change a sales figure.

Step three: Showing gross profit

As you probably know already, gross profit is equal to sales less variable costs. What you've done so far is create a projection showing month-by-month sales listed across 12 columns, followed by your variable costs for each of these months.

Refer to Figures 9-3 or 9-4, and you can see how I've created not only subtotals for sales and variable costs, but also a new row at the bottom called Gross Profit. I calculate this automatically by setting up a formula in each column that simply subtracts total costs from total sales.

If you like, you can even insert an extra row here that calculates the gross profit margin (to do this, divide total gross profit by total sales for each month, and multiply this by 100).

Step four: Adding expenses and revealing the bottom line

Earlier in this chapter, in 'Forecasting expenses for the year ahead', I explain how to create a 12-month projection for business expenses.

Now is the time for you to grab this projection, and copy and paste the information into the work you've done so far. You're almost there! Here's a summary of what you've done so far and how to pull this last section together:

1. **Start with a monthly sales projection for the next 12 months.**

   Refer to 'Step one: Starting with sales' earlier in this chapter. Ideally you'll have a few lines detailing the different kinds of sales, with a row for Total Sales at the bottom.

2. **Add a monthly cost of sales projection for the next 12 months.**

   Refer to 'Step two: Adding variable costs' earlier in this chapter. The detail required here depends entirely on the kind of business.

3. **Calculate the monthly gross profit projection for the next 12 months.**

   Total Sales less total Cost of Sales equals Gross Profit. Set up this calculation so it happens automatically.

4. **Add details of monthly expenses for the next 12 months.**

   You probably have at least a dozen or so rows here, if not many more, in order to show a good level of detail. (My example in Figure 9-5 is pretty simple in this regard, but again I'm sure you get the idea!)

5. **Calculate the monthly net profit projection for the next 12 months.**

   Total Gross Profit less Total Expenses equals Net Profit. Set up this calculation so it happens automatically, and there you have it! A month-by-month prediction of your bottom line.

	B	C	D	E	F	G	H
		Jul	Aug	Sep	Oct	Nov	Dec
7	**Total Sales**	12,000	12,500	12,300	13,000	13,100	13,800
9	Less: Variable Expenses						
10	Cost of Books for Resale	7,200	7,500	7,380	7,800	7,860	8,280
11	Postage and Packaging	1,800	1,875	1,845	1,950	1,965	2,070
12	**Total Cost of Sales**	9,000	9,375	9,225	9,750	9,825	10,350
14	**Gross Profit**	3,000	3,125	3,075	3,250	3,275	3,450
16	Accounting Fees	0	500	0	0	500	0
17	Insurance	0	0	350	0	0	0
18	IT Expenses	320	320	320	320	320	320
19	Marketing Expenses	250	250	250	250	250	250
20	Motor Vehicle Expenses	350	350	350	350	350	350
21	Office Expenses	80	100	120	70	80	100
22	Professional Development	0	0	0	200	0	350
23	Software Subscriptions	220	220	220	220	220	220
24	Staff Wages	850	850	850	850	850	850
25	Superannuation	81	81	81	81	81	81
26	Travel	0	0	220	0	75	0
27	**Total Expenses**	2151	2671	2761	2341	2726	2521
29	**Net Profit**	849	454	314	909	549	929

FIGURE 9-5: Compiling a monthly profit projection.

Understanding the Whole Deal

While many people learn how to create financial projections quite quickly, I find that the figures they produce often bear little relationship to reality.

Probably the biggest area of error is in predicting sales, particularly for new businesses with no history of trading. I cannot stress enough the importance of being conservative in regards to sales growth and what is achievable in the first year of trading. Adding a random 10 per cent growth in sales per month without considering how you plan to achieve this increase is a recipe for failure.

WARNING

The second biggest area of error relates to calculating the costs of each sale. I find that manufacturers consistently underestimate the true cost of building or creating products. Similarly, service businesses often overestimate how many hours the owner can realistically bill for, and consequentially underestimate the cost of subcontract labour.

On a positive note, most business people are quite accurate when it comes to predicting expenses. However, one of the bugbears is understanding the impact your choice of business structure makes upon your profitability projections. Here's the rub: If you're a company structure, your wages and superannuation show in your financial projections as an expense. If you're a sole trader or partnership, wages don't show as an expense; rather, your projected net profit represents the wages you earn.

TIP

Last, the only way to get better at creating financial projections is to compare your forecasts against actuals each month, learning from your mistakes as you go.

Factoring Personal Expenses into the Equation

If you're starting a new business and you have very little savings or start-up capital, you may find you have very little to live on while building up your business. In this scenario, I strongly recommend you create a budget not only for business expenses, but for personal expenses, too.

Here are the kinds of traps you want to avoid:

TRUE STORY

>> I knew a couple who started a business at the beginning of the holiday season and had a few bumper months of trading. They drew all the available cash out of the business in order to survive, but then had no available cash when the business needed to get through lean times.

>> Former clients of mine started up a business that did very well right from the start. However, they hadn't created a realistic budget for personal spending and, despite the business thriving, it didn't generate enough profit in that first year to cover mortgage repayments and school fees. Although they did muddle through in the end, that first year of trading was very stressful and left a legacy of huge credit card debt.

>> A friend of mine started up a business that soon built to generate a steady but modest income. Being a happy-go-lucky personality, she spent money from her business pretty much as soon as it came in. However, 18 months after she opened doors for trading, she lodged her first tax return. She hadn't set any money aside for tax, and had to take out a personal loan to cover the debt.

Scrutinising one's personal spending has to be one of the more depressing ways to spend a rainy afternoon. Alternatively, a rough-and-ready way to figure out how much you need to live is to write down how much you've earned in the last 12 months, look up how much you've saved or how much savings you've used, and calculate the difference. Unless your personal circumstances have changed, this difference is going to be approximately the same as how much you need to live.

However, if you're starting or growing a business and you're willing to live a little leaner while things get off the ground, this method isn't good enough. The only way to really get a handle on your finances is to make a budget and try to live by it. This is the only way to see if you're spending more or less than you can afford.

You can find heaps of great apps online to help you manage your personal finances. If you haven't done so already, I recommend you start today! The simple act of recording every dollar you spend is one of the most powerful ways of taking control of this aspect of your life.

Chapter **10**

Calculating Your Break-Even Point

U nderstanding your break-even point is as essential to your business toolkit as food is to a teenage boy. (Three guesses as to who's in my family.)

Break-even calculations help you to decide prices, set sales budgets and assess the health of your business model. You can figure out how far sales can drop before you start to make a loss, how much extra you have to sell before you turn a profit, how changing sales affect profits or how much you need to lift sales in order to compensate for an increase in costs.

Sounds handy? In this chapter, I explain how you can calculate the break-even point for your own business. So grab your calculator, hang a 'do not disturb' sign around your neck and get ready to go . . .

Identifying Your Tipping Point

Your *break-even point* is the number of dollars you need to earn in any given period in order to cover your costs. Or, to put it differently, the total sales you have to make in order that you make neither a loss nor a profit.

Most business textbooks talk about your break-even point only in terms of *the business* breaking even. In other words, the break-even point is the point at which sales are high enough to cover the costs of your business. However, you can also think of your break-even point in terms of covering not only your business costs, but your personal expenses, too.

In real life, I find that people use the word *break-even* to refer to three totally different things:

>> **Business break-even point:** When you calculate your *business break-even point*, you calculate the sales the business has to make in order to meet its business expenses. In other words, if the business breaks even, it makes neither a profit nor a loss. This calculation is most relevant for businesses with a company structure where directors' salaries (owner salaries) are factored into the fixed expenses of the company.

>> **Business/personal break-even point:** When you calculate your *business/personal break-even point*, you calculate the sales the business has to make in order to meet business expenses and pay you — as the business owner — enough to cover your personal expenses.

Most business guides don't include any reference to personal expenses when calculating break-even, but I think that doing so is important for small businesses with a single owner-operator. After all, even if your business does make a profit, this profit may not be enough if the business is your sole source of income, and the profit generated isn't enough to cover your basic living expenses.

>> **Cash break-even point:** When you calculate your *cash break-even point*, you calculate the sales you have to make in order for your cash out to match your cash in over a specified period of time (usually 12 months). In this scenario, cash out could include things such as new equipment or business set-up costs, and cash in could include business loans or money that you have set aside in savings.

Calculating your cash break-even point provides a simpler approach to doing a proper cashflow (a topic I cover in detail in Chapter 17). However, a cashflow is a more accurate and detailed approach and is preferable if your business offers credit to customers or has inventory.

In the first part of this chapter, I cover how to calculate business break-even, and business/personal break-even. I look at break-even from a cash perspective towards the end of this chapter (see the section 'Looking at Things from a Cash Perspective').

Understanding the concept of break-even

The basic formula for calculating your business break-even point is easy:

Break-even point = Fixed expenses divided by gross profit margin

Imagine I have a friend (I'll call her Annie) who has a cafe on the main street. Her fixed expenses are $4,500 per week (one waitress, one kitchenhand, insurance, rent and so on). Overall, on average she makes a gross profit margin of about 60 per cent. (In other words, if she sells a focaccia for $10, the ingredients cost her $4; if she sells a coffee for $4, the ingredients cost $1.60.)

Annie's business break-even point is going to equal fixed expenses (that's $4,500 per week) divided by her gross profit margin (60 per cent), which is $7,500. In other words, she has to generate $7,500 in sales just to break even and cover her basic expenses. Figure 10-1 shows this principle in action.

	A	B	C	D
1				
2	Average Gross Profit Margin	60%		Based on ingredients costing 40 cents for every dollar sold
3				
4	Fixed Expenses Business	$4,500.00		Staff, rent, insurance and so on
5				
6	Break-even Point	$7,500.00		Equals fixed expenses divided by gross profit margin
7				

FIGURE 10-1: Calculating business break-even point.

Think this through to see how it works out. If Annie generates $7,500 in income, she'll have to pay out $3,000 in supplies (that's the cost of food at 40 cents in the dollar). This leaves $4,500 gross profit, which is exactly the amount she needs to cover her fixed expenses. This figure is Annie's business break-even point.

Factoring personal expenses into the equation

The break-even chat in the preceding section is all very well, but if your business has a sole trader or partnership structure, you probably need to do more than cover your business expenses, in that you'll need to generate enough income to cover personal expenses as well. (I'm assuming that if your business has a company structure, you already pay yourself a wage, and so your wage forms part of your fixed expenses.)

To bring personal expenses into the picture, you need to repeat the business break-even calculation, but this time include the amount of cash you need to generate to cover personal expenses.

Building on the example earlier in this chapter, here's how to calculate break-even in this kind of situation. Imagine that:

>> Annie has a cafe with fixed expenses of $4,500 per week. These expenses don't include any wages for herself.

>> She needs to generate a minimum of $500 per week in order to cover her personal living expenses.

>> She makes an average gross profit margin of 60 per cent.

The formula is the same; however, this time fixed expenses need to include not just business expenses but personal expenses also.

Break-even point = Fixed expenses (including personal expenses) divided by gross profit margin

You could see how the sums pan out in Figure 10-2. Annie needs to earn an additional $833 per week (that's $8333 in total) in order for her business to break even and for her to generate enough to live on.

	A	B	C	D
1				
2	Average Gross Profit Margin	60%		Based on ingredients costing 40 cents for every dollar sold
3				
4	Fixed Expenses Business	$4,500.00		Staff, rent, insurance and so on
5	Fixed Expenses Personal	$ 500.00		The minimum personal funds Annie needs to survive
6	Total Fixed Expenses	$5,000.00		
7				
8	Break-even Point	$8,333.33		Equals fixed expenses divided by gross profit margin
9				

FIGURE 10-2: Calculating break-even point to cover both business and personal expenses.

Putting theory into practice

Are you ready to calculate the break-even point for your own business? Just before I launch into a step-by-step explanation, I'm going to quickly recap the difference between variable costs and fixed expenses. (For more on this topic, scoot back to Chapter 9.)

>> *Variable costs* (also sometimes called *direct costs* or *cost of goods sold*) are the costs that go up and down in direct relation to your sales, and typically include commissions, the cost of the goods you buy to resell to customers, raw materials and subcontract labour.

>> *Fixed expenses* are expenses that stay constant, regardless of whether your sales go up and down. Typical fixed expenses for your business may include accounting fees, bank fees, computer expenses, electricity, insurance, motor vehicles, rental, stationery and wages.

Got all that straight? Then here goes:

1. **Open a new worksheet in Excel (or any other spreadsheet software).**

2. **Enter your gross profit margin on the first line, similar to Figure 10-2.**

   To calculate your gross profit margin, grab your average gross profit (per unit, product, service provided, month or per year), divide this by sales (again, per unit, product, service provided, month or per year) and multiply by 100. If you're not sure how to do this calculation, make your way back to Chapter 9, where I explain how to calculate your gross profit margin in detail.

   By the way, if you are an owner-operated service business with no employees and no variable costs, your gross profit margin will be 100 per cent.

TIP

   Format your gross profit margin as a percentage. To do this, simply click the % button on the main toolbar.

3. **Add the fixed expenses for your business to the next line of the worksheet.**

   If you're not sure how much your fixed expenses are, Chapter 9 focuses on calculating the fixed expenses for your business. I usually like to calculate break-even and think of fixed expenses on a monthly basis, but you can choose any period of time that makes sense to you.

4. **If your fixed expenses don't include any wages for yourself, add whatever you need for living expenses to the next line of the worksheet.**

   Again, Chapter 9 includes tips about building a personal budget so that you're realistic about how much you need to survive.

5. **Total up your business and personal fixed expenses.**

   Figure 10-2 shows the general idea.

6. **Add a row that calculates break-even point, dividing total fixed expenses by the average gross profit margin.**

   In Figure 10-2, the formula for the break-even point is **=B6/B2**. Simple. You now know what you have to achieve in sales in order to meet your business expenses.

7. **If it suits, express the break-even point in a different time period.**

In Step 3, if you express your fixed expenses as total expenses for a month, consequently your break-even point calculates what you need to achieve in sales per month. However, maybe it makes more sense to you to look at your break-even point per day, per week or per year.

8. **If relevant to your business, express the break-even point in units sold, or the number of services provided, rather than dollars.**

For example, if your break-even point is $10,000 a week and you're selling custom-built handmade guitars at $5,000 a pop, you know you have to sell two guitars a week to break even. Or if your break-even point is $4,000 a month and you're mowing lawns at an average of $50 a lawn, you know you have to mow 80 lawns a month to break even.

WARNING

Calculating a break-even point using the method shown in the preceding steps gives you a general indication of how much income your business needs to generate in order to make neither a profit nor a loss over a sustained period of time. However, this calculation doesn't take into account the cash requirements for a business. A business can make a profit but still have negative cashflow (and vice versa), because of factors such as set-up costs, extending customer credit or building inventory. For a more detailed explanation of cashflow management, see Chapter 17.

TECHNICAL STUFF

ALLOWING FOR PERSONAL AND COMPANY TAX

Are you wondering whether you should include personal income tax or company tax in your break-even calculations? The answer depends on whether your business is structured as a sole trader, partnership or company.

If you're a sole trader or partnership, you're responsible for paying tax on any profit that the business makes. The amount of tax you pay depends on many factors, including whether you have any sources of income other than the business. Depending on your circumstances, you may wish to allow for personal income tax when calculating how much you need to draw from your business to cover a living wage for yourself.

If your business has a company structure, your own wages are almost certainly included in company expenses. For this reason, you don't need to include company tax expense when calculating break-even: If the company is making neither a profit nor a loss, company tax isn't an issue.

Changing Your Break-Even Point

If you find that your business is trading unprofitably, and despite your best efforts you can't get your sales high enough to meet your break-even point, your only option may be to change your break-even point.

Using the principles of break-even calculations, you have three possible solutions:

>> Raise your prices (which is often not an option if you're finding it hard to make enough sales).

>> Cut your variable costs (that is, the costs of production or providing your service).

>> Cut your fixed costs.

For example, if I go back to the cafe owner whose calculations are shown in Figure 10-2, I can see that Annie needs to generate $8,333 per week just to pay expenses. Imagine that the local council is planning major road works and Annie knows that her turnover is going to be affected. She reckons she'll probably generate only about $6,000 a week while the work is going on.

Annie goes to the worksheet where she calculated her break-even and experiments with the different scenarios, shown in Figure 10-3.

>> In Strategy One, Annie can see that she'd have to increase her gross profit margin to 83.5 per cent to break even if sales dropped to $6,000 per week. She knows she can't cut food costs or increase prices this much, so this strategy doesn't seem practical.

>> In Strategy Two, she keeps her margins the same but cuts her expenses by $1,400 a week. This seems to work, but she doesn't know if she can cut expenses by this much and still stay open.

>> In Strategy Three, Annie increases her margin by 5 per cent and cuts her expenses by $1,000 a week. She can see that this will work, and thinks that cutting her expenses by this much is probably possible, especially if her landlord agrees to a temporary reduction in rent.

AHEAD OF THE PACK

The handy thing about understanding your break-even point in this kind of detail is that you can take pre-emptive action if you know that costs are going to increase or sales are going to decrease.

	A	B		C	D	E
1	CURRENT BREAK-EVEN POINT				STRATEGY ONE	
2	Average Gross Profit Margin	60%			Average Gross Profit Margin	83.5%
3						
4	Fixed Expenses Business	$	4,500.00		Fixed Expenses Business	$ 4,500.00
5	Fixed Expenses Personal	$	500.00		Fixed Expenses Personal	$ 500.00
6	Total Fixed Expenses	$	5,000.00		Total Fixed Expenses	$ 5,000.00
7						
8	Break-even Point	$	8,333.33		Break-even Point	$ 5,988.02
9						
10	STRATEGY TWO				STRATEGY THREE	
11	Average Gross Profit Margin	60%			Average Gross Profit Margin	65%
12						
13	Fixed Expenses Business	$	3,100.00		Fixed Expenses Business	$ 3,500.00
14	Fixed Expenses Personal	$	500.00		Fixed Expenses Personal	$ 400.00
15	Total Fixed Expenses	$	3,600.00		Total Fixed Expenses	$ 3,900.00
16						
17	Break-even Point	$	6,000.00		Break-even Point	$ 6,000.00

FIGURE 10-3: Understanding your break-even point enables you to plan ahead for changes in trading conditions.

MONEY STUFF

WHAT DOES SOMETHING REALLY COST?

One of the things that can do your head in when working with costings is the question of how to apportion the fixed costs of your business across every item sold or every service provided.

Think of a business selling homemade fudge. The cost of ingredients for fudge stays the same for every packet sold, but the fixed costs (premises rental, equipment rental, insurance and so on), when calculated on a per packet basis, go up or down depending on the number of packets of fudge made.

For example, if the fixed costs are $700 a week and the business makes 700 packets of fudge that week, the fixed costs are $1 per packet. But if the business makes 1,400 packets of fudge, the fixed costs are only 50 cents per packet.

For this reason, arriving at the 'true' cost of an item can sometimes be hard. For you as a business owner, the challenge in this respect is twofold: First, be ever vigilant about controlling your fixed costs; second, always try to maximise production to make as full use of resources as you can. This may mean making full use of rented premises, keeping staff productive and, of course, ensuring that sales are as high as they can possibly be given this level of expenses. By maximising resources in this way, you keep the fixed costs per unit as low as possible.

Looking at Things from a Cash Perspective

When I was teaching at our local business college, one of the exercises teachers were asked to do with the new students (all of whom were planning their new businesses) was to do a break-even analysis from a cash perspective for the first 12 months of trading.

At first, I was a bit sceptical of this somewhat simplistic approach, because the only way to be really sure how things stand from a cash perspective is to do a proper cashflow, a topic I cover in Chapter 17. However, if you don't offer credit to customers and you don't carry inventory, this cash break-even analysis can be a very powerful and relatively simple-to-use technique.

The idea is that you don't look simply at business profitability, but also at how much cash you have in the bank to begin with, how much cash you intend to spend on setting up and how much money (if any) you intend to borrow.

You can see how this analysis looks in Figure 10-4, where I take the figures for Annie's cafe business (the example I use earlier in this chapter), but imagine that she's in her first 12 months of trading. You can see that when I factor in her existing savings and the fact that she's borrowing slightly more than she needs to spend for the set-up, her break-even point drops from $8,333 to $7,467 per week. What this means, in practical terms, is that although in the long-term Annie does need to generate $8,333 in sales every week in order to break-even, she only has to average $7,467 per week for the first 12 months. This is probably a good thing, because most businesses need some time to build up trading.

	A	B	C	D
1	Calculating the 'Cash' Break-Even Point for Annie's Café for First 12 Months			
2				
3	Annie's Average Gross Profit Margin	60%		
4				
5	**Incoming or Outgoing First 12 Months**	Amount		Explanation
6	Annie's savings available	-$ 20,000.00		Annie's savings before she starts the business, entered as a minus amount
7	Other sources of income for the first 12 months	-$ 5,000.00		Loan from Annie's parents, entered as a minus amount
8	Proceeds from business loan	-$ 80,000.00		Loan from bank, entered as a minus amount
9	Money required for setup expenses	$ 75,000.00		
10	Total fixed expenses (business) for the first 12 months	$ 234,000.00		Annie doesn't include variable costs or wages paid to herself, but does include loan repayments
11	Total personal expenses for the first 12 months	$ 26,000.00		Annie reckons she can just survive on $500 per week
12	Goal to have as balance in the bank	$ 3,000.00		Annie reckons she needs at least $3k in the bank so she can sleep at night
13	Total	$ 233,000.00		Net outgoings
14				
15	Break-even point over 12 months	$ 388,333.33		Level of sales required to break even, from a cash perspective, over the next 12 months. (Equals net outgoings divided by average gross profit margin)
16	Monthly break-even point	$ 32,361.11		
17	Weekly break-even point	$ 7,467.95		
18				

FIGURE 10-4: Calculating what you need to do to break even in the first 12 months.

IN THIS CHAPTER

» Describing what lies at the heart of your business

» Shaping up to your customers' vital statistics

» Converting dreams into figures, ideas into goals

» Building strategies to realise your goals

» Ditching the computer and venturing out in the world

» Setting up systems to stay on track

Chapter **11**

Creating Your Marketing Plan

Marketing isn't about selling, nor is it about advertising. Rather, I reckon marketing is about an attitude; namely, the ability to put yourself in your customers' shoes. When you can see your business from an outsider's perspective, acquiring genuine empathy for your customers, you can provide your customers something that they truly want.

However, this ability to see yourself as others see you is easier said than done. Small businesses don't have big marketing departments devoted to market research, customer focus groups or complex surveys. On the contrary, lack of time, along with the healthy desire to succeed and make a dollar or two, tend to conflict with the ability to see things from a customer's point of view. If you're not careful, you can end up spending too much time selling something that customers don't really want, or that they're not prepared to pay for.

REMEMBER

Every marketing activity you undertake is an expression of your overall business strategy (and if you're not yet clear about what this strategy is, I suggest you return to Chapter 2). In this chapter, I talk lots about developing this big-picture attitude to marketing and explain how a marketing plan is a reflection of your business identity, values and direction.

Laying Down the Elements of Your Plan

If you browse through a dozen business books, you're likely to find a dozen different formats for marketing plans. Here's a format that works well for smaller businesses:

>> **Introduction:** Start with an engaging introduction that explains who you are, what you're selling and what it is that makes your business different. See the following section for details.

>> **Target market:** Who are you selling to? Is your typical customer young or old, nerdy or sporty? Later in this chapter, the section 'Defining Who Your Customers Are' explains how to research this information.

>> **Competitor analysis:** In this part of your marketing plan, you describe who your competitors are, and how you compare against them. See 'Analysing Your Competitors', later in this chapter, for details.

>> **Sales targets:** How much are you going to sell? When? Who are you going to sell to? What will be your pricing policy? See 'Setting Sales Targets' for details.

>> **Sales strategies:** Setting sales targets is all very well, but what strategies do you intend to put in place to support these targets? Later in this chapter, 'Building Sales Strategies' and 'Expanding Your Reach Offline' outline a few possible tactics.

>> **Review process:** In the perfect world, a marketing plan concludes by explaining how you plan to monitor your sales results, and tweak sales targets and strategies along the way if necessary. The last section of this chapter, 'Keeping Yourself Honest', deals with this topic.

Going to the heart of the matter

Perhaps the first step in any marketing plan is to return to the heart of what you do. Why are you in small business? What are your values? Why do you believe that people will benefit from the products or services you sell?

For example, an animation company may seem to be in the business of creating animation, but what they're really doing is trying to spread joy and playfulness. A horticulturalist may seem to be running a gardening business, but what they want to do is find ways to build sustainable gardens without chemicals. A financial adviser may seem to be offering straight-up financial advice, but what's driving this person is a feminist ethos keen to help women become financially independent.

Think about what you're selling and the values that underpin what you do. How do these values create a difference between you and your competitors? Write these values down and think about how you might communicate these values to your customers, and how you can embody these values as core to your marketing strategy.

REMEMBER

One more thing. If you're reading this and thinking to yourself that values aren't a defining element in your business — perhaps you work in a relatively 'ordinary' industry, such as construction, fashion, freight or retail — then think again. Scratch the surface, and all of us have a set of values that define who we are and what we do. Communicating these values and connecting them with your business strategy is key to developing a successful brand.

Expressing your difference

In Chapter 2, I suggest you spend time developing a strategic advantage statement that explains how your product or service benefits your customers, and what differentiates your business from its competitors. As I explain in Chapter 2, this strategic advantage could be many things, including having lower costs, a brilliant new idea, specialist skills, or a right to use certain intellectual property.

The next step is to express both your strategic advantage and the values that lie at the core of your business in a few short words that customers can readily understand. These words (sometimes also referred to in marketing as a *tagline*) become your *USP* — your unique selling point.

For example, a carpentry business might have a strategic advantage of having both CAD software and interior design skills, and the owners are passionate about creating sustainable spaces. Their USP could be as simple as 'beautiful home renovations designed to last'. Or a naturopath with a strategic advantage of qualifications in both naturopathy and counselling who believes strongly in the connection between physical and mental health may have a USP of 'a holistic service connecting body and mind'.

AHEAD OF
THE PACK

The neat thing that happens when you take the time to develop your own USP is that you home in on the thing that makes you different from your competitors, which is an infinitely better approach than trying to be all things to all people. Have a think about what you want your USP to be (or what it already is) and how you can best integrate this into your overall marketing campaigns.

TIP

If you're struggling to express your business identity succinctly, open up your web browser and search for businesses similar to your own. For example, maybe you offer an organic vegie home-delivery service. Search for similar businesses all around the world and check out their marketing slogans: 'Direct from farm to your door', 'Where good food doesn't cost the earth', 'Organics undressed with nothing added'. I'm not suggesting you pinch someone else's selling point, but you can use this material for inspiration.

Defining Who Your Customers Are

Traditionally, the second part of a marketing plan is about defining your target market — namely, who your customers are or who you want your customers to be. For established businesses, defining your target market is largely about analysing who your current customers are, and maybe refining this a little. For businesses just getting started, defining your target market is about describing who you hope your customers are going to be.

REMEMBER

Take time to draw up a description of your ideal customer, even if you don't have a single customer who falls into this category yet. Be ambitious, and don't hesitate to make this definition quite specific. A pitfall for many new businesses is trying to be all things to all people, rather than defining a specific type of customer and focusing all efforts on that.

When defining the type or types of customers you want to reach, or that you already service, ask yourself how sensitive these target markets are to external events such as interest rises, changes in government policy, exchange rate fluctuations or environmental changes. For example, maybe you service a mix of overseas and domestic tourists, but you find that exchange rates play havoc with your overseas trade, making for a stressful boom-and-bust cycle. In this case, you may wish to shift your marketing to focus on domestic trade, thereby stabilising your business.

This deeper understanding of who your customers are, and which customers you want to reach, has never been more important. In the days of print advertising, marketers were consigned to a scattergun approach, placing ads in newspapers or magazines and having to deal with all kinds of responses. However, online advertising enables you to identify your target market with great precision. When you place an ad in Facebook, for example, you typically define the audience for your ad according to many variables, including customer location, age, gender, education and interests.

Analysing your customers

How do you go about describing your customers (either the kind of customer you already have, or the kind of customer you hope to have)? Try to use the following categories when painting this picture:

>> **Psychographic:** What kind of lifestyle does this customer aspire to? What motivates them? How do your values connect with their values?

>> **Demographics:** How old is this customer, what is their age, culture, gender, income bracket, family size or place of residence?

>> **Geographic:** Where is this customer located? How many people live in this area? What is the climate?

>> **Behavioural:** How often does this customer purchase from you? Are they loyal to your business?

Sometimes, pigeonholing your customers in this way can feel confusing, especially if you service a diverse range of people. However, things get simpler if you narrow your target market down to the customers you want to have, rather than the customers you actually have. Similarly, I find that if I focus on psychographics — that is, what motivates my customers and binds them together — the similarities between my customers are easier to identify. (And subsequently easier to create marketing campaigns for!)

TIP

Most social media channels allow advertisers to define their target market not just according to age, gender, location and so on, but also according to interests. Common interests are often key to finding the kind of customers who are the best fit for your business.

Understanding what it is your customers really want

So far in this chapter, I've talked about what it is that you want to achieve with your business. I've mentioned being clear about your strategic advantage and your values, and articulating these in what's commonly referred to as your unique selling point.

However, pause for a minute, and ask yourself what your customers really want. Returning to one of my earlier examples, think about the carpentry business with an aspiration to build beautiful homes. Imagine this business is operating in one of the wealthiest suburbs in Sydney. Is it possible that a typical customer isn't simply looking for a beautiful home, but rather is seeking an elevation in their social status, where friends admire the renovations and envy the money that has been clearly spent? If this were the case, the owners of this business might choose to design a marketing campaign that reflects the desire people have for status and recognition, and not just beautiful timberwork.

When you design a marketing campaign, you are essentially making promises to your customers. Your job is to ensure that the promises you make are a good match for what customers really want, and that you understand the deeper needs that drive the behaviour of your customers.

Thinking creatively about channels

Part of understanding who your customers are includes knowing where your customers are likely to seek out your products or services. For this reason, I suggest you devote some space in your marketing plan to channel analysis. Sounds horribly technical, but channel analysis is simply a description of each channel that you plan to sell through.

Here are a few examples of channel analysis:

>> Katie has a dress shop in the suburbs. However, she also sells some clothes online. Her shop is one channel; online sales are another.

>> Oz Pine Imports sells through three different channels: Small retail stores, large retail Australia-wide chains such as Harvey Norman and Domayne, and online portals.

>> Alice makes jewellery. She sells some at the markets herself, some to a local gift store and some through a party plan. Each of these outlets is a channel.

>> A publisher specialising in outdoor books sells to four different channels: Bookshops, online portals such as Booktopia and Fishpond, camping stores and direct to customers.

Do you sell to more than one channel? (And if not, maybe you should!) Ensure you devote some of your marketing plan to describing each channel. Analyse what proportion of your sales goes to each channel, and whether this channel is growing or declining.

A fundamental marketing decision for your business is choosing the very best location or place for your customers to find your product or service. Always be prepared to think creatively in this regard. Do you need to sell from a different location? What online channels are going to work best? Should you use a distributor? Maybe you should not try to sell your product at all, but instead sell the intellectual property to a bigger business?

Researching the market

If your business is very new or hasn't even started yet, I suggest you include some market research in the first section of your marketing plan. Market research sounds like such a technical term, but can be very simple in practice.

Here are some examples:

>> A friend of mine was thinking of opening a shop selling eco-products. She tested her idea at local markets and was able to discover what products sold well, what kind of person was most interested in her products, and how sensitive people were to price.

>> Years ago, I was finding it hard to choose between two possible commercial leases for a retail venture. I did some market research by standing outside each location and doing headcounts of passing foot traffic.

>> One of my family members is planning to set up a business selling chilli sauce. Part of her research process involves making different sauces and giving them to friends and family, and then asking for feedback about taste and packaging.

REMEMBER

Market research is an essential element not only for clarifying marketing strategies and target markets, but also for minimising your business risk.

BLINKERED VISIONS

One of the dodgiest ways to approach a new small business venture is to think of something you want to sell, and then try to figure out how to get customers to buy it. This approach is called *supply-driven marketing*, and often fails to adequately consider market realities.

Look around you and you will notice heaps of businesses that are obviously supply-driven. That tucked-away house up a bush track selling wooden toys to tourists — you can bet the owners run their business this way because they like making toys and working from home. Or the high-end fashion retailer with a shop in a town with high unemployment and below-average incomes — the owner may live in that town and want to own a business close to home, but many other locations may be more suitable.

In contrast, the other way of looking at marketing is to think about what customers want and, then, how you can give it to them. (This approach is called *demand-driven marketing*.)

Analysing Your Competitors

From time to time, I teach business planning at a local college, as part of a government scheme to help long-term unemployed people start their own businesses. I not only enjoy the experience but also always walk away with new insights about the challenges of starting a business venture from scratch.

One of the things I've noticed during this time is how reluctant many people are to analyse potential competitors. After all, if you're just getting started, you may feel daunted about how your fledgling business will be able to compete with more established competitors. However, analysing competitors as part of your marketing plan is crucial.

I talk in detail about competitor analysis in Chapter 2, but for the purposes of a marketing plan, a neat summary of key competitors will suffice. I show one possible approach in Table 11-1, where I list each competitor, how long they've been on the scene, their estimated annual turnover, how they compare in price, and what they do better and what they do worse. My analysis is for a wholefoods store, but the same principles apply to almost any business. If you can't find out some of the information, just leave that bit blank.

TABLE 11-1 **Example Competitor Analysis**

Name of Competitor	How Long Established	Estimated Turnover	Price Comparison	What They Do Better	What They Do Worse
Wholefoods Direct (online wholefoods)	2 years	Maybe $1 to $2 million	More expensive	Home delivery	No retail outlet
The Organic Bean (local outlet)	10 years	Probably $500,000	More expensive	Good local loyalty	Limited stock range
Coles and Woolworths (national supermarket chains)	Years	Billions	Cheaper for most things; more expensive on some organics	You can get all your groceries in one location	Limited organics range; not such good quality control on products
Orient Stores	6 years	Maybe about $1 million	Cheaper on almost everything	More Asian cooking supplies	No organics

REMEMBER

Your competitors aren't necessarily businesses that are doing exactly the same thing as you are. For example, in Table 11-1, the main competitor for the wholefoods store isn't actually other wholefoods stores, but rather the big supermarket chains. Similarly, many businesses are now finding that competitors are increasingly outside of their local area, as customers choose to buy not only goods online, but services also.

TRUE STORY

Be imaginative when thinking who your competitors could be. For example, many years ago my husband set up a boutique recording-studio business and, as part of his planning, we did an analysis of local competitors, listing all recording studios within 100 kilometres. What we didn't realise was that John's main competition would actually be from musicians recording their music at home, using equipment that was increasingly affordable due to changing technology.

Setting Sales Targets

Your marketing plan needs to explain the detail that lies behind the sales levels from your financial projections. These targets might be measured in units sold, services delivered or number of customers reached. However, targets can also be measured in other terms, such as conversions made, customer satisfaction ratings received, or the kind of new customers acquired.

Expressing sales targets in dollars and cents

In Chapter 8, I talk about creating sales projections for 12 months ahead. Your marketing plan needs to reflect these sales projections, and should include details regarding number of units sold, number of products sold, sales by region or sales by market segment, as well as short descriptions explaining how you arrived at these figures. The idea is that your plan generates a sense of confidence in whoever reads it — even if this audience is just yourself — and that these sales targets should be both achievable and realistic.

However, in some situations, especially for businesses with separate sales teams, you may want to develop two versions of your sales targets:

>> The first version of your sales targets matches the financial projections in your business plan, and is relatively conservative in its sales estimates. Such caution is important when growing a business, because you don't want to end up overspending should sales not be as high as you had hoped. This first version forms the 'real' budgets that senior management and finance staff know must be met, and is usually the version that is incorporated into your marketing plan.

>> The second version of your sales targets includes a decent amount of s-t-r-e-t-c-h, with total sales perhaps a good 15 per cent higher than the first version, and forms the budget for sales staff. This highly specific budget expresses targets in terms of units sold, sales to each region or number of services delivered. Details of bonuses or commissions payable if targets are met may also be included.

While running two sets of targets may sound duplicitous, this method acknowledges the importance of balancing financial conservatism against the need to inspire entrepreneurialism and creative drive.

Expressing sales targets in other ways

Of course, marketing isn't just about selling stuff. For this reason, I sometimes like to set sales goals that aren't just expressed in dollars or units sold, but in other attributes as well. (This strategy makes sense when you think about it: Customers don't rate your services or products simply on price; they look at lots of other traits of your business as well.)

You may want to express sales goals in terms of expanding geographic reach, converting more enquiries to sales, increasing your repeat business, increasing customer satisfaction, or many other things besides. In addition, as I discuss in 'Analysing your customers' earlier in this chapter, you may want to set goals about how many 'ideal customers' you manage to reach, and whether these customers are happy with the service you provide.

In Table 11-2, I list a few examples of sales goals that aren't measured in dollars. In the first column, I list long-term goals; in the second column, I list short-term goals; and in the third column, I list the strategies the business intends to employ in order to support these goals. Non-financial goals vary hugely from one business to another, but the important thing is that you think of what goals might be relevant for you, and that you measure your performance against these.

TABLE 11-2   Supporting Sales Goals with Strategies

Long-Term Goal	Sales Goal for the Quarter	Strategies to Support the Goal
Acquire new customers who have similar values and priorities to us	Acquire at least one new 'ideal customer' each month	Redesign our branding and marketing campaign to reflect the core values of our business more strongly
Increase online sales to be at least 50 per cent of turnover	Grow online sales by 5 per cent	Targeted social media advertising; refresh website; expand blog and online presence
Improve booking rates from enquiries	For every 25 quote requests, aim for 10 sales	Automate email responses for quick replies; engage copywriter to review landing page and email templates
Increase repeat business	Repeat business to be 35 per cent of total sales	Review email campaigns for subscriber lists; create monthly special offers; survey customers after each sale to measure satisfaction
Increase customer satisfaction ratings	For all customers who respond to surveys, over 90 per cent say that they would buy from us again	Review of product quality control; implement 24-hour order turnaround

Remember that every goal you create needs to be SMART: **s**pecific, **m**easurable, **a**chievable, **r**ealistic and **t**ime-specific. Ask yourself:

>> **Specific:** Is your goal really precise about what it hopes to achieve?

>> **Measurable:** Can you measure this goal? (Dollars sold, units sold, new customers gained, email enquiries received and so on.)

>> **Achievable:** Is this goal achievable?

>> **Realistic:** Is this goal realistic? Do you definitely have enough time and enough funds to ensure the goal can be met?

>> **Time-specific:** In what time frame do you aim to achieve this goal?

Building Sales Strategies

For every sales target you set, you need to implement marketing strategies that support these targets. Some strategies can't be specifically matched to targets (for example, building up brand recognition is something that supports all sales targets), but other strategies can (for example, social media advertising restricted to a specific location is a marketing strategy that supports a sales goal to increase local business).

In this section, I talk pretty broadly about marketing strategies, including brand awareness, pricing strategies, social media strategies and customer engagement.

Growing a brand that people want

Brand marketing is very different from direct or transactional marketing. With brand marketing, you're trying to change how customers perceive your company or product, as opposed to trying to make a sale.

Businesses tend to have two types of image:

>> Business image (sometimes also called *corporate branding*)

>> The image of the things they sell (sometimes called *product branding*)

Think of your business as having its own identity, personality and image, and that this identity closely reflects your business strategy (refer to 'Expressing your difference', earlier in this chapter). This image is made up of lots of things, but includes your name and logo, marketing taglines, the design ethos of your marketing collateral, your company dress code, the quality of your products or services, the style of your communications, and the general culture of your company.

AHEAD OF
THE PACK

Branding is one of the most important elements in your marketing strategy. For this reason, I recommend you avoid doing things on the cheap when choosing a business name, getting a logo designed or developing marketing materials. It takes years of experience and training to develop an eye for design, shape, proportion and colour, as well as a high level of skill to understand how these elements interact with your business strategy and vision.

Don't dismiss the concept of branding as only being relevant to big corporates. For example, I have a friend who inherited his father's plumbing business. The business was low-key, run from home with an old, battered van, little advertising and no employees. My friend transformed the whole image of his father's business, modifying the name, leasing a new vehicle, advertising online, employing new staff and radically improving customer service standards. All of these actions were part of my friend creating a very successful brand for this small but growing business.

AHEAD OF THE PACK

Franchises are typically very good at delivering a clear image and a strong brand. If you know of a franchise group that operates in the same kind of business as yourself, have a close look at what they do and how effective their brand marketing is. For example, if you're thinking of starting a cleaning service, check out the image of a couple of successful cleaning franchises. (You, too, can have a snazzy pink and blue uniform.)

Finally, do ensure your brand has adequate legal protection, so that another company isn't able to use your company name, product names or even taglines. I talk much more about brand protection in Chapter 7.

Pricing things right

Pricing your goods or services is another key marketing strategy. In Chapter 8, I explain how any price strategy boils down to one of three things: Cost-based pricing, competitor-based pricing or value-based pricing. I also explain how companies with clearly different kinds of customers may use hybrid-pricing, using one of these three strategies for one kind of customer, and another strategy for another kind.

TIP

MARKETING A SEASONAL BUSINESS

Seasonal businesses can be among the hardest to market. I remember a guesthouse operator saying to me, 'I can sell each room ten times over when it comes to Easter time, but midweek, eight months a year, it's dead as a dodo'.

Here are some tips to ride the highs and lows of a seasonal business:

- Be careful with prices and don't be scared to charge peak rates for peak times — the time when you can really make some profit.

- Offer premium services to maximise peak income — some people just want to spend their money!

- Figure out ways to promote your business in quiet times (for example, midweek specials, offers to schools, corporate events).

- Consider a complementary business to run in tandem with your existing business. I know a firewood delivery business that's flat chat in winter, but when quiet times hit in summer, they have their lawn mowing business to fall back on.

REMEMBER

Although price is a key tool in any marketing kit, the way you position and sell your products and services should always be based on a combination of many different factors, such as quality of product or quality of service, competitor positioning, delivery times, location, availability and ambience, and never just price alone.

Defining your social media strategy

When updating this chapter, I hesitated when deciding how much space to dedicate to social media strategy. After all, whole books are dedicated to this topic, and arguably even then, these books are insufficient to provide all the information you need.

So, in the interests of staying relevant but concise, I want to share five pieces of advice about developing your social media strategy as part of your marketing plan:

>> **Don't pretend social media isn't a thing.** If your business doesn't already have a presence on at least one social media channel (Facebook, Instagram, LinkedIn, Messenger, Pinterest, Tumblr, Twitter, WeChat, YouTube are all examples of channels that are strong tools for business), then you need to get started now. A marketing plan without a social media strategy isn't a real marketing plan.

>> **Understand that each channel serves a different purpose and target market.** If you're selling fashion, Facebook is going to work better than LinkedIn; if you're a high-end consultant, LinkedIn works better than Pinterest. If you don't understand the differences between the main social media channels, and why one might serve your business better than another, seek advice from a marketing expert. Don't just leap into using the channel with which you're most familiar.

AHEAD OF THE PACK

>> **Be clear about whether your posts are aimed to build engagement or generate sales.** Social media is ideal for generating conversations with customers, building loyalty and attracting followers, and this customer engagement is an essential precursor to securing sales. Most businesses find that they need to create a mix of posts that engage customers with news and interesting information, and other posts which are designed to make a sale. You need to be clear about the difference between these kinds of posts, and what you're trying to achieve with each one.

>> **Narrow your market, and then narrow again.** Social media is not about mass marketing; rather, it's about defining your market in a super-specific manner and then creating messaging designed specifically for this audience. Spend time narrowing down your market, defining the audience likely to view your posts, and tailoring your messaging.

>> **If you're not really good at this whole game, pay for help.** One of the traps with social media is that everybody thinks they are an expert. However, speak to professionals immersed in this industry, and you quickly realise that doing social media well requires a great deal of knowledge, time and creative flair.

Engaging customers and building trust

I'm updating this book in the middle of the COVID-19 pandemic (well, hopefully the middle, not the beginning!). One of the struggles many businesses have had during this time is how to maintain their relationships with customers, especially if they've been forced to close down. Right at the beginning of the first lockdown, a marketing consultant advised me that I shouldn't aim to make profits during this period, but rather I should find ways to stay relevant to my customers at a time when they might need my support.

TRUE STORY

At first, I couldn't quite picture how to put this advice to stay relevant into practice, but I've seen many examples over the past few months. A local restaurant, forced to temporarily close, shared on social media that it was now making meals for homeless people, and invited customers to drop off donations of ingredients. The staff in a beachside resort, which was again forced to close, posted daily whale-watching reports and videos. At the writers' residency where I work, we offered free online daily writing sessions to our writing community, who weren't able to travel to Katoomba during lockdown.

Each of these examples shows ways that businesses can engage with customers, even in the most fraught of circumstances. In short, customer engagement is less about making sales, and more about building and maintaining trust.

Here are my top tips for engaging with customers:

>> **Ask questions.** People love to be asked things, whether it's a quiz, a poll, a chance to test their knowledge, or a chance to share their expertise.

>> **Ask for reviews.** If you have an ecommerce site, build in the facility where customers can post their reviews. Not only do you receive timely feedback about your products, but you also provide your customers with an opportunity to have their say.

>> **Create clubs or memberships.** You know the kind of thing — a loyalty club with monthly special offers, or a membership offering exclusive benefits.

>> **Involve your customers.** Find ways to make your customers feel that they are part of your company, and that they have a say in what you do.

>> **Offer things for free.** Find ways to recognise loyal customers. (Giving away services or products for free doesn't have to cost you money, depending on how you organise such offers.)

>> **Run competitions.** Most folk love a chance to win, and you can have great fun with competitions — whether it's asking customers to write their own flash-fiction murder mysteries in order to win a weekend pass to a writers' festival, or offering a weekend away to the first customer who successfully solves a complex riddle.

TIP

>> **Share information that's useful or news that captivates.** A solar panel business might share info about cleaning your panels after a dust storm, for example, or a tutoring business might share tips about managing your child's anxiety before exams.

Finally, don't forget that in the ideal world, customer engagement is about sharing your love of what you do, and having a bit of fun along the way.

TIP

USING DIRECT EMAIL CAMPAIGNS

Emailing customers directly with promos for new products or special offers is an excellent sales strategy. By communicating directly with customers who have already purchased from you or expressed interest in your products, you reap the benefits of highly targeted advertising to a market where you have already established trust.

If you don't have a customer mailing list, I suggest you start right now, collecting contact details from every person who makes an enquiry or buys your goods and services. The best way to organise this information is to use a CRM (customer relationship management) database, a system that is designed to manage all of your company's relationships and interactions with customers. CRM systems typically record customer contact details, sales history and track all communications.

Reputable Australian CRM systems include ActiveCampaign, Hubspot, Microsoft CRM, Netsuite and Salesforce, among many others. Alternatively, you could use a simpler solution that focuses solely on email campaigns and templates, such as MailChimp or Moosend.

The best solution varies according to specific business needs, but if you do choose a full CRM system, ensure you subscribe to something that integrates with your accounting software. This way, whenever you record a sale, this transaction is automatically logged in your CRM.

Again, if you're new to this game, don't hesitate to spend some money getting the help of a professional, particularly at first. Designing strong email campaigns requires good design sense, strong copywriting skills and technical know-how. For example, an expert can advise you as to the best time of day to send your marketing emails, how many words to use as the subject line, how to design landing pages on your website for each campaign, and ways to organise your mailing list into specific target markets.

Do avoid using your regular email software (such as Outlook or Gmail) to send marketing emails to customers. If you send hundreds of emails in one go from an email server, your ISP is likely to interpret your communications as spam, and block sending these to your customers. Also, be careful not to breach anti-spam laws — you can only send marketing communications to customers who have agreed to receive communications from you, or who have 'inferred permission' to receive communications. For more info about Australian legislation, do a search on the *Spam Act 2003* or visit www.acma.gov.au.

Expanding Your Reach Offline

While online sales strategies are undoubtedly powerful, the online space is becoming increasingly crowded as competing voices struggle to be heard. For this reason, I suggest that you guard against confining your sales strategies to online mediums alone. In order to maximise your reach, consider other more traditional marketing techniques as part of your sales strategy mix, including face-to-face networking, public relations, and developing marketing alliances.

Networking (yes, actually in person)

As I write this, still in partial lockdown, the idea of going somewhere to meet other business people where I can smell their perfume, hear the click of their shoes on the floor, or even check out what they're wearing from the waist down, feels positively foreign. However, I know that not all meetings will be held forever on Zoom, and that for many different kinds of businesses, meeting people face to face is key to growing new connections.

An unseemly number of business networking functions tend to take place at some ungodly hour of the morning. Unfortunately for me — a committed night owl — getting up at 6 am to put on my best clobber and be super-friendly to a roomful of strangers is something approaching anathema. However, at risk of sounding like a hypocrite, I know that such meetings are remarkably effective. Almost every time I put myself through the torture, I find that I make a contact or two.

Try to avoid thinking of networking as being exclusively about marketing. If you run a pet grooming business, don't stop talking to someone as soon as you realise they don't like dogs; if you're a builder, avoid making a beeline for the person you know has just bought a new house. Networking is about the long game — building relationships, sharing and listening to people — not about doing a hard sell. With true networking, the name of the game is not to approach the world around you with the attitude 'what can I get?' but with the attitude 'what can I give?' If you're generous with your ideas, knowledge and referrals, you soon reap the rewards. As the law of reciprocity states, what you give out is what you get back.

Of course, growing your business through networking isn't just about joining business groups. Every club or social activity in which you participate is a chance to build a new network, whether this be a parents' group, Rotary, the bowling club or netball. By developing a wider social network, you increase the chance of business referrals.

Investing in public relations

Public relations (PR) is all about discovering little ways to make your customers feel good and improve the image of your company seen from the perspective of the broader community. One of the best examples of good PR that I can think of is my local greengrocer. He always has a smile and a free piece of fruit for every child who walks through the door. Kids love him, parents love him, and for about ten cents a pop, he has the best possible advertising.

Here are some other simple examples of good PR:

REMEMBER

>> Involving customers in the testing phase of your new products

>> Participating in trade shows

>> Remembering customers' birthdays

>> Sponsoring school or community sporting events

>> Submitting press releases to local media outlets

>> Throwing a birthday party for your business and having a sausage sizzle

>> Volunteering in the community

>> Writing guest blogs about topics relevant to your industry

In short, public relations is about how you, your company and your brand are perceived by your customers and the wider public, and is a long-term game of building a strong and positive reputation.

TIP

FOUR CONTACTS A DAY KEEP YOUR WOES AWAY

In the book *Up the Loyalty Ladder*, Murray Raphel describes a 15-minute-a-day ritual that he says is 'virtually guaranteed' to bring wealth, fame and friends. He claims to have received hundreds of letters affirming the success of his technique.

Raphel's technique is this: You make four contacts every day, by phone, email, text message or in person. You commit yourself to doing this, in the same way as you have a coffee break or reply to emails, until it becomes so routine that you don't even think about it.

Creating marketing alliances

Look for businesses that complement your own. I know of a naturopath who sends all her clients to a particular health food store; in return, the health food store displays her business cards on the counter. Similarly, I know of a computer trainer who teams up with his local computer retail outlet so that, in tandem, they provide hardware, software, support and training.

Who can you form a strategic alliance with? Think of cinemas and restaurants, plumbers and electricians, nurseries and landscapers, newsagents and bookstores. Which businesses also service your customers, both before they arrive at your door and after they leave you?

Keeping Yourself Honest

The last part of your marketing plan is where you get to explain how you're going to keep yourself honest. How did your actual sales results shape up against your targets? If your marketing campaign fell flat as a tack, can you pinpoint a reason? In order to do this kind of analysis, you do need to put a few systems in place, right from the start.

Comparing targets against actuals

One of the quickest ways to play the reality versus dreams game is to express your sales targets as dollars (if they're not already) and enter these totals as sales budgets in your accounting software. This way you can compare actuals versus budgets every month quickly and easily.

BEING BRAVE WHEN CUSTOMERS LAPSE

A mistake made by many a small business person is to think of marketing as being about ways to generate new customers. Marketing, though, isn't just about generating new customers; it's also about keeping the ones you've got. (Keeping existing customers happy is almost always much cheaper than generating business from scratch.)

Think of the clients or customers you had one year ago, two years ago, maybe three years ago, and compare this list to the list of clients you have now. Who's dropped away? Who hasn't contacted you in months? Don't wait any longer for them to contact you. Instead, you contact them.

By the way, I'm not just talking about the stereotypical sales rep kind of business when I talk of chasing lapsed customers. Keeping in touch with customers (and if they've gone elsewhere, finding out why), is crucial to the success of heaps of businesses — everything from tyre services to dentists, and consultants to acupuncturists.

WARNING

The downside of simply using totals when comparing actual results against budgeted targets is that you can only evaluate the overall success of your sales targets, and you don't get to see the detail that lies behind. For example, your total sales might be close to the combined total of your sales targets, but if you analyse the whole deal more closely, you could find that actual sales via your website exceeded targeted website sales by 20 per cent, but actual sales made via the weekend markets fell short by about the same amount. Alternatively, perhaps your marketing campaign didn't yield a whole lot of sales, but did manage to engage many new customers, some of whom are now following you on social media.

Measuring conversion rates

Marketing folk talk a lot about conversion rates, an expression that sounds terribly religious, but actually refers to the gentle art of converting queries into sales. Increasing conversions rates is one of the most cost-effective and successful methods of increasing sales.

For example, if you sell kitchens and you do ten quotes in one week and two of these quotes are accepted, the conversion rate is 20 per cent. Or, if you're a computer consultant and you receive enquiries over the phone, and an average of six out of every ten enquiries yields a booking, you've got a conversion rate of 60 per cent. Similarly, if you're selling your wares online, and one in every hundred people who visit your site buys something, the conversion rate is 1 per cent. (Online conversion rates are typically very low, averaging between 1 and 5 per cent for commercial sites.)

REMEMBER

From time to time, take the time to measure the effectiveness of your conversion rates and spend time figuring out how to improve on these. (Tools such as Google Analytics, when configured correctly, are excellent for tracking online conversion rates.) Even better, network with colleagues in industries similar to your own to find out what their conversion rates are.

4

People Power

IN THIS CHAPTER

» Committing to a culture where customer service comes first

» Delivering beyond all expectations

» Measuring customer service objectively

» Making customers feel they're the bee's knees

» Encouraging customers to complain

Chapter **12**

Making Service Your Business

' I bring you flowers,' he cried, 'I wine and dine you,' he mumbled, 'and I tell you that you're beautiful,' he moaned. 'Yet still you do not love me. Oh woe, oh woe, is me.' 'My darling,' she replied, 'the flowers, the wine, the compliments, these are not the things I long for.' But her protestations were lost as her lover stared miserably out to sea.

Thus goes the tale, not only of unrequited love, but also of the human condition. For only when people learn to listen to others — whether to their lovers, their children or their customers — can they genuinely respond. As Florence said to Dougal in *The Magic Roundabout* (three guesses as to my age group), 'There's none so deaf as will not hear.'

And this, dear readers — drum roll, drum roll — is the theme of this chapter. Customer service is about *listening* and *responding* to your customers: Finding out what they expect, what they long for, what they experience. After all, unless the customer tells you what's good and what's bad, how can you ever know?

Creating a customer service culture

Ask successful business people what they think their secret is, and chances are they say something about their customers. In fact, the majority of established businesses list customer service right at the top of attributes vital to their success.

REMEMBER

Customer service means different things to different people. I've heard excellent service described very simply as 'being at your best with every customer' or 'figuring out new ways to help people'. Regardless of the description, the principle remains the same for all businesses — excellent service means always doing the right things, in the way a customer wants.

When you look after customers well, they remember. And, if customers do stray to the competition and aren't given the same red-carpet treatment there, what happens? They soon return to you, appreciative and cheerful. In short, when you offer a superior customer service to that of your competition, you earn yourself loyal customers who not only trust you but also recommend your business to others.

Asking for feedback at every touchpoint

In order to deliver excellent customer service, you need to deliver consistent customer service at every point where a customer interacts with your business. Not only that, but ideally you also need to get feedback from customers as to their experience for each of these touchpoints.

In order to identify these touchpoints, ask yourself: How do customers discover your business and how do they make their decision to purchase? What happens during each transaction? What contact do they have with your business after each transaction?

Here are some suggestions about possible touchpoints and what you may want to assess about each one:

>> **Pre-purchase:** Quality of product information, relevance of advertising, ease of creating an account, helpfulness of reviews, efficiency of live chat, responsiveness to enquiries.

>> **During a sale:** Experience of your premises (accessibility, signage, presentation, parking), ease of navigating your website, positive engagement with your social media posts, interactions with staff, speed at checkout or of delivery, relevance of product information, ease of payment processing.

>> **Afterwards:** Speed of email confirmation, efficiency of billing process, quality and fit of the product or service itself, post-sale marketing emails, quality of post-sales service and online help, timeliness of follow-up.

Don't be daunted by asking customers what they think. Indeed, the responses you receive may surprise you. I know that I've found that many of my customers' suggestions have been surprisingly easy to respond to, and have highlighted ways that I can improve customer service with minimal cost and inconvenience.

TRUE STORY

When the Mini Cooper was released in the US, one of the biggest complaints revealed by independent market research was how unhappy people were with the cup holders, which were too small for American 'super-size' coffees. Market research discovered that many thousands of customers had already decided against buying Minis for this simple reason, and had even been warning friends of this issue. Faced with evidence that demonstrated how one simple change might improve sales so profoundly, the engineers at Mini Cooper finally took heed and changed future models to incorporate a larger cup holder.

Being prepared to listen

What happens if you ask customers for feedback, but you don't like their response? Over the years, I've seen many business owners baulk in the face of customers' suggestions, arguing that such changes would be too expensive or difficult to deliver. However, in order to build the trust of your customers, you must be prepared to develop the capabilities to serve customers how and when they want to be served.

TRUE STORY

A few years ago, a chamber of commerce in Western Sydney that I was working with ran a competition for the Best Small Business Award. As part of this process, nominated businesses were requested to distribute customer surveys asking for feedback on their services or products.

The results from these surveys were fascinating and included both good feedback and bad. The CEO of the chamber saw this as an excellent opportunity for businesses to learn and to improve their service, but was astonished by the response when he shared this feedback with the businesses concerned.

'Customers complain that your coffee is cold,' he told one cafe owner, who responded, 'Customers don't know what they're talking about; our coffee is as hot as can be.' Speaking to a consultant, he shared, 'Customers complain you don't return their calls.' The consultant replied, 'I always return calls; that's not true.'

The moral of this delightful tale? It's not enough to ask customers for feedback; you have to be prepared to listen to this feedback as well!

Cultivating a positive workplace

While you may be naturally adept at delivering excellent customer service, guaranteeing that your employees behave the same way is much more challenging. The secret lies in cultivating a positive workplace where customer service is clearly the number one value.

AHEAD OF THE PACK

>> **Recruitment.** As with almost anything to do with employees, recruitment is key. When interviewing, look for staff who are approachable, empathetic and communicate well.

>> **Treat your employees well.** You can't expect employees to deliver above-average service to customers unless you first create an environment where they feel good about their job.

>> **Invest in staff training.** Even a one-day customer service training course can make a difference and, if all staff participate, demonstrates to staff how strongly you feel about serving your customers well.

>> **Be clear about your values.** If you haven't already, draw up a values statement for your business. Prioritise the importance of respect, inclusiveness and listening.

>> **Recognise and reward.** If a customer tells you of a particularly positive customer service experience, recognise the employee or employees who were part of this, and share the story with others.

>> **Enable employees with the authority to respond to customers.** Avoid micro-managing your employees. Instead, ensure employees feel enabled to initiate actions that resolve customer queries or go the extra step to building customer satisfaction.

REMEMBER

KEEPING WITHIN THE LAW

Behind the principles of customer service lie several laws that you're best to get acquainted with. In Australia, one of the most important federal laws is the Competition and Consumer Act (CCA), a law that pretty much mirrors the various state Fair Trading Acts. (The provisions of these Acts are virtually the same, with state Fair Trading Acts generally used within each state, and the Competition and Consumer Act used for national or cross-border issues.)

Whichever scrap of legislation you refer to, the principles are similar, and refer in a commonsense way to the rights of the consumer, and the responsibilities of you as the seller. For example, anything you sell must be fit for the purpose for which it's sold: You can't sell someone a miracle cure for cancer unless you can provide scientific evidence backing up your claim, nor can you sell someone an entertainment unit when you know the speakers are faulty. The law also forbids you from giving false impressions of your products or services or taking unfair advantage of vulnerable consumers.

Going the Extra Mile

Excelling at service doesn't mean providing a five-star, all-singing, all-dancing experience for every customer — a simple caravan park can excel at service without turning itself into the Hilton. Often, excelling at service simply means meeting customers' expectations, regularly checking out your competitors to see what they're doing better than you, and asking yourself how you can improve your own customer service. This extra level of attention to detail is what attracts your customers' attention and gives you that all-important competitive edge.

Delivering on your promises, and more

Whenever you communicate with your customers, you create expectations of one kind or another. As I mention in the preceding introduction, the expectations of the average tourist booking into a caravan park are pretty different from those of a tourist booking into a five-star hotel. However, the trick for both these businesses is to have some understanding of their customers' expectations and then to deliver beyond them.

PLAYING TRUTH OR DARE

How does your customer service rate? Ask yourself the following questions (no fibs, please).

When was the last time . . .

- A customer was confused about what it is you actually do?
- A customer complained about stuff being late or the wrong goods turning up?
- A customer grumbled that they had trouble contacting you?
- A customer misunderstood your rates and queried the bill?
- An employee had a run-in with a customer, leaving you to pick up the pieces and smooth the way?
- A customer didn't book a second time and you didn't contact them to find out why not?
- You were late by ten minutes or more arriving at an appointment and you didn't contact your customer to let them know?
- A customer complained and ended up even madder after speaking to you or your staff?
- You felt that you didn't know what your customers really wanted?

Your score? Give yourself ten points if your answer is never, zero points if the answer is more than six months ago, and minus 20 points if the answer is six months ago or less.

50 points or over: You're an angel and your customers are blessed. Decorate your halo.

0 points to 40: As my Year 9 teacher used to say: 'Could try harder.' Consider enforced exile to a cold and barren island.

–10 or less: Icy showers and daily jogs at dawn for you, dear reader, followed by a diet of brown rice and beans for at least a month. (This is a truth or dare quiz, after all.)

AHEAD OF THE PACK

Finding a way to exceed your customers' expectations is often remarkably easy. The caravan park owner may provide birdseed so guests can feed the parrots; the boutique hotel may remember, with the aid of its database, a customer's preferred kind of coffee. Have a think about how you can do this for your business:

TIP

>> **Communicate and keep customers informed:** For example, imagine your reaction if a plumber messaged you to advise of a ten-minute delay. (I think I'd die of shock and delight, on the spot.)

>> **Deliver the same quality of service, every single time:** Delivering great customer service every now and again isn't enough. In order for customer service to be exceptional, a customer needs to have the same experience every time.

>> **Over-deliver on your promises:** Deliver early and finish the project before the deadline.

>> **Pay attention to small details:** The wording of emails, packaging of products, or presentation of your business premises are examples of details that matter.

>> **Think of ways to make your customers feel special and important:** Send handwritten thank you cards with your online orders, seek advice from customers about possible changes to your business, or provide help carrying heavy baskets or bags to the car park.

THE PHYSICAL THING

You don't have to look like Cate Blanchett or Chris Hemsworth, but if your business involves meeting customers face to face, projecting a good image is vital.

Ask the following questions about yourself and your employees and see how you rate:

- **Do you smile and look customers in the eye when you first see them?** Eye contact, along with a winning smile, is a wonderful thing.

- **When did you last see soap and hot water?** This means clean hair, clean fingernails, clean clothes and not a single cabbage leaf behind an ear.

- **How do your greetings rate?** You know, stuff like, 'Good morning, can I help you?' or 'G'day, how's it goin'?' (Anything is better than looking up with a blank expression waiting for the customer to say something.)

- **What expression do you wear when you're serving customers?** Maybe get someone else to give you feedback on this. Happy and interested is in; boredom and indifference are out.

- **Do you manage to thank the customer and say goodbye when you're done?** The basics — 'Thank you' and 'Goodbye', along with a chirpy Aussie equivalent to 'Have a nice day' — are all that's needed.

Understanding how to build trust

For me, the most important element of customer service is being able to trust the person or the people I'm dealing with. Key to building this trust is authenticity, expertise and consistency.

This quality of authenticity is often what strikes me first. I'm quick to sense whether the person helping me believes in what they're doing, and genuinely wants to assist. Of course, a sense of humour doesn't go astray either, especially when it comes to complex or time-consuming interactions.

Expertise is perhaps next on my list. If the person I'm dealing with is knowledgeable, then I'm quick to appreciate that, particularly if they're willing to share this knowledge and take the time to make sure I understand what they're trying to communicate. Similarly, if I'm transacting online, if I know that a company's information is always detailed and accurate, this helps me trust their products.

Finally, I guess for me to grow trust in a brand or a business, I need to experience a high level of consistency. Even though I recognise the challenges of delivering great service every single time, particularly for relatively new companies with a small number of employees, I know that it only takes one or two poor experiences to erode my confidence.

Brainstorming how you can do better

It may seem a bit wacky, but one way to brainstorm customer service, especially if you have three or more staff, is to get into some role-playing with your staff (kind of like charades except hopefully you're all sober). The idea is that you get together and ask one person to act out a particular role — maybe a customer who's new, confused, cranky or even all three — and appoint someone else to take the role of the person on the receiving end. Everyone else watches and, after the role-play is finished, they give feedback and comments. Sometimes it's good to act out what terrible customer service looks like, as well as excellent customer service.

I also like to ask staff how they would improve customer service if they were the boss. (I find something about this question sparks a certain candidness in the response!)

In short, role-play allows you to put yourself in someone else's shoes. Not everyone finds this an easy thing to do but, regardless of this fact, role-play is a great trigger for getting staff to think about what it's like to be on the other side of day-to-day transactions.

TIP

You can emerge from role-play exercises with an agreement among staff and yourself about how to deal with certain customer situations. (If you're unsure about how to initiate customer service exercises, search online for 'customer service e-learning tools'. It may be that an online self-paced tutorial is a practical way to build the skills of yourself and your employees, and provide some ideas for role-play.)

TRUE
STORY

I know of a gym that used role-play games to explore how new customers felt when they made enquiries or joined up. As a result, employees now operate with checklists detailing everything staff ought to cover when they receive a customer enquiry, a new customer membership or a membership renewal. The checklists mean that all customers receive the same high standard of attention and service — and guess what? The system is working really well!

Appreciating the need for speed

Customers expect speed, especially when it comes to any early interactions they have with your business. After all, if you don't get back to customers straight-away, your competitors are only a mouse click away.

I realise that replying within the hour isn't always possible, especially if you're a small business owner who is not only serving customers, but also chief bottle washer, bookkeeper and marketing director to boot. Here are some ideas to help respond to customers swiftly, even when resources are limited:

AHEAD OF
THE PACK

>> **Automate as many routines as possible.** If you find yourself typing data from one place into another (for example, whenever you receive an online sale you have to enter the details of this sale somewhere else as well), then look at automating these processes. If This Then That (IFTT) is a super handy app that specialises in getting different bits of software to talk to one another.

TIP

>> **Configure your website and social media channels so that you send automated replies to all enquiries received online.** You know the kind of thing — a message that tells the customer their enquiry has been received and you'll get back to them shortly.

>> **Consider employing a virtual assistant (VA) to deal with online enquiries for times that neither you nor your staff are available.** VAs may sound super high-tech, but are actually an accessible and affordable option for many small businesses.

>> **Look for industry-specific apps.** For example, I run an Airbnb and recently came across a neat app which automates almost all my responses to book-ings, including confirmations, reminders and follow-ups. At only $5 a month, this app saves me two to three hours per week.

>> **Provide customers with tracking information.** If you're selling goods online, you may find a large proportion of enquiries relate to the status of orders. Let customers know as soon as their order is shipped and, wherever possible, provide tracking numbers so they can look up the status of their order themselves.

Continuing service after the sale is made

Last year, I purchased a venetian blind online for the bedroom skylight. Even with help from my son, I really struggled to install the blind and once I'd finished, I found the blind was very tricky to open and close. In short, I wasn't super happy with the product or the company. However, a couple of weeks later I received a phone call from their marketing department asking if I was happy with the blind, and how I'd gone with the installation. When I explained what was happening, the technician realised that the blind was missing a bracket. She posted the bracket to me that day which I then attached to the blind, and now everything works just fine.

I guess what impressed me so much about this call was that the company made the effort to provide me with service *after* the sale, even though I hadn't made contact with them at that point. For your business, the best way to follow up with customers might be a phone call, an email, sending a link to complete a survey, or providing the ability for customers to leave reviews on your website. Following up sales in an active manner means you're able to respond to feedback more promptly, fix problems and, of course, increase your chances of securing this customer's business next time.

Evaluating Your Performance

Ensuring high standards of customer service requires a commitment to evaluating how you're going. In the ideal world, you not only invest in measuring customer service using clear metrics, but also benchmark your results against others in the same industry.

Designing surveys

Customer surveys can be deceptively tricky to design. Here are some pointers to help navigate these murky waters:

TIP

>> **Be clear about why you want the feedback:** Refer to 'Asking for feedback at every touchpoint' for ideas. Don't try to measure everything at once, but instead focus on a particular area and limit the number of questions you ask.

>> **Be specific:** Don't simply ask, 'How do you think we could improve our customer service?' Rather, focus in on likely problem areas, perhaps asking, 'Do you have any comments or suggestions about our product warranty service?'

>> **Include scope for customer comment and feedback:** Don't limit yourself to gathering ratings out of ten or providing a selection of boxes for customers to tick. Instead, ask customers for comments, suggestions and ideas — people are often incredibly generous with their time and input.

>> **Measure specifics:** See 'Reflecting on other service benchmarks' later in this chapter for some ideas.

>> **Use software designed for the job:** Specialist survey software radically simplifies the process of distributing surveys, collating responses and analysing results. In addition, the better software solutions also provide lots of pointers for good survey design. I recommend SurveyMonkey (www.surveymonkey.com) as an accessible and affordable tool.

Measuring your speed

Earlier in this chapter, in 'Appreciating the need for speed', I talk about the importance of speed as an element of customer service. With this in mind, I recommend you measure in minutes, hours, days or weeks every element of your customer service. For example, you might measure the average time it takes you to respond to a phone call or email enquiry, how many days your company takes to send somebody a quote, how long the average customer spends in your waiting room, how long it takes you to complete a job, the time between a customer placing their order and receiving their goods, or how quickly you resolve problems.

Try to shorten times wherever possible by improving processes and training staff. Also, in the ideal world, see if you can compare the speed of your service to that of your competitors, and take action to stay one step ahead.

Reflecting on other service benchmarks

As well as speed, I like to use three other benchmarks for measuring customer service: customer satisfaction score, net promoter score and customer retention rate.

Customer satisfaction (CSAT)

The CSAT is one of the most straightforward ways to measure customer satisfaction. You measure CSAT simply by asking, 'How satisfied were you with your experience?' and then asking your customer to rate you on a scale of 1 to 5 or 1 to 10.

**AHEAD OF
THE PACK**

One neat thing about CSAT is its wide popularity as a measure of customer service, meaning you can readily compare yourself with others in the same industry. Typically, a good CSAT score (in other words, the average of all your customer responses) falls between 75 and 85 per cent. For example, if you score 75 per cent and you're using a scale of 1 to 10, this means that three out of every four customers have given you a score of 6 or higher.

Net promoter score (NPS)

The NPS measures customer loyalty, and specifically measures how likely your customers are to refer you to someone else. Compared to the CSAT, the NPS asks customers about their intentions, not just their emotions. Accordingly, how customers respond is less influenced by their mood at that particular moment, making this measure particularly significant.

You measure NPS by asking customers how likely they are to recommend you on a scale from 1 to 10. If someone scores your service with a 9 or a 10, they are a promoter; if they give you a 7 or an 8, they are a passive; if they score you 6 or less, they are a detractor. To calculate the NPS, you calculate the difference between the percentage of promoters and detractors. For instance, if you have 45 per cent promoters, 25 per cent passives and 30 per cent detractors, your NPS is +15.

Again, a neat thing about measuring your NPS is that you can benchmark against other companies in your industry. For example, in 2020, education and training companies enjoyed an average NPS of 71, where healthcare providers rated much lower with 27. Leading customer loyalty companies such as Apple typically reach scores of 75 to 85 per cent.

Customer retention

This measure refers to the ability of your business to retain customers over time and is typically calculated on a monthly or annual basis. In the following example, I calculate the measure for one month. The maths is a little grisly, but here's how it's done:

1. At the end of the month, add up how many customers you have.

2. Subtract the number of new customers you acquired during the month from this total.

3. **Divide the result from Step 2 by the number of customers you had at the start of the month.**

4. **Multiply the result from Step 3 by 100.**

   In other words, if I had 100 customers at the end of April and 90 customers at the beginning of April, but I acquired 19 new customers during the month, then my customer retention rate would be 90 per cent.

TIP

While you may be able to compare your customer retention rates against others in your industry, this measure is also useful to monitor on a regular basis so that you can observe how your customer satisfaction increases or decreases over time.

Showing That You Care

Some people reckon that caring is something you either have in your nature or haven't. Pish tosh. Most people relate to others in a way that's 90 per cent habit and 10 per cent genuine response, in a manner so ingrained that they don't even think about it.

The wonderful thing about most bad habits is that you can change 'em, given a little willpower and a few nicotine patches. So, in this very warm-and-fuzzy section, I talk about ways to show your customers that you care.

'I appreciate how you feel'

The phone rings at an insurance company. A clerk dons their headset and accepts the call. A distraught voice calls out . . .

Caller: My house has just burnt down! Everything has gone. I'm ringing to find out about my insurance.

Clerk: Right, no problem. Can I have your policy number please?

Hmm. Apart from the fact that any record of this policy has probably just gone up in smoke, the thing that's so terribly wrong about the clerk's response, of course, is the lack of *empathy*. You want to communicate your appreciation of the person's problem — a sentiment that's just as important as finding a solution.

TIP

You can teach yourself and your staff to be empathetic by becoming conscious of the way *you* use language. If a customer approaches you with a problem, get into the habit of replying using a sentence that begins with the words, 'I understand . . .', 'I'm sorry . . .' or 'I can appreciate . . .'. Role-play games work well to help change habits and learn new ways of communicating.

You can practise empathy in lots of little ways, at work and at home. Maybe, when your partner/colleague/daughter next hassles you about the washing-up, you can answer, '*I understand* you're upset about the washing-up. It's a real bummer. *I'm sorry* I haven't washed up for the last six months. *I can appreciate* it's a problem and you must feel bad.' (Just remember to duck.)

'I've done that sometimes!'

Wherever you are, in whatever situation, trying to find a common bond with someone is innately human. The same thing is true in business, where most customers are keen to build a relationship with you, of one kind or another.

Maybe you're on a Zoom meeting, and a client says, 'I can't make our appointment next week — I'm off to London with the kids.' You can say, 'Ah, London, that's where I was born!' or 'Gee, that's a long flight with children, how old are they?' Or perhaps someone says in your shop, 'I just love that dress, but yellow makes me look sick.' You can reply, 'Yellow makes me look dreadful as well. I find pale colours suit me best.' The idea is to build rapport and demonstrate common ground. In short, *be interested* in your customers and who they are!

'Let me confirm what you just said'

'Hi,' says the lady at the restaurant. 'I'd like a Greek salad please, but with no onions, no shallots and the dressing separately on the side. And a little bit of salt and no anchovies. Thanks.'

'All right, I think I've got that,' answers the waitress with a vague expression as she scribbles in her pad. 'Oh, what's that about salt?' Five minutes later the salad arrives, complete with dressing on the top and anchovies mixed in. The waitress looks taken aback when her customer complains.

The following week, the lady tries again, at a different restaurant this time. 'Hi,' she says quietly. 'I'd like a Greek salad please, but with no onions, no shallots and the dressing separately on the side. And a little bit of salt and no anchovies. Thanks.'

'No problem,' answers the waitress. 'But let me confirm that: A Greek salad with no onions, shallots or anchovies, a separate dressing and just a little salt. Is that right?' 'Thanks,' comes the reply, and five minutes later a happy customer munches into her rather odd Greek salad.

TIP

Listening is a technique, and people who are good at listening like to confirm they understand the other person. They use phrases such as 'Let me confirm what you just said . . .' or 'You're looking for so-and-so? Is that right?' or 'I'd like to summarise your request.'

When you build these special *listening* phrases into your vocabulary, they become habits in the way you respond and listen to your customers. A simple trick, perhaps, but one method that certainly works.

Can I help you with anything else?

Consider how you can fit this question (or a similar question) into your business, using whatever expression you or your staff are most comfortable with. You don't have to say it in exactly the same way; the following phrases are also perfectly okay:

» What else can I do for you today?

» How else can I help you?

» Are you looking for anything else?

» Do you have any other questions I can answer for you?

Extending customer interactions in this way helps create a sense for the customer that you have time and space to provide them with the service that they need.

FUN AND GAMES

AHEAD OF THE PACK

Here's one way to get staff thinking creatively about customer service. At your next staff meeting, ask everyone to recall and share an example of great service they experienced recently, along with an example of not-so-good service.

What happens is that someone tells a positive tale and everyone else says, 'Wow, that's *fantastic*.' They may even suggest ways to match this service in your business. Then someone comes up with a negative tale (maybe something simple, like a shop assistant dumping the change on the counter) and everyone jumps on the bandwagon: 'Yuck, that's *terrible*. I hate it when someone does *that*.'

This simple technique reinforces within the group what's okay and what's not. As well as taking merciless advantage of the powers of peer pressure, group discussions also create a culture where everyone has to think regularly about the experience of customer service.

Dealing with Complaints

While discouraging to receive, more often than not, a customer complaint presents an opportunity for you to improve your customer service and secure the edge on your competition. Indeed, complaints are so helpful, I reckon all businesses need to ensure they create accessible platforms where customers can provide feedback quickly and easily.

REMEMBER

Successful businesses are prepared to listen to customers, follow up on every bad customer experience, fix things for that customer as much as possible, and then take steps to correct systems so that these experiences don't happen again.

Why complaints are serious

Think back to the last time you experienced poor service and ask yourself whether you complained to the business in question. Next, think about how many people you told (if any) of your negative experience.

If you're anything like most people, you didn't complain to the business but you've not been shy in telling others about your experience. This kind of response is because over 80 per cent of people who receive mediocre or poor service don't complain — unless, of course, the business is wise enough to actively seek feedback. However, what most people do is share their poor experience with colleagues, friends, neighbours and family.

WARNING

A person with a complaint is likely to tell an average of nine others about their bad experience, and happily name the offending business in *every* telling of the tale.

Extrapolate these delightful statistics and, well, having a hernia on the spot ain't out of the question. For example, if you received four complaints in the last 12 months, multiply this number by five to come up with an estimate of how many unsatisfied customers you actually have. (This calculation makes 20, by the way.) Then, multiply 20 by nine (you get a whopping 180) and you have the number of people hearing bad things about you. I show how the maths works in Table 12-1.

How to respond to complaints

Some people are great at dealing with disgruntled customers, smoothing their ruffled feathers and wooing them back to happiness in the blink of an eye (and actually enjoy the process). Others find customer complaints incredibly difficult, responding to aggression with hostility and to criticism with defensiveness.

TABLE 12-1

How Many Complaints Have You Received This Year?

Number of Complaints You Hear About	Number of Actual Complaints	Number of People Who Hear the Bad Things
1	5	45
3	15	135
5	25	225
10	50	450

Here's my five-step process for dealing with tricky customers:

1. **Take your customer's complaint seriously.**

   As I show in Table 12-1, every complaint you receive represents up to 45 people who, unless you can resolve this complaint, might otherwise hear negative things about your business through word of mouth.

2. **Listen to your customer.**

   If you receive a complaint in person or on the phone (rather than via email or online), immediately pause what you're doing and take the time to really listen to what the customer is saying.

3. **Put yourself in the customer's shoes, and use empathetic language.**

   Try to understand the problem from your customer's point of view, putting yourself in the customer's shoes. Use sentences that begin with *I understand*, *I appreciate* and *I'm sorry*. Don't be tempted to hurry the customer straight to the solution stage. The customer wants to feel heard and understood almost more than anything else.

4. **Respect your customer.**

   Sometimes it's easy to minimise customer complaints by poking fun at them once they are out of earshot. Instead, it pays to respect that others have different values from yourself, and respecting such differences is core to understanding good customer service.

5. **Take steps to rectify the problem or compensate the customer.**

   Wherever possible, offer immediate action.

6. **Review your processes and decide how you can avoid this problem occurring in the future.**

7. **Share with the customer what steps you have taken, or are about to take, so that this problem won't happen again.**

REMEMBER

This last step is the single most important step you can take. If a customer knows you not only took their complaint seriously, but have also changed how you do things so that others won't experience this problem, they will know that you have genuinely listened to them. Such customers may even return to your business to trade with you again, which is a significant turnaround from being in a position where they felt motivated to submit a complaint.

Chapter **13**

Becoming an Employer

I remember the great feeling I had when my small business grew big enough to be able to afford my first employee. I was able to not only give someone else a job, but also take the first tentative step towards preparing my business for the time when (hopefully), it didn't need me there 24 hours a day, 7 days a week (okay, maybe I exaggerate my working hours a little).

You may find the number of laws surrounding employment a bit daunting when you first start employing people. Suddenly, you need to understand tax, superannuation, insurance, workplace safety and much more.

I understand that all this bureaucracy can be a tad overwhelming at first, and so, in this chapter, I set out to explain everything employer-employee related in the simplest way possible. With any luck, you can soon enjoy the liberation of being an employer without feeling weighed down by tedious legalities.

Becoming an Employer: The First Steps

The employee checklist in Figure 13-1 lists everything you need to know in order to hire your first employee, with individual items from this checklist explained in more detail throughout the rest of this chapter. (Note that this checklist sets out your minimum obligations as an employer. In contrast, a best-practice checklist would also include things such as health and safety checklists and induction procedures, topics that I discuss further in Chapter 14.)

Becoming an Employer Checklist

Getting started

- Have all employees completed a Tax File Number declaration?
- Have you supplied all new employees with a Fair Work Information Statement?
- Have you taken out a workers' compensation insurance policy so that your employees are covered in the event of an accident?

Pay day

- Is your payroll software Single Touch Payroll (STP) compliant and do you submit pay details to the ATO with every pay run?
- Do you provide payslips with every employee pay that include all of the necessary information, such as employer name, date and period of payment, any deductions and superannuation payments?
- Do you maintain and keep all necessary employment records, including wage rates, leave history, superannuation details, nature of employment (for example, full-time, part-time or casual) and hours worked?

Staying the right side of the law

- Does your business comply with all relevant awards?
- Do you have a copy of all relevant awards at your workplace available for employees to read?
- Have you double-checked with your accountant whether any contractors should really be considered employees for taxation, superannuation and/or workers' compensation purposes?

Covering your back

- Do you have a written workplace safety policy?
- Do you have a sexual harassment policy?

FIGURE 13-1: Your employer checklist.

If all these steps feel overwhelming, do consider hiring a bookkeeper to help, if only for a few hours every fortnight. A bookkeeper can not only help you to manage payroll, but also help keep many aspects of your business admin in order, leaving you free to get on with doing what you do best.

Getting employees to fulfil their part of the deal

The very first step with your new employees is to get them to fill in a form outlining their personal details. No, not *that* personal, just a bit personal:

1. **On the employee's first day, provide the employee with a Tax File Number declaration.**

   You can order this form online from www.ato.gov.au or by phoning the ATO on 1300 720 092.

2. **Ensure the employee completes this declaration before their first payday.**

   I suggest you provide an incentive: Say, 'No form — no pay.' Why? Because if an employee *doesn't* give you a completed declaration by the time payday comes around, you have to deduct tax at a rate of 49 per cent.

3. **If the employee is entitled to any tax offsets, provide a Withholding declaration form.**

   Some employees claim reduced tax rates by anticipating an entitlement for zone tax offsets, invalid carer tax offsets and so on. However, if someone who is entitled to a tax offset *doesn't* complete a Withholding declaration, and you deduct tax at the standard rate, the employee gets a refund at tax return time.

REMEMBER

4. **Post or electronically lodge the Tax File Number declaration to the Tax Office within 14 days of the employee completing the form.**

   You have no idea how often employers forget to send off these forms. So dare to be different, and get your form(s) to the Tax Office without delay.

5. **Store your copy of each employee's tax declaration in a private place.**

   No, I don't mean your undies drawer. Rather, store employee declarations in a place where other employees can't find them.

WARNING

The *Privacy Act* places immense obligations on an employer to protect the tax file numbers of their employees. They must not be available to anybody who does not have a proper and authorised reason to access them.

Covering employees for accidents

As an employer, you must ensure that your employees are insured in the event of an injury in the workplace. The idea behind workers comp is that all employers pay insurance to cover for the event of an employee getting injured at the workplace. This insurance means the employee receives compensation if unable to work.

If you're a business owner, you must take out a workers compensation insurance policy, even if you only hire one casual and they only work for you every now and then. Otherwise, you will be personally liable should any kind of accident occur in the workplace.

REMEMBER

Be careful how you — or your insurance broker — categorise your business when you first sign up for workers comp or accident cover. Premium rates vary enormously depending on what industry you're in, ranging from below 1 per cent for bank tellers (the only thing injurious to their health is terminal boredom), up to an eye-watering 11 per cent for NSW professional footballers.

MONEY STUFF

The best way to keep premiums down is to be proactive about safety in your workplace — one employee accident and your annual insurance premium may well skyrocket. (I talk lots more about occupational health and safety in the section 'Playing Safe and Playing Fair', later in this chapter.)

Ensuring your software is up to speed

If you're hiring your first new employee, you need payroll software that can deal with Single Touch Payroll (STP). The idea of STP is that whenever you pay an employee, the software automatically submits details of this payment to the ATO.

In case you're wondering, you can't do this by logging onto the ATO and entering this information manually — the only approach that the ATO accepts is that you use third-party payroll software that is approved as 'STP-ready'. You first use this software to record your pays, and then the software sends a summary of wages, super and tax to the ATO.

If you're just getting started with a small business, this requirement can seem pretty onerous. However, any regular accounting software sold in Australia is able to deal with STP (and if isn't, beware!). Also, if subscription costs are your concern and you have four employees or fewer, you can find a list of approved payroll software solutions on the ATO website that all cost less than $10 per month (just go to www.ato.gov.au/STPsolutions).

Subscribing to super

The whole superannuation rigmarole gets a little overwhelming for new employers. To keep up to date (after all, the information that I write here could have changed by dinner time, let alone by the time you're reading this), I suggest you visit www.ato.gov.au/business and make your way to the Super for Employers page. However, at the moment, the superannuation samba steps go like this:

1. **Figure out whether you need to worry about super at all.**

   If you have any employees who earn more than $450 a month, in any one month of the year, you have to pay super on their behalf. Also, if you pay contractors under a contract that is wholly or principally for labour, you have to make super contributions for them, even if they quote an Australian Business Number (ABN).

2. **If necessary, sign up to a default super fund.**

   Sometimes employees don't already belong to a super fund or are slow to provide this information. If an employee fails to provide you with details of their super fund by the date their super is due, you have to pay the super into your *employer-nominated fund* (also referred to as your *default fund*). You can choose what this fund will be, so long as it is a 'MySuper' product (for a list of approved products, go to www.apra.gov.au).

3. **Unless the employee first provides you with details of their super fund, supply all new employees with a Standard choice form.**

Depending on the award or employment agreement, most employees are entitled to choose their own superannuation fund (rather than having to pay into your employer default fund). Unless an employee has already provided you with their preferred super fund, you need to provide them with a Standard Choice Form within 28 days of starting employment.

4. **Ensure you have complete super fund details for each employee.**

In order to pay super on behalf of an employee, you need the name of the fund and that employee's membership number.

5. **With the aid of your payroll software, figure out how much you owe.**

Superannuation is a handsome 9.5 per cent of gross wages. (This rate is set to increase to 12 per cent by 2025.) So, for example, if you pay an employee $500 a week, you pay an additional $47.50 a week (which is $500 multiplied by 9.5 per cent) into a complying superannuation fund on the employee's behalf. Remember the threshold, however: If an employee earns less than $450 in a month, you don't pay super that month.

REMEMBER

Stay clear of heavy fines and pay super for everyone who's entitled to it, even if you've hired and fired an employee by the time you come to pay super.

6. **Double-check you're not paying super on any payments exempt from super.**

You only have to pay super on *ordinary time earnings*. In other words, you don't have to pay super on things such as some kinds of annual holiday leave loading, one-off bonuses and overtime. I provide a summary of the definition of ordinary time earnings in Table 13-1.

Also, if an employee is under 18 and works 30 hours a week or fewer, you don't have to pay super. Some domestic workers such as nannies and housekeepers are also exempt if they work fewer than 30 hours a week. (Why housekeepers, who are saints sent from heaven as far as I'm concerned, should be a unique category deprived of super beats me, but there you go.)

REMEMBER

7. **Pay up.**

You're obliged to pay superannuation on the 28th day after the end of each month or quarter (the minimum frequency is per quarter, but some super funds specify that you have to pay monthly).

TABLE 13-1   When You Have to Pay Super (and When You Don't)

You Must Pay Super on . . .	You Don't Have to Pay Super on . . .
An allowance that is unlikely to incur additional expense (such as a first-aid allowance)	An allowance that is likely to be fully expended by the employee (such as motor vehicle allowance where the employee is obliged to use their own car)
Annual leave loading if referable to lost opportunity to work overtime	Other annual holiday leave loading
Bonuses	Accrued leave on termination
Casual or shift loadings	Ancillary leave such as jury duty
Payments in lieu of notice	Benefits subject to FBT
Government wage subsidies	Maternity or paternity leave
Holiday pay	Overtime payments
Long service leave	Redundancy payouts
Personal leave/carer's leave	Reimbursement of expenses
Regular wages	Workers compensation payments (where no work is performed)

Meeting Minimum Pay and Conditions

As an employer, you're obliged to offer employees certain minimum pay and conditions such as annual leave, personal leave and additional loadings for casual employees. You also need to know about the limits that are in place for the number and arrangement of hours you can require people to work. Minimum pay and conditions vary depending on where your business is located, the industry in which you're operating and your legal structure.

REMEMBER

The main thing to be aware of is that the onus is on *you* as the employer (rather than on the employee) to understand what the minimum legal pay and conditions are.

Understanding what laws apply

One of the first things that you need to research is what award or awards are relevant to your employees. An *award* is a special document that outlines minimum wages for employees in a particular industry or occupation. If an award exists for your industry, you as an employer have to stick by it. You can't contract out of an award by getting an employee to agree to lesser conditions or agreeing to ignore their award.

TIP

As well as researching employee minimum wages, you must also research minimum employment conditions, such as annual leave and maximum working hours. In all states other than Western Australia, employment conditions for private businesses are covered by the National Employment Standards (NES). In Western Australia, the award itself covers minimum employment conditions for sole traders and partnerships.

Figuring out what legislation applies to your workplace and location can be tricky, and something that is difficult to summarise in this book due to the frequent changes that arise. Accordingly, I start with a clear caveat: At the time of writing, my information is up to date. However, the onus is on you to double-check that what you read here still applies.

With this in mind, here are some pointers to ensure that employees are paid correctly:

1. **Check that Fair Work Australia is the correct source of information.**

   At the time of writing, if you're a company structure or you operate from any state other than Western Australia, contact Fair Work Australia (phone 13 13 94 or visit www.fairwork.gov.au) for information about pay scales and employment conditions. However, you may want to check with your industry association or local chamber of commerce that this reference is still correct.

   If you're a sole trader or partnership based in Western Australia, visit www.commerce.wa.gov.au or phone 1300 655 266 for information about pay scales and employment conditions.

2. **Review the pay, leave, awards and entitlements that apply to your industry.**

   Go to the Pay, Leave, Awards & Agreements, and Employee Entitlements pages at www.fairwork.gov.au. With pays, if you're not certain what award applies to your business, seek further advice.

REMEMBER

   The awards that apply in your workplace are a vital reference for any payroll officer. Carefully read through every award relevant to where you work. Whenever you have a query about an employee's pay, keep in mind that these documents are a primary reference.

3. **Check that your workplace complies with National Employment Standards.**

   The National Employment Standards (NES) provide a safety net that outlines ten minimum entitlements for all Australian employees, including maximum weekly hours of work, parental leave and annual leave.

   The beady-eyed among you may spot that this document refers to *minimum* entitlements. Beware: Certain industry awards require you to provide more generous conditions than those described in the NES.

TECHNICAL
STUFF

WHAT ABOUT WORKPLACE AGREEMENTS?

Although awards may seem restrictive in their conditions of employment, employers and employees can still seek flexibility with the use of enterprise agreements or individual flexibility arrangements (IFAs).

Enterprise agreements are agreements made between employers and their employees about conditions of employment, including things such as rates of pay, annual leave, allowances and dispute resolution procedures. These agreements typically follow a bargaining process between the employer, employees and union representatives, and must be registered with the Fair Work Commission within 14 days.

In contrast, *individual flexibility arrangements* (IFAs) are smaller in scope and are only able to vary working hours, overtime and penalty rates, allowances and leave loading, and may be negotiated with individual employees. Neither employer nor employee can force an IFA upon the other. The employer doesn't have to register IFAs with the Fair Work Commission.

Sounds simple enough, but if you're running a small business you probably have enough on your plate just understanding the minimum pay and conditions relevant to your industry. My suggestion is that you first focus on understanding the current awards that apply to your workplace before you spend precious time and energy setting up an enterprise agreement or negotiating IFAs.

WARNING

Don't be hoodwinked into thinking that you can pay above the minimum for some things and below the minimum for others, justifying this juggling act by saying the two cancel each other out. The only time trading pay or benefits is okay is if an employer negotiates some kind of registered workplace agreement, and registers this agreement with the relevant industrial relations body.

Choosing between part-time, full-time or casual

The basis on which you employ someone is an important consideration. Generally speaking, here are your employment options:

>> **Casual employment:** The most flexible and open-ended of all employment options, as well as being (theoretically) the easiest to terminate. However, casual rates are higher than permanent rates and long-term casuals are often entitled to many of the privileges that apply to permanent staff (such as long service leave and security of tenure). In addition, some Australian awards now require that if a casual works regular shifts for more than six months, you

convert employment to a part-time basis. I suggest you only use casual employees for ad hoc shifts and relief work. This approach avoids the risk of a disgruntled long-term casual lodging a claim for sick or holiday pay or getting burnt out because of not getting a decent break. After all, if work becomes scarce in the future, you're legally able to reduce hours or make positions redundant.

>> **Fixed-term employment:** A part-time or full-time position, but for a finite period of time (for example, six or 12 months). You must have a robust reason for only offering a fixed term, such as a specific one-off project, or a parental leave position.

>> **Full-time employment:** Probably the easiest and most cost-effective option, from an administrative point of view. However, if you have a downturn in trading, varying hours or terminating employment may be both difficult and complex.

>> **Part-time employment:** Works well in that you can secure staff commitment and reliability, but the main drawback in comparison to offering somebody casual employment is the lack of flexibility for you, the business owner. (You still have to offer work, even if business is quiet.)

WARNING

CASH ECONOMY — BEAUTY OR BEAST?

If you're tempted to pay an employee cash in hand, I suggest you pause for a moment and think carefully. When an employer pays cash wages to an employee, the employee receives all the benefits (in that they don't pay tax on their wages) but the employer faces extra expense as well as significant risk.

The extra expense eventuates because you can't claim this employee's wages as a tax deduction. For example, what may appear to be cheap wages at only $20 per hour could cost you more than an employee who you pay $30 per hour, simply because you can't claim cash wages as a tax deduction.

In addition, you carry the risk that this employee could have an accident while working for you. If you haven't put this employee through the books, they won't be covered by your workers compensation and you, as the employer, will be held personally liable.

Playing Safe and Playing Fair

Although it would probably take you about 15 years to read through all the handbooks and regulations concerning workplace safety, also known as workplace health and safety or WHS, this area of the law isn't as complicated as you may think. Scratch a little deeper and you see that workplace safety is really a consciousness-raising exercise (I'm sounding pretty seventies now), encouraging both employers and employees to be responsible.

Workplace safety isn't just about preventing people from getting their legs chopped off in sawmills or being run over by tractors. Instead, workplace safety covers all types of workplace environments, discussing such things as the length of time employees should sit at a computer without a break, how hot the urn in the kitchen should be or ways to organise work schedules to reduce stress.

The buzzwords with workplace safety are 'proactive' and 'preventative'. The idea is that you try to integrate safety practices into your business, supplemented by some kind of written workplace policy. As time goes on, safety becomes a habit, with both you and your employees working together to keep your workplace safe on an ongoing basis.

Being practical, not pedantic

Here are some practical options you can work towards, to make your workplace as safe as possible:

WARNING

>> Set limits on lifting weights. From a workplace safety perspective, claiming 'it was my employee's choice to lift the heavy sack' simply doesn't keep you free from prosecution.

>> Display clear operating instructions next to any machinery — even the food processor in a kitchen or that urn in the back office.

>> As required, make sure staff are supplied with and use personal protective equipment (PPE). (**Remember:** PPE must be used in accordance with the manufacturer's instructions.) Always have a first-aid kit that is adequate for the sort of injuries and situations you're most likely to encounter on the premises. Try to make sure at least one employee has a first-aid qualification.

>> Provide a smoke-free workplace.

>> Ensure you have measures in place to prevent common injuries such as slips, trips and falls, and manual handling, ergonomic and repetitive strain injuries (these last two items apply particularly to staff working on computers all day).

>> Ask employees to actively watch for risks and dangers in their workplace. Place health and safety on the agenda of regular staff meetings and document these discussions as proof that you work actively on your health and safety procedures.

>> Provide all new employees with a health and safety overview as part of their induction.

REMEMBER

The preceding list is brief — my aim is to provide a starting point so that you can get a feeling for your obligations. Stiff penalties may apply if you breach workplace safety regulations, so I do recommend you take the time to find out a little bit more. Visit the website for the relevant Workcover or Worksafe authority in your state.

AHEAD OF THE PACK

Keeping your workplace safe requires ongoing commitment. Figure 13-2 provides an overview of how to approach your business health and safety strategy.

Health and safety review cycle

Find out all the legislation and regulations that you have to comply with (these can vary depending on your location and industry, so be sure to check with your relevant state authority or industry body).
⇩
Determine your own workplace health and safety policy, including how you consult with staff about health and safety issues, and ensure your policy is understood and communicated.
⇩
Choose someone to focus particularly on workplace safety as part of their role within your business.
⇩
As a team, make a list of all possible risks in your workplace and ensure everybody understands their responsibilities in relation to workplace health and safety.
⇩
Prioritise these risks according to their likelihood and possible consequences, and start a program to deal with each one.
⇩
Ensure adequate employee induction and training in regards to safety.
⇩
Record your progress in writing.
⇩
Review policies and workplace safety regularly.

FIGURE 13-2: Workplace health and safety is an ongoing process.

Blonde jokes are over

You probably know by now that *any* kind of harassment in the workplace — whether teasing, initiations, practical jokes or ethnic taunts — is completely out. And, of course, sexist jokes, unwelcome invitations and unsolicited touching are all no-go activities, whatever your gender.

TIP

The easy way to avoid any problems is to draw up a simple anti-harassment and anti-bullying policy, where you make it clear what behaviours are okay and what behaviours aren't. Communicate this policy to staff — stick it on the wall if necessary. Also, plan to make it part of what you cover with new employees on the day they start with you. *Note:* Your business policy also needs to include appropriate use of the internet and email.

IN THIS CHAPTER

» Getting clear about what's needed

» Casting your net wide to attract bees to your honey

» Interviewing and picking the best match for the job

» Understanding leadership and creating a workplace where people want to be

» Managing staff and reviewing performance

» Dealing with difficult employees

Chapter **14**

The Art of Management

While small businesses are often credited as innovators, the paradox is that the poor managerial skills of owner-managers prevent many small businesses from achieving their full potential.

Even if your workplace is relatively small and you only have one or two employees, you still need to set high standards for yourself when managing staff, and aim to build a workplace that is as positive and productive as possible. The best workplaces are where employees feel involved in the day-to-day running of the business, where the values and aims of the business are clear, and where employees feel they can have fun and learn new things.

If you're new to running a business, defining the ingredients of being a good people manager is tricky. In this chapter, I talk about recruiting good staff, building great relationships with your employees and creating a workplace where people really want to be. I also talk about the 'pointy' end of management, and share tips and ideas about how to manage tricky employees.

Drawing Up a Position Description

When recruiting new staff, drawing up a position description (also sometimes referred to as a 'job description') is an important first step. At this point, you want to include aspects such as the purpose of the role, skills or qualifications required, hours and location of work, key areas of responsibility, specific duties, and relation to others (either reporting or managing). You have a much better chance of recognising the perfect applicant when you see them if you've already thought carefully about the essentials of the role.

A recruitment expert who helped with this chapter explains the concept like this: If you're in the market for a 'new' second-hand car and you write out a list of criteria at the beginning such as 'four doors', 'big boot' and '4WD', you're much less likely to be sucked in by a beautiful (but completely unsuitable) bright pink sports car that you stumble across at the car yard.

Position descriptions also provide a clear set of management expectations, so that employees are clear about where their job responsibilities begin and end. If you're not sure how to write a position description, don't worry. The bare bones of a position description are simple:

1. **Start with the title of the position.**

   Include enough information in the title so that it indicates the nature of the work as well as the level. Be careful with the words you choose. For example, don't give someone the title of 'Manager' unless you're prepared to delegate and let that person actually be a manager.

2. **Specify who this employee reports to, and who reports to this employee.**

   If this employee is below someone else in the pecking order, make it clear from the start. Similarly, make it clear if this employee will have anyone else reporting to them or if they are going to be responsible for the supervision of others.

3. **Write a couple of sentences that describe the purpose of this person's role.**

   In short, why does this job exist?

4. **State how many hours a week the job involves, the employment basis, and any non-standard conditions such as weekend work, working in very hot or very cold environments, or heavy lifting.**

   By employment basis, I mean whether this position is full-time, part-time or casual.

5. **List the duties that the job involves.**

    Itemise everything the person is responsible for doing, from opening the shop at the beginning of the day to putting the sign out, from preparing financial reports to managing stock levels.

    For more senior roles, document the key responsibilities, such as supervising staff and managing budgets, instead of trying to capture every specific task. Outline the areas where the manager is allowed to delegate: 'May authorise expenditure up to $5,000' or 'May call in casual staff to meet service demands'.

TIP

6. **List the outcomes that you expect this employee to meet.**

    You may find this clause overkill if you're a small business just getting started but, on the other hand, setting outcomes does pave the way for clarity in any relationship. For example, if you include debt collection as part of the duties of a bookkeeper, you could include an objective such as 'Ensure no more than 5 per cent of debtor accounts are more than 90 days overdue'.

7. **List what qualities you're looking for.**

    At this point, I recommend not having too many requirements, but instead focus on the essentials by listing no more than five key aspects. For instance, if you're recruiting a person to work in accounts, they're going to need attention to detail, competence with technology and accuracy under pressure. Friendly customer service is a bonus rather than essential in this role.

8. **List the minimum qualifications, education, skills and experience required for this role.**

    Of particular importance here are any licenses or documents legally required as part of the role — for example, a Working With Children Check.

REMEMBER

Make sure your position description allows you room to move. I like to add a clause that says something like, 'The duties in this position description may be modified and updated by the employer from time to time following agreement with the employee. The employee also agrees to perform all other reasonable duties and comply with reasonable instructions issued by the employer.'

Playing the Recruitment Game

Take a moment and think about your previous workplaces and the different people you encountered. Visualise the very best employee you worked with, and then visualise the very worst. The gap between the two can be pretty huge, can't it? This gap is precisely the reason, when working for yourself, you must invest time and care when recruiting new employees.

Although being a good judge of people isn't something you learn overnight, creative recruitment and good interview techniques all combine to make the process of choosing new staff more likely to be successful.

Reaching the best applicants

When recruiting, I reckon it pays to cast your net as widely as possible. After all, the more applicants you reach, the better your chance of finding excellent staff.

The most obvious starting point is usually to advertise, placing an ad in a prominent jobs website such as SEEK. I also suggest you advertise the position in your social media channels and on your website. For less skilled jobs, your local newspaper or even a sign in the window may be an alternative.

However, one limitation of advertising is that the best people are often already in employment. To counter this limitation, try to find ways to attract the *passive job seeker* — the person who isn't actively seeking work but may be interested in working for you — so that you maximise your chance of getting the best applicants. To attract passive job seekers, start by letting friends, families and colleagues know about the vacancy and, at the same time, use social networking tools such as LinkedIn and Facebook. For example, I subscribe to the recruiter version of LinkedIn, which lets me contact people with specific skills or professions within my regional area, letting them know that I have a vacancy available.

If both social recruitment and traditional recruitment fail to deliver the employee you're looking for — maybe you live in a regional area or you lack experience interviewing and choosing staff — a recruitment agency may be a good way to go. Although agencies can be relatively expensive, this fee will be money well spent if you can find the right people you need to grow your business.

Selling the position

Here's my number one tip when advertising for a new employee. Ask yourself: '*Why* would an employee want to work here, and what makes us so special?' Bear in mind that the best employees probably already have a job, and if you advertise a vacancy simply by saying, 'Shop Assistant Wanted. Minimum Wages Paid', you're unlikely to yield great results.

TIP

When I write a job ad, I tend to visit the SEEK jobs website first and behave as if I'm a job seeker, searching for jobs like the one I'm about to advertise. I then read through a dozen or so ads, and pick the best ideas from each one. With this in mind, I get ready to create my own ad. Things to include in your ad are:

- » **The basics:** Include the job title, a brief description of the work involved, and whether this position is full-time, part-time or casual. (In regards to pay, I either mention a pay range or skip specifying this at all, because I leave this to be negotiated in the interview.)

- » **Why this job is so great when compared to others:** Figure out what you can offer that makes your job more appealing, such as a great location, opportunities to learn new skills, study leave or flexible working hours. Highlight these points in bold right at the top of your ad.

- » **Essential and desirable criteria:** List the skills, experience and attributes essential for the job, as well as those that are desirable. The more specific you are about what you're looking for, the easier it is to weed out applicants and find the best ones to interview.

- » **How to apply:** Depending on the volume of applicants, you may wish to simply supply an email address. However, for more professional or hard-to-fill positions, I suggest providing a contact name within your business, along with a phone number. You want to make it as easy as possible for prospective candidates to contact you.

Throughout the recruitment process, remember that the aim of the game is to get the very best employees you can. Keep 'selling' the position whenever you speak to prospective employees, so that they feel attracted to you and the workplace you offer. However, at the same time do be careful not to oversell the position. For example, be careful not to give misleading information on salary potential when advertising, especially in situations where staff sell on commission or via referral selling.

Picking the Best

So, you've advertised the position, gone through the applications, and you're ready to start the interview process. In this next section, I talk about what questions to ask (and not to ask!) during an interview, and how to be confident about selecting the right person.

REMEMBER

If a job applicant has been recommended to you through word of mouth, even if they are a friend or a member of your family, don't be tempted to shortcut the recruitment process. You still need to request a full application and resume, conduct an interview and follow up this person's referees.

Asking the right questions

Because staff requirements vary so much from business to business, I can't tell you exactly what questions to ask. However, here are some ideas to get you started:

TIP

>> **Keep questions relevant:** Make sure your questions relate to the essential and desirable criteria listed in the position description, and for the most part ask each applicant the same questions — that way, you're comparing apples with apples. Take written notes of the replies, rating these replies out of five or ten so that you can keep an objective measure of your response.

>> **Be specific:** If the job has a technical aspect, don't be scared to ask specific questions that test their knowledge. You can take advantage of special tests that are available for most jobs, such as typing speed tests, mechanical aptitude tests, using an Excel spreadsheet to calculate something or asking the candidate to watch a short YouTube clip and then take notes.

>> **Check out creativity:** Ask applicants an off-beat question such as: 'If you were prime minister for a day, what would you do?' (I'd ban lawnmowers on Sundays, roadworks on public holidays and any speeches lasting longer than ten minutes.)

>> **Check out problem-solving abilities:** Ask the applicant to think of a tricky situation that they've faced in the past, and to describe how they dealt with it. If faced with that situation again, what (if anything) would they do differently?

>> **Go digging for toxic behaviours:** Ask for one or two things the applicant liked least about his or her last (or current) company. If this applicant complains about their past or current employer or colleagues during the interview, take this as a warning. History has a habit of repeating itself.

>> **Remember practicalities:** Remember practical stuff such as when the applicants are able to start, the kind of pay they're looking for, what hours they can work and how flexible they are. At this point, don't forget that in the same way as this applicant is 'selling' to you, you are also 'selling' to them. If you can be flexible with hours, choice of workdays or work location, now is the time to say.

Avoiding the wrong questions

Although I'm sure you are well aware of equal opportunity and anti-discrimination legislation, here are a few practical examples of the kinds of topics to avoid:

WARNING

>> Be super careful about family issues. Questions such as, 'Do you have any children?' or 'Are you married?' or 'Do you have any plans for more children?' are totally unacceptable.

>> Never ask about someone's childcare arrangements. If the job requires travel and/or extended hours and you want to check the applicant's availability, ask something like, 'This job requires someone to travel overnight for a couple of nights every month, and to work the occasional weekend. Is there anything that would prevent you meeting those demands?'

>> Even more inappropriate than personal and family history are questions or comments about topics such as religion and nationality.

>> Health issues are also tricky (although you can ask 'Are there any health issues that may prevent you from doing this work?'). If the applicant mentions a health problem, don't automatically exclude this person from further consideration, but instead assess whether the problem would prevent the applicant from doing their job properly.

>> Questions about drug use or sexual preference are definite no-go areas.

TIP

One catch-all question that *is* okay to ask, and which often results in applicants offering up personal information, is 'Do you have any other commitments that may affect your work or availability?'

Matching people and positions

Here are some ideas to help you make the final decision about who is the best person for the job:

TIP

>> **Think about capabilities, not just about skills.** By skills, I mean the knowledge of how to complete a task, such as how to lay a tile floor, update a database or complete a tax return. By capabilities, I mean an aptitude for learning or a capacity to innovate, such as the ability to quickly learn how to tile a floor, or the ability to figure out how to update a database. If you're in an industry that's facing rapid change, capabilities become more important than skills.

>> **If you're still not sure, ask for a second interview.** If interviewing more than one person for a second time, ask similar questions of each interviewee and rate their replies to each question out of five or ten. After the interview, add up the totals and see who gets the highest score. This somewhat clinical approach contributes objectivity to the process.

REMEMBER

>> **Don't underestimate the importance of attitude.** You can't judge a person by skills and work experience alone; personality is important too. Think about how well this person is likely to fit into your existing team.

>> **Speak to at least two of the applicant's referees.** I suggest you only follow up referees right at the end of the recruitment process, after you've pretty much decided to offer somebody a job. Checking references is a vital part of the recruitment process, providing you with the opportunity to explore any concerns or lingering doubts you may have. However, I do feel that referees are so important that sometimes, when I can't decide between two applicants, I seek references for both before making a final decision.

Also, make sure at least one reference is from a person who has previously supervised the applicant. If applicants don't give you the details of their supervisor in their job immediately prior to this one, ask them why. I remember doing a reference check once, just before offering someone a job, and the voice at the end of the line said, 'What? He gave *my* name as a reference? I can't believe it . . .'

Offering Someone a Job

So, you interviewed Fred or Sheila or Bruce (or whatever the applicant's name is) and you reckon you've found the perfect person for the job. What do you do next? Don't just phone 'em up and ask if they can start tomorrow. Instead, make contact, offer the job and, if the person accepts, write a handsome and professional letter of appointment.

Sending an offer of employment

Exactly what you include in a letter of appointment depends on what you included in the position description, and whether you wish to include a separate employment agreement. However, look to the checklist in Figure 14-1 for the key elements that you need to include in either the letter of appointment or the employment agreement. (This checklist may seem a tad bureaucratic, but the good thing is that it lays sound boundaries and expectations, right from the start.)

Offer of Employment Checklist

Essentials to include in either your letter of appointment or your employment agreement

- ❑ Your business name and the location of your workplace
- ❑ The employee's name and details
- ❑ The title of the employee's position
- ❑ The proposed starting date
- ❑ The rate of pay and any allowances payable, including details of the relevant award and classification (if applicable). (Indicate whether or not the pay rate quoted includes compulsory employer superannuation contributions.)
- ❑ Employment status (full-time, part-time or casual)
- ❑ Actual hours, including meal breaks, tea breaks and overtime
- ❑ Details of holiday and other leave entitlements
- ❑ Duration of any probationary period
- ❑ Termination provisions — cover under what circumstances you can terminate the employee's employment, and what period of notice the person would receive
- ❑ How much notice you require from the employee if they resign
- ❑ Space for the employee to sign acceptance to the terms and conditions of your offer (make sure you get this signed copy on or before commencement)
- ❑ A full job description that outlines duties and responsibilities, and clearly states the need for all employees to comply with your business policies and procedures

Other non-essential things

- ❑ Comments regarding confidentiality of information and trade secrets
- ❑ Basic employee details form, detailing important stuff such as bank account details, emergency contacts and super fund details
- ❑ Restrictions on setting up a competing business during the term of employment or for a reasonable time afterwards
- ❑ Your company policies regarding equal opportunity, workplace safety, harassment, bullying and so on

---

FIGURE 14-1: Checklist for what to include in a letter of employment.

Setting a probationary period

I recommend that you start all new employees with a probationary period and that you state the conditions of this probationary period clearly in your letter of offer. The great thing about probationary periods is you get to observe how an employee fits in and whether they have the skills you require. (Fair Work Australia recommend that probationary periods are limited to three months, but can last longer depending on the nature of the job and if agreed in writing.)

TWO EARS, ONE MOUTH — USE THEM IN THAT RATIO

Sadly, most people in our society are much better at talking than they are at listening. However, unless managers learn to listen to staff, they risk missing out on valuable feedback and ideas.

When discussing issues with employees, try rephrasing what someone has just said and saying it back to them, using a sentence that starts with, 'So, do you mean . . . ?' Ask questions to clarify what someone is saying or encourage a response with comments such as, 'I'd like to hear more about that.'

Active listeners learn to tolerate silences in a conversation (murder for a chatterbox like me!) and to acknowledge what someone has said in a reflective manner; for example, saying, 'That must be very challenging for you.' In essence, being good at active listening means you know how to let the other person feel heard.

For more active listening tips, type 'active listening' into YouTube (www . youtube . com) and check out some of the many hundreds of free tutorials on this topic.

WARNING

Just because an employee is on probation doesn't necessarily mean you can dismiss this person with no explanation or warning. During a probation period, the onus is on you, as the employer, to clearly communicate your expectations and try to assist the employee if these expectations aren't met. I advocate that you give probationary employees a performance review interview at least once every four weeks throughout the duration of the probationary period.

Learning to Lead

Many people tend to think of business leaders as visionary CEOs responsible for transforming large companies. In reality, especially for small business, this kind of top-down, directive style is rarely successful, and most experts would agree that small business owners who rely upon a more consultative leadership style achieve the best long-term profitability.

A consultative leadership style involves coaching rather than directing, mentoring rather than instructing, and encouraging rather than criticising. This kind of leadership style not only helps employees to do their job better, but also necessitates a change in the way you think about your employees. Because coaching is your responsibility, you are less likely to blame staff for their mistakes, and you're more likely to reflect on how you could do a better job leading and mentoring. This in turn tends to result in a more productive and positive workplace.

Daring to delegate

No matter how fantastic you are, even if you're a multi-tasking, multi-skilled, perfect-demographic-kind-of-super(wo)man, you have only so many hours in the week that you can work. At some point or other, you're going to have to let go and trust others to do some of the work for you.

This step can be kind of tricky for control freaks, because in order to delegate work to others, you've got to be able to trust a little. You've got to have faith in your staff and trust they can do their jobs (and not immediately bite off their heads when they don't). However, the beauty of trusting in this way is that if your staff can get on with things without you, and get a kick out of doing their jobs well, they're going to want to carry on doing this to achieve even better results.

REMEMBER

All the delegation in the world doesn't do you any good if your staff don't know what they're meant to be doing (which is where clear position descriptions come in), and if your staff don't know how to do their jobs (which is where training and good systems are so vital). As a leader and as a delegator, keep your team well informed and give people the support they need.

Building a positive workplace

If you can build a positive workplace with staff who want to come to work and make your business as successful as it can be, you also build your own freedom. You build a business where you can afford to take holidays, get sick, go bush; indeed, do all the things that normal people do.

Here are some ideas about making your business somewhere that employees really want to be:

>> **Ask for staff input in regards to day-to-day decisions:** Asking for input is different from delegating decision-making power. Ask staff what they think, and take the time to find out the opinions of those who never speak up. Even if you don't agree with them, employees are likely to appreciate the opportunity to have a say, so long as you're sincere in seeking their opinion.

TIP

>> **Be clear about your values:** What does your business really value? Innovation and creativity, ethics and compassion or contributing to the community? Be clear about what your values are, and consider formalising your values with a values statement and a code of conduct.

- » **Be fair:** Sounds so easy, but being fair can be surprisingly tricky, especially in family businesses when children are also employees.

- » **Fix problems forever:** Encourage everyone to fix problems so they stay fixed; draw up new policies or procedures if need be so you can avoid repeating your mistakes. Announce that the boss is NOT always right and you're prepared to admit you make mistakes like everyone else.

- » **Foster an environment where learning is highly valued:** Most employees are happiest if they have an opportunity to learn and grow. This doesn't necessarily mean running training courses or spending hours coaching staff members, but can be as simple as encouraging everyone to share information and knowledge with one another.

- » **Help build positive working relationships between staff:** Don't tolerate any kind of bullying or verbal aggression, particularly from your managers towards your staff. Provide opportunities such as staff BBQs or pizza lunches for staff to get to know each other.

REMEMBER

- » **Support and acknowledge staff achievements:** Openly celebrate achievements in staff meetings, such as a staff member completing their studies, someone receiving positive feedback from a customer or a deadline being met. (Remember that salespeople are not the only heroes!)

Communicating every way you can

Close your eyes and think of people you know who are naturally good communicators. Then think of people you know who are real shockers. Now look at yourself from the outside and ask yourself where you fit in the scale of things.

Sure, communication is a skill that's more natural to some than others. However, anyone can improve their communication skills by doing simple things:

- » **Be honest:** Don't hold grudges or pent-up frustrations. If something annoys you, spit it out (but nicely!).

- » **Communicate early and often:** Most managers don't communicate early enough or often enough with staff members. If employees do well, say so. If they stuff something up, show them how to do it better. Be specific in your feedback so that employees know precisely what to keep doing or stop doing!

AHEAD OF THE PACK

NO TIME TO MAKE TIME

Don't postpone training staff because you're so strapped for time that you think, *It's much quicker to do the job myself, rather than show someone how to do it.* The problem is that you end up doing everything and thinking that you're completely indispensable.

So, next time when you think you can do something quicker yourself, press your pause button and ask, 'If I spend an hour teaching my employee to do this today, how many hours can I save over the course of the next year?'

Chances are, you're going to save heaps of hours and earn great dividends on the time you invest.

>> **Don't put up with grouchy staff:** If a member of staff is sullen and grouchy, find a private moment to ask the person what the problem is. Be prepared to listen to the response — honesty is a two-way street! — and offer help if you possibly can. This kind of conversation doesn't mean you need to take on the role of life coach or counsellor to your staff — it just means lending an ear in the event staff want to talk, and giving them some reasonable time and space to work through their issues.

>> **Share a little of yourself:** Be human. Tell your employees that your only social life is your customers, your staff and the dying pot plants at home. Rave on about your sporting obsession or dance around the office when you're happy.

Don't Worry, Be Happy

Happy employees make for happy workplaces. As an employer, you need to reward employees properly for their input, help them evaluate their progress and be aware of how difficult managing change is.

Rewarding with more than money

Fortunately for the average cash-strapped small business, keeping staff happy doesn't necessarily have to mean doling out big bonuses, extravagant company cars and paying for school fees. Instead, you can help to keep your staff happy in many everyday ways:

REMEMBER

TIP

>> **Be nice:** Remember employee birthdays, acknowledge staff achievements or offer to make everyone a cup of tea. Have a mufti day for a charitable cause.

>> **Be as flexible as you possibly can:** If you can, offer part-time employment, not just full-time, and be flexible about start and finish times, particularly for those with children. Consider offering time-in-lieu, rostered days off, additional annual leave or leave without pay.

>> **Let people work from home, if practical:** If COVID taught us anything, it taught us just how much employees can actually do when sitting at home in their pyjamas.

>> **Offer discounts for company products:** Again, this option probably doesn't cost you much (maybe you can even make additional sales!) but employees appreciate it.

MONEY STUFF

>> **Offer flexible pay conditions:** You may have some flexibility with pay rates or conditions so long as you keep the legal minimums in mind.

Reviewing performance regularly

Whatever your perspective, and no matter how small your enterprise, providing some kind of formal performance review process for your employees is important.

I've changed the way I approach employee performance reviews. I used to think of performance reviews as a chance to appraise employees and provide some measured feedback, with a sprinkling of judicious criticism where required. Now, I see performance reviews as a two-way process: Yes, I do give employees some feedback, but equally important is finding out how the employee feels about working for me. I like to ask employees to rate their employment from 1 to 10 on a whole heap of factors, including whether they feel involved in the business, whether they think management listens to feedback and how happy they are coming to work.

AHEAD OF THE PACK

Although performance reviews offer an opportunity for you to discuss any minor concerns that you have, reviews shouldn't hold any big surprises for an employee. If you're really concerned about an employee's performance, you should address these issues as they occur, and not wait until their review falls due. (See 'Managing Difficult Employees', later in this chapter, to find out more.) Instead, the emphasis in a performance review should be how you can work together to improve productivity, how to organise priorities, and what additional staff training may be required.

Managing change

You probably know the maxim that goes, 'The only thing constant is change'. Well, the saying that should go hand in hand reads, 'Where there's change, there's resistance'.

TIP

Here are some tips to help employees manage the challenge of change:

>> If employees fear change because of the unknown, reassure them about what is to happen and precisely how these events may affect them. If systems or processes are going to change, ensure employees receive enough training for these changes to flow through successfully.

>> If employees fear change because they feel that they lack control, involve them as much as possible in the process, and encourage them to talk with you about their concerns as the change progresses.

>> If your employees are worried about the time and effort involved in changing, try selling the outcome of the change to them, explaining how it may be good for them.

>> Always acknowledge that change is difficult, so express your appreciation for your employees' efforts.

REMEMBER

Some employees are always going to be cynical about change, no matter how well you present things, so don't waste too much time or effort on trying to convert them. You may even need to cut to the chase, and clearly state the reasons for the change as well as your expectation that they cooperate with the change effort.

Managing Difficult Employees

So, you thought your employee was the bee's knees, the cat's pyjamas, a true ruby-dazzler and more. But time has passed and your dream employee is driving you bananas.

As tempting as it may be to hand this employee a final pay on Friday with a warning never to darken your doorstep again, the much smarter move is to act with more caution. Too often, inexperienced employers tend to blame employees when things don't go well, instead of looking at how they could help employees by providing additional training, matching their skills better to the tasks required or providing more clarity about what the job requires.

Figuring out whether the problem is actually you

If you find yourself unhappy with an employee's performance, don't go straight to a complaining mindset. Instead, ask yourself two simple questions:

>> **Does this employee lack the skills or training to do the job properly?** If so, you either need to give this employee different tasks or provide the employee with more training.

>> **Did the employee make a mistake because the procedure wasn't documented properly?** Could you create a procedure for this employee to follow so that if this situation occurs again, the same error wouldn't happen?

If your answer to either of these questions is 'yes', the problem is as much yours as it is the employee's. Your focus needs to be on providing the employee with the skills or procedures necessary to do their job properly; in the meantime, don't waste precious energy criticising your staff.

Knowing when to draw the line

Although I emphasise the importance of training, employee support and positive management, I also realise that sometimes you get an employee with very difficult behaviours or blatant disregard for their position description. In these situations, you need to be both fair and firm.

Here are some tips that I've found to be helpful:

AHEAD OF THE PACK

>> **Act early and act often:** As soon as you experience a problem with an employee, pull them to one side to discuss what's happening, ideally on the same day. Never postpone discussing problems until the employee's annual review meeting.

>> **Always give the employee a chance to tell the other side of the story:** One of the biggest mistakes is not providing an employee the opportunity to express their view of the situation.

>> **Build a dossier:** If an employee always pushes the boundaries of acceptable behaviour but doesn't quite warrant a formal warning, document all the little behaviours you perceive to be a problem, making diary notes for things such as personal phone calls in work time, lateness or being curt with a customer. Then, if you do decide to issue a warning, you can justify your action more readily.

- **Don't rely on warning letters:** Only use letters as a follow-up on face-to-face meetings. If you think that a warning letter could lead to this employee's dismissal, see the next section.

- **Ensure the employee understands precisely what is expected from their position description.** Refer to 'Drawing up a position description', earlier in this chapter, to find out more.

- **Prevention is better than cure:** Minimise staff problems by focusing carefully on your recruitment process, as discussed earlier in this chapter.

TIP

Ensure that your employment policies distinguish between poor performance (which normally results in a counselling and warning process) and *serious misconduct* (which may result in *summary dismissal* and the dismissal of an employee without notice). Typically, examples of serious misconduct include theft, fraud, violence and serious breaches of workplace health and safety procedures. A word of warning, however: Even if you have clear policies in place that define serious misconduct, never dismiss an employee on the spot without first getting legal advice!

Giving an employee a warning

If an employee displays serious disregard for their position description or continues to underperform even when given adequate support and training, one course of action is to request a meeting with this employee and issue a formal warning. Be careful to document both the conversation and the warning properly. You can find good templates for employee meetings and written warnings at FairWork Australia (`www.fairwork.gov.au`).

Here are some things to remember when issuing a warning to an employee:

REMEMBER

- **Always provide the employee with the opportunity to respond to whatever the stated problem is:** If this employee mentions other issues that may be affecting their performance (for example, an elderly parent in need of care, hence the recent absences, or a lack of training), you must consider these issues when determining future actions.

- **Ask for written confirmation if someone threatens to resign:** If an employee responds by saying they want to resign, ask for a letter of resignation. This way the employee can't later claim to have been sacked. If your request is refused, make a file note of exactly what occurred and what was said. (But don't ever write a letter of resignation on the employee's behalf!)

>> **Consider who else should attend the meeting:** Depending on the seriousness of the underperformance, you may want to have someone else in the room as an observer or offer the employee the opportunity to bring a support person to the meeting.

>> **Explain clearly the improvements you expect:** Be specific and, ideally, refer to the details within the employee's position description. Provide a date by which you expect improvements to be made and indicate how you intend to assess performance over that period.

>> **Set a meeting date to review the progress of improving work performance:** I often find a second meeting is more constructive than the first, as the employee has had time to reflect on what has occurred.

>> **Tell the employee what the consequences may be if he or she doesn't improve:** For example, 'If a clear improvement in your attitude to your supervisor isn't seen by such-and-such a date, you may receive another warning and, ultimately, your employment could be terminated.'

REMEMBER

Giving a formal warning to an employee is a relatively drastic step, and usually indicates a failure in recruitment, induction, day-to-day management or training. In other words, if you find yourself issuing an employee with a warning, take this as an opportunity to reflect on how you could have done better as a manager, and how you could avoid this happening again in the future.

Terminating an employee

Sometimes an employee simply doesn't work out, and the best choice for your business is to terminate this person's employment. At this point, I suggest that you seek advice from your industry association or legal adviser before proceeding further, so that you can be sure you do not expose yourself to the risk of an unfair dismissal claim. (The laws regarding unfair dismissal are complex and vary according to the number of employees, legal structure and location of your business.)

Whatever the situation, you must be careful to follow a clear and fair process: The main reason employers receive unfair dismissal claims isn't because of *why* they sacked someone, but rather *how* they sacked someone.

WARNING

Don't be tempted to force an employee into leaving by pretending you don't have the work, demoting someone to junior tasks or making an employee uncomfortable. These strategies can be construed as unfair dismissal if the employee feels that they have no option but to 'resign'.

REMEMBER

If you do end up terminating an employee's position, make sure you give the person proper notice or, alternatively, payment instead of notice. (Check with the relevant government agencies or your industry or employer association for how much notice you're required to give.)

Unfair dismissal laws differentiate between employers with fewer than 15 employees, and employers with 15 or more employees. You can find information about both situations at Fair Work Australia (www.fairwork.gov.au) but in this section, I focus on how the law applies to businesses with fewer than 15 employees. (Note that this information is not relevant if you operate from Western Australia and you're a sole trader or a partnership.)

The crux of the Small Business Fair Dismissal Code is that employees can't make a claim for unfair dismissal in the first 12 months following employment. Furthermore, if an employee is dismissed after 12 months and the employer has followed the Small Business Fair Dismissal Code, the dismissal will be deemed to be fair. Note, however, that you can never terminate someone's employment due to discriminatory reasons such as race, gender, religion, marital status, sexual preference, disability or age.

For more information about the Small Business Fair Dismissal Code, and how it applies to you, go to www.fairwork.gov.au.

5

High Finance

IN THIS PART . . .

Figure out how much finance you need to get your business started.

Stay on track with efficient bookkeeping systems.

Discover how to read financial statements, understand trading results, and use budgets to plan ahead and build strong profits.

Manage your taxes wisely.

Chapter **15**

Financing Your Business

How much cash does your business need? Lots of it, of course! And however much you have, there's usually not quite enough . . .

Banks are often reluctant to lend to businesses, especially start-ups, so many people end up with personal or investment loans, using their home loans as the security. Unfortunately, this difficulty in securing finance often means that businesses are undercapitalised right from day one. All too often I see people starting a new business with only a couple of thousand dollars in capital.

In this chapter, I talk about the different kinds of finance available, and how to go about applying for a loan. But before you get this far, read through the start-up checklist at the beginning of this chapter, so you can be clear about how much dosh you *really* need in order to get started. The last thing you want is a business that has everything going for it, but runs short of capital and is forced to close before getting properly established.

Budgeting Enough for Start-Up

Business start-up costs are often much higher than you imagine, with things such as council fees, insurance, legal fees and rental bonds being just some of the expenses that people forget to budget for. This section looks at budgeting for start-up expenses, making sure you have enough to live on, and assessing how much you may need to borrow.

Creating a start-up budget

If you're still at the initial planning stage of your business, read through the following lists, which itemise many of the key expenses you need to budget for when starting a new business:

>> **New equipment or tools:** Expenses here include IT systems and peripherals, motor vehicles, office furnishings, retail equipment (cash register, point-of-sale software), and tools and other equipment.

>> **Premises fit-out:** Budget for council fees, fit-out of new premises, lease agreement fees, and rental bond and rent in advance.

>> **Other start-up expenses:** Accounting fees (advice for new set-up), consultant fees, incorporation of company, insurance (public liability/business indemnity/property insurance), internet connection and networks, legal fees, licence fees, marketing and branding (including business logo and registration of business name), security bonds for electricity and gas, signage, stock for resale, training of staff, and website design all may need to be budgeted for.

Of course, service businesses tend to have fewer start-up costs than retail businesses (a retail fit-out typically costs well over $100,000) and, if you're purchasing a franchise, you need to add in the franchise purchase price as well as the ongoing monthly retainer while you're still getting things off the ground.

AHEAD OF THE PACK

While your budget for start-up expenses is an essential first step, this budget doesn't necessarily provide a clear indication of how much you need to borrow — you only know that for sure when you complete the rest of your business and personal budgets.

TRUE STORY

A CAPITAL AFFAIR

A few years ago, a friend of mine decided to open a gift shop. She signed a lease in the main street and, while the shop stood empty for two months, she spent up big on fitting out the premises, and installing designer lights and top-of-the-range point-of-sale and security systems. The shop looked absolutely beautiful. The trouble was, by the time she was ready to open, she didn't have enough capital left to purchase adequate stock, nor enough capital to live on for the next 12 months while her business established itself. Within six months, she had to cut her losses and close down.

Adding enough to live on

Most businesses don't make any profit in the first six months and, in fact, many businesses make a loss during this time. For some businesses, the period before you see any profits may be a year or even longer. You may find that you not only need to borrow funds to get your business up and running, but also need some additional funds in order to finance your living expenses in the first few months.

Quite how you budget for living expenses depends on your circumstances, and whether you're continuing to work another job while your business gets established (I talk more about this topic in Chapter 9). If need be, I suggest you ask for help from your accountant or business adviser to create a personal budget.

Assessing how much you really need

By now, you should have an idea of how much money you require for equipment, vehicles, office or shop fit-out, as well as how much you need (if anything) for opening stock. In addition, you've started thinking about whether you need additional funds to cover your living expenses while you get yourself established.

At this point, you can start thinking about three things:

>> If you don't have the necessary savings, will you be able to borrow the money?

>> How much finance will you need, and what will the likely repayments be?

>> Will these repayments be affordable in the first year or two of your business — or will this level of borrowing bring an unacceptable level of risk and/or stress?

Depending on the answers to these questions, you may want to review your start-up budget. Although you don't want to risk business failure by being under-capitalised, you may find that you can pull back or delay on some spending without the business suffering unduly.

Here are some tips for pruning your start-up budget:

>> **Consider leasing rather than buying assets outright.** Finance that's secured against an asset such a vehicle is usually pretty easy to obtain, and preserves your cash so that it can be used as working capital instead.

>> **Be realistic about spending precious funds on a new car.** You may want that brand new speed-machine, but unless your vehicle is an essential part of the brand and image of your business, you can almost certainly do without.

>> **Consider buying stuff second-hand.** Again, second-hand stuff isn't as glamorous as new and shiny stuff, but may do the job just as well.

>> **Look at renting equipment.** If your budget includes new equipment, consider whether you could rent this equipment on an occasional basis while your business builds up.

TIP

Always guard your *working capital* (that is, the difference between your current assets and current liabilities) as a tigress guards her cubs. Even if you think you have enough cash to purchase everything your business needs to get started, if your business is successful and grows at any kind of pace at all, the growth itself is likely to gobble up your ready cash.

Separating Start-up Expenses from Operating Expenses

If you're new to business, you may find it hard to differentiate between start-up expenses and operating expenses. This difference is crucial in order for you to calculate how much start-up finance you require.

REMEMBER

A *start-up expense* is a one-off expense related to starting your business or purchasing an asset that your business requires. An *operating expense* is an ongoing expense that will feature as a regular part of running your business.

Dealing with initial start-up expenses

One of the tricky questions when planning for a new business is how to treat initial start-up expenses. For example, if you spend $500 painting your new office, does this count as a business start-up expense, or is it just repairs and maintenance?

The answer — in terms of your business plan and financial reporting, but not necessarily your tax return — is that if something's a one-off expense that's related to getting your business started and you don't expect to have this expense again as part of day-to-day trading (or not for a little while at least), you should treat this as a start-up expense.

Putting theory into practice

I don't know about you, but despite the fact that *For Dummies* books are about as chirpy as can be when dealing with some pretty dry topics, I still tend to glaze over when reading about costs versus assets, profit and loss forecasts and budget estimates. So I'm going to take a real-life business and show how a budget for startup expenses interacts with financial forecasts.

In this scenario, my friend Eva is starting up a small retail business. In Table 15-1, you can see what she reckons she's going to have to pay in the first four weeks of starting up her business (including the money she'll have to pay before she even opens her doors for trading).

TABLE 15-1

First Four-Week Budget for Retail Business

Expenditure	$
Accounting fees for advice regarding starting a new business	1,600.00
Advertising for the first month	200.00
Cost value of stock purchased for resale	20,000.00
Insurance for the first 12 months	2,400.00
Lease payment for air-conditioning unit	400.00
New shelving and computer equipment	15,000.00
Rental bond (eight weeks' rent)	4,800.00
Rent in advance (four weeks)	2,400.00
Signage and marketing brochures	1,500.00
Wages for the first month	3,000.00
Website design including first month's hosting (hosting is $100 per month)	1,100.00
All other expenses for the first month (bank fees, electricity, internet, motor vehicle, telephone and so on)	800.00
TOTAL	**53,200.00**

Imagine that Eva sells $10,000 of goods in her first four weeks of trading. What do you think the projected Profit & Loss should be in her business plan for this period?

At a simplistic level, you could say that Eva is going to receive $10,000 as income, and she'll spend $53,200 in expenses, which would equate to a $43,200 loss.

However, this basic approach doesn't give a true representation of what's going on, and no bank or investor is going to want a bar of a business that shows this kind of loss.

What Eva needs to do is separate her start-up expenses from her operating expenses. Table 15-2 shows how she does this.

TABLE 15-2 **Start-up Expenses versus First Four Weeks of Operating Expenses**

Expenditure	$
Start-up Expenses	
Accounting fees for advice regarding starting a new business	1,600.00
Cost value of stock purchased for resale	20,000.00
Insurance (pre-paid 11 months)	2,200.00
New shelving and computer equipment	15,000.00
Rental bond (eight weeks' rent)	4,800.00
Signage and marketing brochures	1,500.00
Website design excluding first month's hosting (hosting is $100 per month)	1,000.00
TOTAL	**46,100.00**
Operating Expenses — First Four Weeks	
Advertising for the first month	200.00
Insurance for the first month	200.00
Lease payment for air-conditioning unit	400.00
Rent in advance (four weeks)	2,400.00
Website hosting	100.00
Wages for the first month	3,000.00
All other expenses for the first month	800.00
TOTAL	**7,100.00**

Can you see how, if you view Eva's figures from this perspective, the projected Profit & Loss looks very different? If Eva makes 40 cents gross profit in the dollar, the business would have $10,000 in sales, $6,000 in cost of sales and $7,100 in expenses. The business would still show a loss of $3,100, but this is significantly less than a loss of $43,200.

AHEAD OF THE PACK

Chapters 7, 8 and 9 look in more detail at piecing your financial projections together, but at the early stages of your business, what's vital to understand is the distinction between start-up expenses and operating expenses. This distinction is important not just from the perspective of creating accurate financial projections, but also from a business management point of view. After all, if you don't understand this distinction, you won't be able to calculate your true profitability with any accuracy in the early months of trading.

By the way, your accountant will almost certainly treat start-up expenses differently for tax purposes, choosing to write off items that you've shown as start-up expenses so that you minimise your tax bills. However, the treatment of expenses from a tax-management point of view is different from how you should treat expenses from a business-management point of view.

Sizing Up Your Finance Options

Just as the idea of heading across the desert in a two-door hatchback would need re-evaluation, you need to consider different types of loans or credit, depending on the stage your business is at, and what you need the finance for.

You may need finance for some or all of the following:

MONEY STUFF

>> **Finance for initial working capital:** A line of credit, business loan, home equity loan or equity partner is usually the best way to raise the initial capital for your business.

>> **Finance for new equipment or motor vehicles:** Leases, chattel mortgages or hire purchase agreements usually work best, with the asset itself providing the security for the loan.

>> **Finance for short-term trading fluctuations:** Overdrafts and credit cards can tide you over in tricky times, although they're an expensive form of borrowing, especially if you're always in the red.

MONEY STUFF

GROWING PAINS

When a business grows quickly it gets hungry for cash — requiring more equipment, more stock and more employees. Often, businesses end up needing finance not because they're struggling, but because they're so successful.

Here are some finance tips for surviving a growth spurt:

- **Don't use up cash buying new assets:** Even if you've got $20,000 sitting in your bank account, avoid paying for things such as cars or new equipment with the cash. (If your business is growing fast, excess cash is soon in high demand to pay tax bills, increase stock or offer more credit to customers.) Instead, sign up for a lease, chattel mortgage or hire purchase and spread the repayments over a few years.

- **Slow down your growth, if you can:** It's exciting when you think you're onto a winning idea, but slow, steady growth is much easier on your cashflow. Go one step at a time and, as much as possible, let the profits from one stage finance the next.

- **Use business loans or lines of credit, rather than overdrafts or credit cards:** A growing business uses up credit in no time at all, and then finds it hard to pay back. When your business is established with good, strong growth, a business loan or line of credit is your best option.

Taking out a business loan

Want the harsh reality? If you're looking for a business loan for a new business, and you don't have some security (such as your home) to offer as a guarantee against the loan, you've got a very slim chance of getting your loan approved. Even if you do have equity in your home, many banks aren't prepared to take a risk until a business is established and you have a proven income stream. (Some businesspeople get around this by securing a loan for 'personal investment' purposes while they're still in regular employment, and use this loan for share trading and similar activities. Then, by the time they seek to go into business, they're able to use some of these funds for start-up working capital. Whether this is an option for you very much depends on your personal circumstances.)

If the bank *does* come good with approving a loan, you're likely to get a choice between a line of credit and a business loan:

>> A *line of credit* works a little like a regular banking transaction account, except the balance is in the red, not the black. You can use the loan for all your business banking, including both deposits and withdrawals. You have a credit

limit on the account, and it's your choice whether you pay off the principal or pay interest only.

>> A *business loan* works more like a regular home loan — you borrow a certain amount and commit to regular repayments over a certain number of years.

What type of business loan is going to work best for you? On the upside, a line of credit is wonderfully flexible but, on the downside, you have to have a disciplined nature to force yourself to pay off the debt (if you never reduce the principal outstanding on your line of credit, you end up paying more interest than on a regular business loan). With business loans, the upside is you get it paid off quickly. The downside is the bank usually offers a relatively short term (five years is quite standard), meaning that repayments are high when the business is least able to afford it.

Almost all banks require some security against borrowings, and this rule normally means the owners or directors put up their own home as collateral. I know how scary putting up your own home as security can be, but the more security you offer, the lower the cost of the loan (interest is normally charged at normal variable rates, plus a risk factor that the bank assesses, which is usually between 1 and 3 per cent).

WARNING

MIXING HOME AND BUSINESS

Redrawing against the equity in your home loan is an easy and common form of business borrowing. However, if you end up with a single mortgage shaped as a combination of personal and business borrowings, calculating how much interest expense is personal and how much is business gets pretty tricky.

The same issue crops up if you redraw funds for personal purposes from a business loan (for example, to pay a personal tax bill or renovate your home). Because you're mixing personal and business borrowing, the interest on this loan is no longer 100 per cent tax deductible and, potentially, the Australian Tax Office can question whether you're able to claim any of the interest on this loan at all.

You can avoid your claims for interest deductions getting knocked back by keeping your home and business borrowing completely separate. If you want to borrow against the equity in your home, ask for a split loan facility, where you end up with two loans using the same security. Similarly, if you have a business loan and you're ahead on the repayments, make a redraw only if you intend to use the redrawn funds for business purposes.

WARNING

Even if the business loan is in your name only, remember that if you guarantee this loan against a property that's jointly owned, *both parties* (that is, both you and your best beloved) are jointly liable. This means that even if the relationship breaks down or one partner suffers ill health or dies, the other person must continue and take over the whole payment.

Finding a new lease of life

The idea behind leasing a new vehicle or new equipment is that a finance company buys the asset on your behalf and then rents it to you. You pay the rent every month for an agreed amount of time, and then, if you like, at the end of this period you can buy the asset from the finance company for a reduced price (this reduced price is usually called a *residual*). All your lease repayments are tax deductible.

Here are a few reasons leasing works well for small businesses:

MONEY STUFF

>> **Leasing terms are flexible:** Your monthly repayment depends on three things: The interest rate, how long the lease runs and the amount of the residual (also sometimes called a *balloon payment*) that you have to pay at the end. (You're best to make this balloon payment as small as possible, so that you don't end up paying out a heap of dough for something that isn't worth much and you can't afford to replace.)

>> **Leases are relatively easy to obtain for existing businesses:** For existing businesses with proven cashflow, leases are relatively easy to get because they're secured against the asset itself. (In contrast, new businesses may find the finance companies unwilling to offer a lease and, if they do, the lease terms are likely to be expensive.)

>> **Leasing is easier when cashflow is tight:** Because leasing doesn't require an upfront deposit, monthly repayments are often more manageable than one big lump sum. If your business is seasonal, you can even arrange lease repayments that allow you to pay more in the busy months and less in the slow months.

TIP

>> **Leasing allows for some flexibility with tax deductions:** You can claim monthly lease repayments as a tax deduction, and if you've got enough ready cash when the end of the tax year comes around, you may even be able to pay 11 months in advance, and receive the whole amount as a tax deduction that year (do check with your accountant first, however!).

>> **Leases may provide a good way to keep your business up to date with the latest technology:** Some leases let you upgrade equipment simply by terminating the old lease and taking out a new lease. However, check the balloon payments and lease conditions carefully, because many leases require a payout higher than the item is worth.

CROWD AROUND

Crowdfunding (also sometimes called crowdsourcing, crowd financing or crowd fundraising) is an increasingly popular way to raise funds for your new business idea.

Crowdfunding operates in one of two possible ways. The first way is rewards-based crowdfunding, which allows people to contribute money to a project that has yet to be completed, or a business that has yet to be started, in exchange for some kind of reward. The rewards vary from project to project. For example, I recently contributed to a crowdfunding campaign for a community arts festival in my town. In exchange for my $50, I receive an invitation to the opening party. I could also have chosen to contribute $500 in exchange for advertising in the festival program.

The other way that crowdfunding operates is through equity crowdfunding, where investors pay to own a slice of a company.

Are you wondering whether crowdfunding is a possible way for you to raise funds for your business? New crowdfunding platforms launch almost every day, but Crowdfunder, Indiegogo, Kickstarter, Patreon and Pozible are all established platforms with high participation rates.

WARNING

You can get hit with a load of penalties when you pay out a lease too early. For this reason, choose the term of the lease carefully and do your sums before deciding to sell a leased asset.

Getting hitched with chattel mortgage or hire purchase

Chattel mortgages and commercial hire purchase are very similar to leasing, but with a few key differences:

TECHNICAL STUFF

>> **Ownership:** With a chattel mortgage (but not with hire purchase), *you* own the asset, not the leasing company.

>> **Tax deduction method:** Instead of claiming the entire monthly repayment as a tax deduction, you're allowed to claim the depreciation on the equipment or vehicle as well as the interest on the loan. Usually, this arrangement means you get a bigger tax deduction in the early years of the agreement than you would with a lease.

>> **No residual:** Chattel mortgages and hire purchase agreements don't usually have a residual. This means when you finish your monthly repayments, you don't have a big lump sum to pay at the end.

>> **Goods and Services Tax (GST):** Depending on the nature of the agreement and the reporting method you use to report for GST, you may be able to claim all the GST back in one lump sum at the point you purchase the new equipment or vehicle. Check with your accountant to find out more.

No hard-and-fast rule exists to help you determine which is the best option — leasing, chattel mortgage or hire purchase. If you're not sure which is best for you, I suggest you chat to your accountant.

Canoodling with credit cards

In the perfect world, credit cards are a handy facility. You can pay bills over the phone, fix up expenses when travelling or use them to tide you over if cash runs short one month.

Most corporate credit cards are set up so you have to repay the whole balance each month, usually via a direct debit from your business bank account. However, many small business people don't have a corporate credit card and, instead, they use their personal credit card to pay for business expenses.

This scenario is where you can get into trouble: Personal credit cards are not only terribly expensive — especially if you're strapped for cash and end up paying the minimum monthly payment only — but also sickeningly easy to get hold of. I remember consulting to a couple who had taken out a new credit card loan every time cash ran short. They ended up with 11 credit cards between them and a cumulative debt of $80,000!

WARNING

Be wary. Credit cards are great as a short-term credit solution, but when used for long-term borrowing, they're an extremely expensive option.

Seeking equity partners

So far in this chapter, I only talk about *debt finance*, meaning that to get cash for your business, you go into debt. However, the other major source of business finance is *equity finance*. With equity finance, you receive funding from an investor in exchange for a portion of ownership of your business. Equity finance is more popular in the United States than in Australia, but the industry is growing fast.

MONEY
STUFF

The idea with most equity finance is that investors — sometimes referred to as *business angels* — buy into your company, offering funds and expertise in return for part-ownership. The investors don't receive interest on these funds, but instead are looking for a return through long-term capital gain. Because the investors are exposed to the risk of your company failing, they usually look for businesses with a strong history of growth and higher-than-average returns.

The advantages of equity finance include the ability to raise funds even if you don't have security or collateral to offer, meaning that your financial structure is more stable. In addition, your business can hopefully benefit from the investor's management expertise. On the downside, an outside investor means that you no longer have complete control of your business. You may find it hard having to consult others before making decisions, especially if you're used to running your own show.

Choosing Your Lender

It's a big, bad world out there — if you want to pay outrageously high interest rates, you can always find someone to sign you up. So don't get sucked in, but instead make sure you get the best possible deal when applying for a loan.

Compare interest rates and loan fees

Comparing one loan against another isn't just about weighing up interest rates, but is also about factoring in all the hidden costs such as establishment fees, loan service fees and exit fees. Unfortunately, arriving at a true comparison is really tricky. For example, an establishment fee of $600 has much more impact on how much a loan really costs when the loan is for three years only, rather than 25 years. More complicated still: Some lenders may say they have no application fees, but then charge you fees for valuation, legal document preparation and risk assessment.

MONEY
STUFF

Although I recommend you try to compare interest rates and fees on a loan *before* you sign on the dotted line, bear in mind that most comparison charts you find on the internet aren't that sophisticated. For example, although honeymoon products automatically revert to an undiscounted variable rate and look bad in terms of comparison rates, some lenders switch you to another product after the honeymoon, which can work very well.

TIP

In short, when choosing a lender, product knowledge is your best friend. Find a reputable broker who isn't wedded to one particular bank, and who can compare the offerings from different banks objectively.

Consider other interest(ing) factors

When you're looking for the loan that's going to work best for your business, remember that the right loan isn't necessarily the one that has the lowest effective interest rate. Here are a few other important factors to consider:

>> **Redraw facilities and conditions:** Although most variable rate loans now offer *redraw* facilities — where you can redraw on the loan when you're ahead of the agreed repayment schedule — some banks make it much harder than others to do so. Some banks require a formal application every time you want to redraw or they stipulate that the redraw has to be a minimum amount. Many banks also charge redraw fees.

>> **Service:** However impersonal your bank, banking locally and developing some kind of relationship with the branch manager offers many benefits. (You can still shop around using a broker to get the best deal, just let the agent know you want to use a local bank. The broker may even be able to introduce you to the manager.)

REMEMBER

>> **Fees for early termination of loan:** Many loans, especially those with special honeymoon rates in the early years or those that have low application or establishment fees, charge whopping fees if you pay out the loan early. Even if you don't envisage having enough cash to pay out the loan within the next few years, keep in mind that you may want to refinance at some point and, of course, this option almost always involves paying out the existing loan.

Watch out for honeymoon periods and interest-free credit

When shopping for items for your new business, you may find that some of the larger retail stores offer incredibly attractive deals to finance your purchases, such as no deposit, two years interest-free, followed by a loan to be repaid over 24 months or so.

WARNING

Finance schemes can be good value, but do read the fine print with the biggest magnifying glass you can find. With some contracts, if you don't make a repayment on time, you can be landed with a whopping 27 per cent or more interest, back-calculated from the day you made the purchase.

TRUE STORY

THE HIDDEN PRICE OF (SOME) FAMILY LOANS

If you're considering borrowing funds from your family, I suggest you think through the possible consequences very carefully first.

Several years ago, one of my clients borrowed a large sum of money from his father to start a business. I had thought that this was a family loan that had worked very well, as my client had repaid his father assiduously over several years. However, I discovered later that my client's sister had been, and still was, very upset about this loan. It turned out that she had approached her father for finance as well, but her father had said he couldn't lend her anything, because he had no money left to lend. The sister had missed out on the purchase of the farm she wanted, and nursed a resentment against her brother for years.

You will find many ways to make money in your lifetime but you will only have one family, and your family relationships are probably more valuable than anything else you have in your life. If you're considering borrowing from your family, pause first to think how other siblings may feel and what would happen if you fail to repay these funds. If your siblings could feel resentful or your family would suffer in any way if you fail to repay these funds (and failure in business, no matter how optimistic you currently feel, is always possible), then think again. You may be better to borrow from a different source, or postpone your business venture.

IN THIS CHAPTER

» **Working out how often you need to do your books**

» **Subscribing to accounting software that works for you**

» **Setting up basic bookkeeping systems**

» **Getting paid on time**

» **Staying on track with bookkeeping deadlines**

Chapter **16**

Cooking the Books

I may sound like a total nut, but I reckon bookkeeping isn't so bad a job. In fact, doing your books is almost interesting, in a perverse picking-the-lint-out-of-your-navel kind of way. You discover the answers to lots of fascinating questions such as exactly how much profit (or loss) you're making, how come you never have as much money as you think you ought to, and why your belly-button lint is always that strange grey-blue colour.

This chapter talks mostly about bookkeeping in the context of keeping track of income and expenses, setting up systems, and choosing a software solution that works best for your business.

If the idea of all this activity just makes you want to curl up on a bean bag and binge on Netflix, I understand. However, don't stick your head in the sand and hope that your books will do themselves. Instead, pay the money, hire a bookkeeper, and get the job done.

Figuring How Often to Do the Deed

So, how often do you need to do this whole bookkeeping game? On the one hand, you don't want to get so behind that you can't produce reports or see what customers owe you but, on the other hand, you don't want to overdo things, working on your books so often that you record only one or two transactions each time.

While you're of course free to chart your own course, here's a look at the pluses and pitfalls of the two most common methods: Doing your books once every few months (see the next section) and doing your books on a regular basis (see the section 'Doing the books regularly', later in the chapter). By the way, if you're weighing up these methods, see 'Meeting Bookkeeping Deadlines', later in this chapter, for more about reporting requirements for most small businesses.

Doing your books just once in a while

Random bookkeeping, punctuated by intervals of months if not years, is what many accountants describe as 'shoebox accounting', harking back to the days when clients might arrive with a year or two of financial records stuffed unceremoniously into an old shoebox.

Shoebox accounting brings a comfortable chaos to any business. As the financial year ticks by, you simply dump all your bank statements, receipts and supplier bills in a messy heap somewhere. Once a year or every few months, usually days before a tax return or Business Activity Statement is due, you retrieve this unhappy heap and attempt to put it in some kind of order.

Shoebox accounting has its advantages:

>> You can ignore the drudgery of year-round bookkeeping.

>> Bookkeeping is sometimes a relatively swift process, because you churn through a whole year's transactions in one hit.

And disadvantages . . .

>> You miss out on the benefits of regularly doing your books, such as up-to-date financial reports or budgets.

>> By the time you do the books, you've forgotten what some of the transactions are, so you waste hours trying to do things such as match up receipts against miscellaneous electronic debits from your bank account.

>> You risk incurring fines for late payments of tax or GST.

In short, I recommend shoebox accounting only for the smallest of small businesses, such as a hobby business, or a business with no GST, no wages, few bills and irregular income.

TIP

Using accounting software that has bank feeds is a great alternative to shoebox accounting. This way, even if you don't connect to your accounting software for a few months, when you do finally log on, most transactions are there, and in many cases, already coded. Also, the ease of cloud accounting often converts even the most reluctant of shoebox bookkeepers into relative enthusiasts.

Doing your books regularly

Most businesses record day-to-day bookkeeping as transactions occur. If you use accounting software, every time you make a sale to a customer, you record the sale in your books. Voilà, the bookkeeping for this transaction is complete. Similarly, when you receive a payment, you record the transaction against outstanding customer invoices and, in the process, you complete the bookkeeping for the transaction.

Here are a handful of tips to ensure you organise your time efficiently, so that you can do your books in the quickest possible time:

>> **Record sales transactions once and once only.** Don't record sales in a word processor or in handwritten docket books. If you need to create invoices on the run, use an app on your smartphone where you can record the sale, take a payment from your customer if possible, and then send this data to your accounting software.

>> **Pay supplier accounts in batches.** Set a schedule for bill payments, and then stick to it. For example, if you have weekly accounts, set one day per week where you settle these bills. If you have monthly accounts, set aside one day per month.

TIP

>> **Set up bank feeds to import transactions automatically.** Configure bank feeds so that every time you log onto your accounting software, all your banking transactions are imported automatically. All you have to do is set up rules to allocate transactions automatically, manually allocate account codes, or match transactions against transactions that have already been entered.

>> **Use software to manage employee pays.** In order to comply with Single Touch Payroll (STP) regulations, you must use accounting software to record employee pays. However, the bonus is that you can use this software to calculate tax, superannuation and generate payslips.

TIP

USE THE RHYTHM METHOD

For small businesses, try to establish a regular rhythm for when you do your books and, if possible, schedule as many bookkeeping activities as possible onto the same day per week. For example, set the same day every week to record both employee pays and weekly supplier payments.

If you find it hard to stick to a routine and find yourself doing your books in dribs and drabs whenever you have a free moment, consider delegating the bookkeeping to somebody else. Many small businesses have a bookkeeper who comes in once per week for a half day just to complete the whole bookkeeping function.

Choosing Software that Fits

In Australia, the most popular accounting software solutions are MYOB, Quick-Books and Xero. All three of these products offer significant benefits that facilitate managing your business properly. If you're agonising about which software is right for you — maybe you've heard about Xero but a friend recommends MYOB — here are a few pointers about finding the perfect dance partner:

>> **Ask your accountant for their opinion:** Just as most mothers never fail with their incisive commentary as regards your future partner, many accountants get pretty vocal about what's best in terms of software. So, if you're tossing up between a couple of products and your accountant much prefers working with one of these in particular, you're likely to minimise accounting fees by following that recommendation.

**AHEAD OF
THE PACK**

>> **Think to the future:** Can this software grow as your business grows? For example, maybe you don't need the ability to connect this software to your ecommerce store right now, but you think you will at some point in the future. Look at the add-on apps that can connect to the software to provide the possible features you will need.

>> **Find out what support options exist, and how much they cost:** Access to quality support is of particular importance if you're living out in the bush. Find out what the local support consists of and which product is supported best in your particular locality.

**MONEY
STUFF**

>> **Calculate the cost of annual fees:** At the time of writing, I find that the main players have a surprisingly large difference in pricing, and one or two are significantly cheaper than others. When costing annual fees, remember to take extras such as payroll or inventory into account, and also don't get hoodwinked into comparing pricing based on the short-term discounts so many companies offer for the first 6 or 12 months.

Whatever solution you choose, do ensure the software has bank feed features, and take the time to enable these features. Bank feeds combined with bank rules mean that data entry virtually becomes a thing of the past.

Bank feeds refers to the process where your accounting software connects to your bank every night and downloads a summary of every transaction for that day. Sounds boring, but not so. The outcome for you is that your transactions appear automatically in your accounts (the date, the amount, who was paid and so on), without you or a bookkeeper having to do a thing.

Bank feeds work together with bank rules. *Bank rules* are the process whereby you can create 'rules' so that transactions are coded automatically to the correct accounts.

In other words, every time you log into your accounts, all your transactions are already entered. All you have to do is review how these transactions have been coded, and click to approve them. In the blink of an eye, not only are your books complete, but you can also generate a Profit & Loss report, create Business Activity Statements or get an up-to-date reckoning of how much customers owe you.

WARNING

WHY CAN'T I USE A SPREADSHEET INSTEAD?

Many business owners spurn accounting software and instead choose to record income and expenses using spreadsheets.

Spreadsheets are one step up from handwritten books, I agree. However, they don't quite cut the mustard. For one thing, spreadsheets are very vulnerable to error: You only need to get one formula wrong, maybe missing out a row at the top or the bottom when adding up a column, and your totals are wrong also. Spreadsheets are also much slower, particularly when compared to the combination of bank feeds and cloud accounting software.

Another problem is that spreadsheets only do half the job. Although you can assemble records for your tax return, you can't use a spreadsheet to generate a customer invoice, a purchase order for a supplier, or employee pay slips. More importantly, you can't use a spreadsheet to generate financial reports. You don't get a Profit & Loss report, a Balance Sheet, a neat report showing how much GST you owe, or any of the other reports that are standard to any accounting software.

In other words, if your business has more than a handful of transactions per month, don't muck around with a spreadsheet but instead subscribe to some decent accounting software.

Creating Recordkeeping Systems

If your business is already up and running and you're doing your own books, you may not need to read this section. However, if you're new to business and wondering where to begin with the recordkeeping side of things, the next couple of pages are made for you. Don't be too anxious — keeping accounts isn't the arduous initiation rite that others may have you believe it is. In fact, the whole deal is surprisingly straightforward.

For more detail about creating bookkeeping systems for your small business, see *Bookkeeping For Dummies*, 3rd Edition, published by John Wiley & Sons Australia, Ltd and written by yours truly.

Keeping track of income

In this section, I list the records you *have* to keep in order to stay legal, even if you don't have time to do your books right now (after all, you're probably flat out running your business). So forget that Scarlet-O'Hara-I'll-do-it-tomorrow excuse. Nothing in this list is very complicated, so you can start all of it today.

>> **Customer invoices:** If customers pay direct into your bank account or pay by cash, do ensure you record an invoice in your accounting software for every payment you receive. Remember that if you're registered for GST, your invoices must say Tax Invoice at the top and clearly indicate whether the sale includes GST, or not.

>> **EFTPOS dockets from customer payments:** If customers pay by EFTPOS, stick the merchant dockets on a spike throughout the day. Clip each day's merchant dockets together and store in a safe place.

>> **Cash register rolls:** Keep hold of the cash register tape, and make sure you total the till every day (often called Z totals).

>> **Electronic point of sale systems:** Save end-of-day sales total reports as PDF files in a spot where you can find them later.

AHEAD OF THE PACK

>> **Web sales:** Ideally, connect your ecommerce site with your accounting software (for example, setting up PayPal as a separate bank feed) so that all sales made from your website can be easily coded direct to income.

Tracking expenses

Remember that every receipt for money spent on your business is a tax deduction, which in turn is money in your pocket. So keep track of the following:

>> **Receipts for expenses that you pay for using cash or personal bank accounts:** If you can, avoid paying for business expenses with anything other than a business bank account. If you do pay for a business expense using cash or a personal account, keep these receipts separate. You can then reimburse yourself, transferring funds electronically from your business account to your personal account. When you come to do your books, code this transfer of funds to the relevant expense. (So, for example, if you reimbursed yourself for a night at a hotel when on business, you'd code this transaction to Travel and Accommodation Expenses.)

>> **Credit card or EFTPOS receipts:** If you receive a receipt for something paid by credit card (a tank of fuel, for example), you need to keep this receipt for tax purposes, because a credit card or bank statement by itself may not be enough of a record to satisfy a tax audit. However, you don't really need to refer to this receipt again for bookkeeping purposes, and so the easiest approach is simply to file these receipts in date order somewhere you can find them again if you have to.

>> **Invoices or receipts you receive by email:** So long as you back up your emails, you don't need to print these transactions. Instead, create a new file within your email software called Electronic Payments. (Alternatively, some accounting systems allow you to attach electronic files to transactions.)

>> **Bank and credit card statements:** Store bank statements logically in date order within a ring binder folder, or create a folder on your computer and store PDF versions of your bank statements in that location.

REMEMBER

>> **Employee records:** Ensure you maintain meticulous records on any documentation related to employees, including declaration forms, timesheets and correspondence. In addition, use payroll software to track employee payments, tax and super.

Storing your business records

For tax purposes, you need to keep most business records in an accessible form (either printed or electronic) for a full five years after your business tax returns are lodged. In addition, if you have claimed depreciation on an asset, you must keep records regarding that asset for five years after the last time you claim depreciation. Similarly, if you acquire or dispose of an asset, you must keep records for a minimum of five years after it is certain that no capital gains tax applies.

Although five years is a requirement for tax purposes, seven years is the *statute of limitations* (the maximum time after an event that legal proceedings based on that event may be initiated) for companies. For this reason, if your business is set up using a company structure, I strongly suggest you retain all business records for a full seven years.

WARNING

If you do your accounts online using accounting software, bear in mind that you may need to export all your historical data should you ever decide to unsubscribe. Many services will not allow you to view your data unless you have a current subscription. For this reason, I also suggest that you save a PDF copy of your Profit & Loss report, Balance Sheet report and full Transaction Journal at the end of each financial year.

Doing the bare basics

What are the bare basics you need to do on the bookkeeping front? Here goes:

» **Keep track of income, along with any GST you collect (if you're registered):** If you're using accounting software, generate customer invoices for all income received, and record payments against these invoices.

» **Stay on top of what customers owe you:** I dedicate a whole chunk of this chapter to this vital topic — see 'Keeping Track of How Much You Owe' later in this chapter.

» **Itemise all expenses, along with any GST paid (if you're registered):** If you pay for most expenses from a business bank account or credit card and you use accounting software and bank feeds, recording expenses is child's play. When the transaction appears in your accounting software, all you have to do is select the correct category (advertising, bank charges, computer expenses, rent and so on), and your work is done.

» **Keep track of supplier accounts and how much you owe:** For smaller businesses, this can be as simple as paying immediately for almost all bills, so that you always know where you stand, or keeping a folder with 'Bills To Be Paid' written on it. For more established businesses with lots of supplier accounts, or for businesses that report for GST on an accrual basis, it makes more sense to enter supplier invoices in your accounting software as soon as you receive them. This way, you always know how much you owe at any given time.

» **Record transactions for any business expenses that don't appear in your bank feeds:** You need to do this if you pay for expenses using cash or a personal bank account.

REMEMBER

>> **Record all employee pays and upload the pay details each pay cycle using Single Touch Payroll (STP):** As I mention earlier in this chapter, it's mandatory to have payroll software if you have employees so that you can upload summary data from pay transactions to the Australian Tax Office for every pay cycle.

>> **Reconcile bank accounts regularly:** Without going into all the technicalities, reconciling your bank account involves matching your books against your bank or credit card statements and checking that the two sets of figures agree with one another. Boring as bat poo, I admit, but this process is absolutely essential to produce reliable figures.

TIP

KEEPING BUSINESS SEPARATE FROM PERSONAL

Here's a simple thing that takes you a few minutes to set up, and saves you countless hours over the lifetime of your business: Open a business bank account and keep this bank account completely separate from your personal bank account. And while you're at it, open up a separate credit card account too. (If you're a sole trader, your bank probably won't let you open a corporate credit account. Don't worry. Simply open another credit card account in your own name, but use this credit card for business purposes only.)

I've run my own business for almost 30 years now, but it took a good 10 years before I finally separated my business transactions from my personal ones. Why? I used to think having separate accounts was too much hassle, and I didn't want to have to transfer funds every time I needed to go to the supermarket or buy a bottle of wine.

However, in the end, I did open a new business bank account, and when I did, I couldn't believe how much time I saved. I could review my bank statements each month and know for sure that everything on the statement related to business. I no longer wasted hours each month poring over receipts trying to remember whether it was printer ink I'd bought in Kmart or a new T-shirt.

So, if you haven't already separated your business affairs from your private ones, do so now.

Keeping Track of How Much You're Owed

If your business offers credit to customers, one of the most important aspects of bookkeeping is to monitor overdue accounts and chase payment when required. If you don't have an outgoing personality or you're not a naturally assertive person, this process can be somewhat gruelling. This reticence quickly turns into a negative cycle, because the longer you leave a debt before you chase it, the more likely it is that the debtor won't pay. The secret to getting paid is to have clear credit terms and make contact with customers the moment they go beyond these.

MONEY STUFF

If you have trouble getting motivated about the idea of debt collection, think of it this way: Imagine your monthly sales are $30,000 and customers pay on average in 60 days. If you can reduce this average from 60 days to 45 days, you generate an extra $15,000 of working capital for your business, interest-free!

With this motivator in mind, I explain a few money-chasing tricks in the next sections of this chapter.

Asking nicely

When a customer's account runs overdue, get in contact straightaway. By overdue, I'm not talking about 60 days or 90 days. If you offer 30-day accounts, start chasing when the account is ten days overdue. If you offer seven-day accounts, start chasing as soon as the account is seven days overdue. The longer you leave a debt before chasing it, the more risk you run of not getting paid.

Although email reminders and statements are an easy and quick first step, they are also very easy for customers to ignore. If a customer doesn't respond to an initial reminder, the best method is often to get on the phone. Over the years, I've refined my telephone technique down to a fine art, so here are a few tips, straight from the horse's mouth:

TIP

>> **Be polite, cheerful and warm:** Get to know who is responsible for accounts by their first name and make sure they know who you are, too. Ask about their family, their holidays — build rapport. (Being friendly is a great way to elicit guilt.)

>> **Know what kind of payer you're dealing with:** Before you call, have a quick look at this customer's payment record. Does this customer usually pay on time or do you usually have to hound them? Are payments getting slower and slower?

>> **Offer solutions:** If someone genuinely can't pay immediately, don't wait for them to tell you when they can pay, but instead provide a solution. Start by

saying something like, 'How about 50 per cent this week and the balance in 14 days?' If the customer rejects this solution, have another (gentler) solution up your sleeve that you can suggest instead.

» **Don't be fobbed off by excuses:** If they've lost the invoice, email them a copy within the hour. If the invoice 'is delayed in the system' ask the accounts person to investigate what stage the invoice is up to. Say you're going to ring the person back the next day.

» **Ask for a commitment:** When somebody makes a vague comment such as, 'I'll be paying that bill next week' or 'I'll attend to your account as soon as possible', reply by saying, 'Thanks so much for that. Does this mean I can expect a payment by such-and-such a date?' If the customer agrees, confirm the response by saying, 'That's great. I'm writing in my diary to expect your payment by (say) 31 March. If I don't receive your payment by 1 April, I'll phone again to check there are no problems.'

AHEAD OF THE PACK

» **Make a note of any promises a customer makes:** If a customer promises to pay by a certain date, note this date and set up reminders for yourself so that you receive a prompt when this date rolls by.

» **Keep a record of every call and piece of correspondence:** I keep a record of all the usual high jinks that happen when chasing one of my customers, such as when I call, what the customer promises and when to contact the customer again.

Getting drastic

You may have been reading through all my debt-collection tips, thinking to yourself: *She's optimistic. None of those strategies would work with so-and-so.* I understand. Some customers are professional payment-avoiders. They know how to take you right to your limit and maybe beyond, and are quite content in the knowledge that some of their suppliers are likely to give up along the way, letting them get off, scot-free.

So here's my strategy for getting blood out of the proverbial stone:

1. **Do all the basic stuff first.**

    Don't go in heavy straightaway, or you may lose a customer. Send statements and emails, make phone calls and send pleasant reminder letters. Offer to let people pay off the account in two or three instalments, if that helps.

2. **Send a final warning letter, along with a deadline.**

    This warning is known as a *letter of demand* and usually says something like, 'We advise that if payment is not received within seven days of the date of this letter, we will instruct our debt collection agency (or solicitor) to issue proceedings against you to recover the unpaid debt together with our legal costs.'

REMEMBER

3. **If the deadline rolls by without payment, carry out your threat.**

   Whatever you threaten, you must be prepared to follow it through. If you threaten to take legal action within 12 days, send the lawyer's letter on the morning of the 13th day. If you threaten to cut off supply within seven days, cut it off on the eighth day.

4. **Get help.**

   If a customer doesn't respond to final warnings, ask your solicitor to send a letter, issue a summons yourself by going to the local court or, alternatively, sign up with a debt collection agency.

Meeting Bookkeeping Deadlines

I suggest that you create your very own bookkeeping calendar, scheduling all the deadlines you need to meet throughout the year. Of course, you may find that not all the following deadlines apply to your business. For example, many smaller businesses don't incur fringe benefits tax, and a business with no employees doesn't have to worry about PAYG withholding tax and other payroll deadlines.

Important dates for your bookkeeping calendar typically include the following:

>> **Fringe benefits tax (FBT):** Usually your accountant is responsible for lodging the FBT annual return (due 21 May each year). However, you (or your bookkeeper) need to ensure that books are up to date as far as 31 March (the FBT year runs from 1 April to 31 March) so that you can give your accountant the information that they require.

MONEY STUFF

>> **GST:** If you lodge BAS statements quarterly, the due dates are 28 October, 28 February, 28 April and 28 July. The February extension is due to the summer holiday silly season. (Don't you love the fact that even the Australian Taxation Office recognises that everything grinds to a halt for weeks on end over summer, and provides extensions to summer deadlines?) If you lodge activity statements monthly, the due dates are 21 days after the end of each month, with no merciful extension of time given in summer.

>> **Income tax:** If you lodge your tax return yourself, the deadline is 31 October each year. If you use an accountant to lodge your return, you usually receive an extension, which can be up to May the following year.

- **PAYG instalment tax:** Companies and individuals often have to pay PAYG instalment tax (income tax instalments paid in advance) either monthly or quarterly. If monthly, payment is due 21 days after the end of each month; if quarterly, payment is due 28 days after the end of the quarter, as part of your regular BAS statement.

- **PAYG withholding tax:** Employers have to pay PAYG withholding tax (tax deducted from employee wages) either monthly or quarterly. If monthly, payment is due 21 days after the end of each month; if quarterly, payment is due 28 days after the end of the quarter, as part of your regular BAS statement.

- **Payroll:** If you're using Single Touch Payroll (STP), you must complete a finalisation declaration by 14 July.

- **Payment summaries:** If you are not yet using STP, or you made any kind of employee payment that wasn't included in your STP reporting, you need to issue employees with a payment summary by 14 July.

- **Superannuation:** Unless a super fund stipulates that you need to pay monthly, super is due 28 days after the end of each quarter (in other words 28 July, 28 October, 28 January and 28 April).

- **Tax file number declarations:** These declarations must be forwarded to the Tax Office within 14 days of you receiving them.

- **Taxable Payments Annual Report:** If you are in the building and construction industry, or provide cleaning, courier, IT or security services, you also need to lodge a Taxable Payments Annual Report (TPAR) by 28 August each year.

TIP

Where a due date falls on a day that isn't a business day (that is, the due date is a Saturday, a Sunday or a public holiday), you're okay to lodge stuff on the first business day after the due date.

IN THIS CHAPTER

» Translating your Profit & Loss report

» Unlocking the secrets of your Balance Sheet

» Understanding the sad tale of why profit doesn't always equal cash

» Making out with budgets

» Predicting if you're going to be in the red . . . or the black

Chapter **17**

Understanding Financial Statements

I n this chapter, I talk heaps about serious money stuff, using sombre words such as profit margins, budgets and cashflow. Don't sweat. Even if you loathed maths at school, navel-gazing your own finances can be quite fascinating.

Why? Because the questions no longer revolve around how Emily and Jack can divvy up 15 Smarties among three friends, or how ten to the power of nothing equals some mysterious amount. No, the kind of maths here is all about *your* money, and how little or much of it you have. No matter how idealistic you are, this topic has got to rank pretty high on the list of what makes for interesting entertainment.

Discovering What Reports You Need (and When)

You aren't the only one who needs financial reports for your business. Other people expect to see reports too, including investors, loan providers and accountants. Here's a quick summary of who is likely to need what, and when:

» **The Tax Office:** You are required to submit a tax return once a year, summarising totals for key income and expense categories as well as a final profit figure for the business.

» **Banks/lenders:** Banks and lenders usually require the last three years of tax returns as part of any loan application. Lenders may also ask for Profit & Loss projections for small business loans.

» **Investors:** Typically, investors require a full range of financial reports, including lists of assets, accounts receivable, accounts payable and inventory. Investors may also require a full financial plan for the next three to five years.

Sounds simple? Maybe. However, in order for your business to flourish you need to generate more reports than this, as well as more frequently. Here's my suggestion for what reports to generate, and when:

» **Weekly:** If you offer customers credit, the most important report to monitor on an almost continual basis is your Aged Receivables report, showing who owes you what.

» **Monthly:** A Profit & Loss report and a Balance Sheet. Used in tandem, these two key financial reports paint a pretty complete picture of your financial health.

» **Monthly:** A comparison of your actual Profit & Loss report against your budgeted Profit & Loss for that period. Only this way can you tell if budgets are realistic and on track.

» **Monthly:** Sales reports, analysing total sales, profit, top ten items, top salespeople and so on. The exact format of your sales report very much depends on the type of business you run.

» **Quarterly:** Budget projections. Although I suggest you create a budget once a year for the 12 months ahead, I suggest you tweak your budgets every few months. Also, if your business is very seasonal, if you import goods or if you make large sales on credit, you need a cashflow report that goes hand in hand with your budget.

> **» Every six months or so:** In addition to the reports listed, I suggest you review your business financial plan on a regular basis. This is a good time to reflect on key business performance ratios such as inventory turnover, receivables turnover and return on investment ratios.

REMEMBER

Don't think that you need to be a super-experienced bookkeeper or an accountant in order to generate these reports. Even with no financial training, you can generate any of these reports yourself, using a combination of accounting software, a spreadsheet and a good dose of common sense.

Telling a Story with Your Profit & Loss Report

A Profit & Loss report is a story, telling you how your business has fared over the past few days, months or even years. It lists sales at the top, purchases and expenses in the middle, and a final profit (or loss) figure at the bottom, giving a quick and simple indication of whether your business is blooming with health or is as sick as a dog. If you're using accounting software, a Profit & Loss report is a completely standard report that you are able to generate at any time.

Understanding how it all works

Although most Profit & Loss reports are pretty easy to understand, don't be tempted into thinking that a profit is cause for partying and a loss is reason for a maudlin drinking bout. The important thing is to understand not only *what* the bottom line is, but also *why* you made a profit (or loss!) in the first place. (See Figure 17-1 for an example Profit & Loss report.)

TIP

To understand your Profit & Loss report, try this: Carve out some space for yourself (easier said than done, I know), sit down and read every single line of your report, slowly and thoughtfully. Think of this process as being rather like one of those spot-the-difference puzzles you did as a kid. But instead of spotting the cat with three legs or the woman wearing a saucepan on her head, look carefully at the following:

> **» Sales figures:** Look at sales for the month and see whether they seem reasonable. By the way, GST isn't included in total sales figures on a Profit & Loss report.

REALISM CITY PROFIT & LOSS REPORT JANUARY				
	This Month ($)	% of Sales	Same Month Last Year ($)	LY % of Sales
Sales — Clothing	32,000	49%	22,500	38%
Sales — Jewellery	27,000	41%	29,500	49%
Sales — Giftware	6,200	10%	8,000	13%
Total Income	63,200	100%	60,000	100%
Purchases — Stock	41,250	63%	34,200	57%
Gross Profit	23,950	37%	25,800	43%
Advertising	750	1%	920	2%
Bank Charges	60	0%	110	0%
Electricity/Gas	370	1%	400	1%
Motor Vehicle	963	1%	1,600	3%
Postage & Stationery	250	0%	270	0%
Rental	3,600	6%	3,200	5%
Salaries/Wages	5,462	8%	4,620	8%
Superannuation	519	1%	460	1%
Total Expenses	11,974	18%	11,580	19%
Net Profit	**11,976**	**18%**	**14,220**	**24%**

FIGURE 17-1:
A simple Profit &
Loss report.

REMEMBER

>> **Any odd figures:** Be critical and double-check that every single line on the report makes sense. No-one knows your business like you do — your gut feeling about which figures are right and which figures are wrong is usually spot-on.

>> **Gross profit margins:** For retailers, wholesalers and manufacturers, your gross profit margin is crucial and should stay pretty constant from one month to the next. (I talk more about profit margins in Chapter 9.)

>> **Relationships between different accounts:** Notice the '% of Sales' column in Figure 17-1? I like having this column in my Profit & Loss report because it shows me how different expenses move in tandem with sales. For example, if wages go up, hopefully sales go up, too.

MONEY STUFF

>> **This year's figures compared to last year's:** Comparing one year against another is a great way to get an overview of where your business is heading. For example, in Figure 17-1, although sales are up compared to the previous year, the profit margin is down and expenses haven't changed significantly, meaning less profit in the final wash-up.

Looking at sales

I'm not going to state the obvious and say what a good idea looking at your sales figures each month is, 'cos I'm pretty sure you're doing this already. Instead, I want to share an idea about how you can look at your sales figures in a bit more detail.

Ask yourself what different types of income you earn, and whether you can split your income into between three and ten different categories. For example, maybe you're a builder who earns money from the work you do on new houses, renovations, extensions and landscaping (there you go — four income categories). Maybe you're like me, and earn money from a combination of writing, consulting and teaching (three categories). Or, maybe you run a newsagency that doubles as a post office and dry-cleaning agency (three again).

As soon as you arrive at some kind of split, modify your bookkeeping to incorporate these different categories. (With accounting software, you simply add new income accounts in your accounts list.) Start to categorise all your income into these groups so that this information can appear on your Profit & Loss reports, similar to how the sales figures for clothing, jewellery and giftware show up separately in Figure 17-1. At a glance, you can see which category is the biggest earner and which is the dead weight, as well as how income patterns change from year to year.

TRUE STORY

I had a client who sold both new and second-hand computer gear, as well as computer accessories. When he split up his income to monitor how much money he generated from each source, he was surprised at the pitiful amount second-hand sales produced. 'They're such a headache,' he said, 'and take up about 80 per cent of my time every week. I can't believe they bring in so little.' He watched the trends for a few more months and, subsequently, made the decision to axe the second-hand goods, a strategy that's worked really well for him.

The other thing to bear in mind when analysing sales is how the split of your sales reflects your overall business strategy. For example, maybe you run a music school and your long-term business strategy is to develop online music lessons with high-profile teachers. You certainly want to separate this income category in your Profit & Loss reports so you can monitor the growth in this area.

Counting the costs

Whatever kind of business you have, you probably have some expenses that directly relate to sales (in accounting jargon, these are known as *variable costs* or *variable expenses* and are called *cost of sales* accounts). The idea is that when sales go up, cost of sales goes up, and when sales go down, cost of sales goes down.

MONEY STUFF

Think about your business and figure out which expenses are truly cost of sales accounts. Expenses that *aren't* cost of sales accounts are *fixed expenses*, and include things such as accounting fees, bank fees, computer gear, depreciation, electricity, interest, motor vehicle, rent, stationery and telephone. These business expenses don't change much from month to month, regardless of whether your sales go up or down.

Expenses that *are* cost of sales vary, depending on what type of business you're running. Here are a few examples to help you figure out what's what:

>> **Service businesses:** If you run a service business, you may not have any cost of sales accounts, because you're not actually producing or selling anything except your time. However, if you employ staff or contractors to deliver the service — maybe you run a kids' party business and you employ other entertainers — these payments count as cost of sales. Everything else gets lumped together under expenses.

>> **Manufacturing companies:** Cost of sales includes things such as raw materials, electricity used in the manufacturing process, production labour and factory rental. Expenses are things such as accounting fees and telephone.

>> **Real estate agents:** Typical cost of sales includes advertising, agent commissions and signage. Expenses are things such as accounting fees, motor vehicle costs and telephone bills.

>> **Retailers:** Cost of sales accounts are the goods that retailers buy to sell again, usually called purchases.

>> **Tradespeople:** Cost of sales includes materials and subcontract labour, while typical expenses include advertising, phone bills and tools.

For more on fixed and variable costs, and how they affect your gross and net profit, refer to Chapter 9.

Weighing up your expenses

Grab your Profit & Loss reports for the last few months and scan them. Highlight your five highest expenses (usually items such as wages, rent, interest and advertising). Write these expenses down and total them up. My bet is that these five expenses combined probably make up around 75 per cent, or more, of your total outgoings.

TIP

Think about how you could analyse these expenses in more detail. For example, maybe you could split wages into service staff and admin staff, or maybe you could split cost of materials into fabrics and accessories. Create separate accounts to enable you to monitor these expenses in a little more detail in your Profit & Loss. This will help with expenses control and future budgeting.

MONEY STUFF

I also like to separate any expenses from which I get a personal benefit of some kind. For example, it's good to separate your own motor vehicle running costs from those of your employees, or your own wages and super from employee wages and super. This way, you can quickly add up the total benefit that you're getting out of the business, something that often gets a little hidden when first looking at financial statements.

Taking a Snapshot with Your Balance Sheet

If your Profit & Loss report tells a story about what's going on in your business over any period of time, your Balance Sheet is a photograph that shows a candid snapshot of how much you own and how much you owe at any point in time. As Figure 17-2 shows, a Balance Sheet starts by listing assets (such as your bank account, stock on hand, furniture and computer equipment), and then moves to liabilities (credit cards, supplier accounts, loans and the like). The bottom line finishes with a flourish, calculating the difference between your assets and liabilities — a figure that represents your stake in the business and that's often described as your *equity*.

More than anything else, your Balance Sheet is the report that shows the value of your assets, your stake in the business, the efficiency of your stock and customer management, and much more.

TIP

If you are using accounting software, a Balance Sheet is a completely standard report that you are able to generate at any time. In contrast, trying to build a Balance Sheet report from spreadsheets is really a very technical process. For more about accounting software, refer to Chapter 16.

Realism City Balance Sheet as at June 30

	$
Current Assets	
Cheque Account	14,306
Petty Cash	100
Trade Debtors	23,500
Non-Current Assets	
Plant & Equipment — at cost	12,500
Plant & Equipment — Acc. Depreciation	(4,000)
Total Assets	**46,406**
Liabilities	
Trade Creditors	13,832
GST Paid	(2,562)
GST Collected	6,254
Visa Card	1,800
Bank Loan	22,000
Total Liabilities	**41,324**
Net Assets	**5,082**
Equity	
Retained Earnings previous years	12,250
Less: Drawings this year	(14,750)
Current Profit this year	7,582
Total Equity	**5,082**

FIGURE 17-2:
A Balance Sheet shows where your business is at.

Understanding the fine print

Like your Profit & Loss report, read every little bit on your Balance Sheet and make sure it makes sense. You may want to go over the nitty-gritty of your own report with your accountant but, in the meantime, here are a few comments to get you going:

TIP

>> Your business bank account appears as an asset unless you have an overdraft, in which case the account shows up as a liability.

>> *Trade debtors* is a fancy accountant term meaning money that customers owe you. Keep an eye on how much you're owed, making sure it doesn't get out of hand.

WHAT IF I DON'T HAVE A BALANCE SHEET?

Your accountant probably doesn't provide you with a Balance Sheet if you're a sole trader with few assets and no employees. However, as your business grows, a Balance Sheet becomes increasingly essential in order to manage your cashflow and to calculate true profitability. I recommend that all growing businesses use accounting software of some kind (such as MYOB, QuickBooks or Xero) so that they can generate their own Balance Sheet reports on a regular basis.

**MONEY
STUFF**

>> On a more solemn note, *trade creditors* means money you owe to suppliers. (Hopefully this figure isn't too high.)

>> *Accumulated depreciation* is yet another weird expression, meaning the amount your accountant has already claimed back on assets that you paid good money for, but for which you were unable to claim a deduction straight-away. I talk more about the convoluted workings of depreciation in Chapter 18.

>> GST Paid on Purchases either appears as an asset or as a minus liability because this GST is an amount the government owes *you* (yippee!). However, some accounting software doesn't distinguish between GST Collected on Sales and GST Paid on Purchases, instead only showing a combined account called Tax Payable.

>> Hire purchase accounts show up in a weird and tortuous way that only accountants understand. (Accountants seem to work on a similar principle to that of lawyers, who avoid using plain English so they don't do themselves out of a job.) However, as long as hire purchase loans appear in the liability section, they're probably okay.

Building documentation to support each figure

If you're conscientious about this whole bookkeeping palaver — and I suggest that you are — you or your bookkeeper should keep records that substantiate every figure that appears on your Balance Sheet. These records very much depend on each individual business, but in this section I provide just some of the support-ing documentation that your accountant or an investor may require in order to 'prove' the accuracy of your Balance Sheet.

TIP

How often you double-check balances in such detail depends on your business, but as a minimum you should go through your Balance Sheet and check every line that has a non-zero balance at least once a year.

Here are some of the accounts you should check, and how you do so:

>> **Bank accounts.** To check bank accounts, generate bank reconciliation reports from your accounting software for all bank accounts, including loans. Compare the ending balance from these reconciliation reports against bank statements for the same period.

>> **Inventory.** The total value of individual inventory items (showing quantities and purchase price for each item) on your inventory reports should match with the total value of Inventory or Stock on Hand in your Balance Sheet.

>> **Accounts receivable.** Generate a receivables report showing how much each customer owes. The total owing from customers on this report should match with the balance of Trade Debtors in your Balance Sheet.

>> **Fixed assets.** To check fixed assets, ask your accountant for a depreciation schedule listing all assets held, including initial purchase price and the written-down value. In the ideal world, the total of each asset category on this schedule should match with the value of this asset category on your Balance Sheet.

>> **GST liability accounts.** If you pay GST on an accruals basis, the amount of GST you owe the ATO on your Activity Statements at the end of the month or quarter should match with the value of the GST liability account(s) in your Balance Sheet for the same date.

>> **Accounts payable.** Generate a payables report showing how much you owe to suppliers. The total owing to suppliers on this report should match with the balance of Trade Creditors in your Balance Sheet.

>> **Payroll liabilities, including superannuation payable.** The balance of these accounts at the end of the month should match with the superannuation and PAYG tax you actually paid in the following month.

TIP

I always double-check the balances in my Balance Sheet, generating proof that each line is definitely correct, before asking my accountant to finalise my end-of-year returns.

Appreciating your net worth (someone has to, after all)

I often get asked about the *equity* section of a Balance Sheet, because it can be a little bewildering at first. Here is my two-minute explanation of how equity all works: Imagine you pitch up in the desert with two mates, Bruce and Wayne. You have ten bucks in your pocket when you arrive; after a fabulous game of poker, you still have ten bucks but you owe Bruce two dollars and Wayne owes you three dollars. You're one dollar ahead! The state of play now is

Cash	$10	Creditors	$2
Debtors	$3		
Total assets	**$13**	**Total Liabilities**	**$2**

Your net worth = Assets *minus* Liabilities = **$11**

Can you see how the idea of equity works? You add up all your assets (including things such as cash, customer accounts owing and motor vehicles), and then add up all your liabilities (stuff such as credit cards, supplier accounts outstanding and loans). Subtract total liabilities from total assets and you arrive at your equity in the business — a figure sometimes also described as *net worth*.

The equity section of your Balance Sheet always equals the difference between your assets and liabilities. If total equity is a positive figure, your business has made a profit over time and you've left some of this profit in the business (either that or you've put your own capital into the business). If total equity is a minus figure, your business has made a loss over time *or* you've taken out more than you've put in (or a combination of both).

Why Profit Doesn't Always Mean Cash

I can't believe how often clients ask, 'Veechi, my reports say I'm making fistfuls of cash, but how come there's nothing in the bank?' Similarly, I occasionally witness clients who are wallowing in cash and living the high life, even though their Profit & Loss reports are decidedly gloomy.

REMEMBER

The long and short of it all — profit doesn't equal cash and cash doesn't equal profit.

Gazing into the deep, black hole

Why is it that your Profit & Loss reports say you're doing well but you have no cash anywhere to be seen? I set out a few possible explanations here:

MONEY STUFF

>> **You've been paying tax:** A tricky habit to avoid (do tell me if you discover how), but the truth is that as soon as you make any profit, you have to pay tax. (Tax payments don't usually show up in Profit & Loss reports for sole traders or partnerships because, cruelly enough, they're not a tax-deductible expense and count as owner's drawings.)

>> **You've bought new equipment or a car:** If you buy new equipment or motor vehicles, you or your bookkeeper have probably allocated this purchase to an asset account, not an expense account. This is the correct treatment, but the upshot is that the purchase doesn't appear as an expense in your Profit & Loss report, explaining why you can be short on cash even if your profitability looks rosy.

>> **You have teenagers:** The most merciless financial cash drain on any individual. (Just kiddin'.)

>> **You repaid a loan:** Loan repayments don't usually show up as expenses, meaning that loan repayments gobble up cash but don't affect your profit.

>> **You're owed more than you were before:** If you bill a customer in April, your Profit & Loss reports show this income in April, even though you may not actually receive the cash until weeks or months later. Therefore, if customers owe you more now in total than they did at the beginning of the period for which you're reporting, this difference has sucked up your cash.

Looking through rose-coloured spectacles

It may be easy to grasp why a business may not have any cash even though the business is turning a profit. However, what about the opposite scenario, where a business is rolling in cash but the Profit & Loss reports look unfavourable? In many ways, this situation is even worse, because you can all too easily get lulled into a false sense of security and spend beyond your means.

Here are some reasons cash might be rosy but your profit grim:

WARNING

>> **You receive a loan:** Loans are both a blessing and a curse. When you receive a loan, the sudden influx of cash can burn a hole in the thickest of pockets.

>> **Your creditors are building up:** You can actually get by for quite a while making a loss but staying afloat, simply by running up outstanding accounts. If

you start to stretch out suppliers to 60, 90 or even 120 days, you not only generate a fair amount of bad feeling, but wads of cash also.

>> **You're running stock down:** If your stock levels go down, you have more cash available. Simple as that.

Doing the sums for sustainable growth

One business paradox is that if you get too successful, too quickly, you can actually send yourself down the gurgler. Just in case you think I'm talking out of my ear, here's my logic.

As your business grows, you need more cash, more furniture, more computers and so on. The amount of money that customers owe to you is also likely to increase. The new assets take up cash; in order to pay for them, you need to first make a profit and, second, invest this profit back into the business. However, if you grow too fast, you need new assets faster than you can make and invest your profit.

**MONEY
STUFF**

This concept of too-fast growth is often called *the limit of sustainable growth*. Without delving too much into the mathematics, as your business grows, your assets have to grow, too. You can either finance these assets by reinvesting profits or you can finance them by taking out a loan. For example, if you can invest enough profit to increase cash, debtors, equipment and so on by 10 per cent a year, your business can comfortably grow at 10 per cent a year.

An example may help. Imagine that your business turns over $250,000 a year, and you have around $50,000 tied up in stock, computer equipment and outstanding customer accounts. If you made a profit this year of $40,000 and you had personal drawings of $35,000, this result means you have only put $5,000 back into the business. Dividing your reinvested $5,000 by $50,000 equals 10 per cent. This year's turnover of $250,000 plus 10 per cent equals $275,000, meaning this amount is the maximum you can grow your business in the next year without having to seek extra finance.

WARNING

STAY AWAY FROM CASH GOBBLERS

Be canny about how you use up your cash. In particular, don't spend big lumps of cash unless you have to. For example, unless you have an enormous cash cushion behind you, don't even consider paying outright for equipment or motor vehicles that you can otherwise get finance for. Similarly, don't pay off loans in advance of your repayment schedule unless you can redraw funds whenever you want.

WARNING

The pace at which a business can comfortably grow *is* limited: To be very successful, too quickly, runs the risk of putting such a strain on your cashflow that, unless you can secure additional finance, your business may not survive.

Budgeting As If You Mean It

A few years ago, inspired by my own preaching, I went home and announced we were doing a *family budget*. On one side, I listed the money that comes in every week (this column was short and sweet). On the other side, I listed our regular expenses, breaking out in a cold sweat as I reached the fifth foolscap page (okay, maybe I exaggerate just a little). I added up the income column, and then added up the expenses column. (Needless to say, we are now reading by candlelight and eating gruel three times a day.)

This chilling realism is what budgets are all about. The budgeting process is vital if you're thinking of starting up a business, both in terms of listing set-up costs and also setting limits for expense spending for the first year or so. For established businesses, budgets are the only way to prioritise spending and set clear targets for sales.

If you're just starting a business, I suggest you use a spreadsheet as a starting point for your budget, as I explain in the next section. On the other hand, if you're a seasoned business owner, and already have accounting software up and running, you may prefer to use the budget features that belong to your accounting software. Software such as MYOB, QuickBooks or Xero enables you to create budgets quickly, using last year's results as the basis for your projections.

Creating your first budget

I do assume a very basic knowledge of spreadsheets in this section but, if you find that I go too fast for you, you can ask a friend or your accounts staff for help to get you started. Here goes:

1. **In a new spreadsheet file, list the months of the year along Row 1, starting at Column B.**

   I assume here that you've fired up your spreadsheet program and created a new, blank worksheet. List the months of the year along the top, starting with the current month. You can see how I do this in Figure 17-3.

2. **List your income and expense categories in Column A.**

Work down Column A, listing first the different types of income you earn, followed by a list of the different expenses your business has. Again, Figure 17-3 shows how this may look (this sample is a fairly simplified version; you probably have quite a few more expense categories).

3. **Complete dollar estimates for income and expenses, month by month.**

MONEY STUFF

Ah, finally, the fun bit: You need to fill in dollar estimates for income and expenses, month after month. Round amounts to the nearest $50 or so — forecasts aren't meant to be a science! — and bear in mind seasonal variations. Allow leeway for unforeseen expenses and, when estimating sales figures, be conservative.

4. **Insert or add rows for Total Income and Total Expenses, and then press AutoSum (if you're using Excel).**

The idea of the Total Income and Total Expenses rows is that they automatically add up all the rows above them. To get your spreadsheet to do this calculation, you have to insert a formula. In Excel, the easiest way to do this is to press your AutoSum button. If you buy goods for resale, you also need to insert rows for Purchases and Gross Profit, as I do in Figure 17-3.

5. **Create a row at the bottom called Budgeted Profit.**

The rule is that Budgeted Profit always equals Gross Profit less Total Expenses. In my example (refer to Figure 17-3 again), Gross Profit is in Row 11 and Total Expenses is in Row 21, so the formula for January's budgeted profit is **=B11-B21**. Repeat this formula for each month of the year.

6. **Save your work, print it and ponder.**

When you're ready to print, click Page Setup and select Landscape as the page Orientation. If you like, you can usually specify how many pages tall and wide you'd like your report to be against the Scaling selection.

When you have your final budget in your sticky hands, spend a generous amount of time checking it over, ensuring it makes sense and is realistic.

Recognising relationships

When reviewing your budget, take time to consider whether any income or expense categories are directly related to one another. For example, purchases, commissions and freight usually go up or down in direct proportion to monthly sales, and superannuation goes up and down in tune with wages.

Realism City Budget for January to June							
	Jan	**Feb**	**Mar**	**Apr**	**May**	**Jun**	**Total**
Sales — Clothing	34,500	36,225	38,036	39,938	37,941	36,044	222,685
Sales — Jewellery	23,400	24,570	25,799	27,088	25,734	24,447	151,038
Sales — Giftware	6,700	7,035	7,387	7,756	7,368	7,000	43,246
Total Income	64,600	67,830	71,222	74,783	71,043	67,491	416,969
Purchases — Stock	35,530	37,307	39,172	41,130	39,074	37,120	229,333
Gross Profit	29,070	30,524	32,050	33,652	31,970	30,371	187,636
Advertising	1,200	1,200	1,250	6,000	1,350	1,400	12,400
Bank Charges	75	75		75	75	75	375
Electricity/Gas	350	350	350	350	350	350	2,100
Motor Vehicle	850	850	850	850	850	850	5,100
Office Rental	3,600	3,600	3,600	3,600	3,600	3,600	21,600
Postage & Stationery	850	850	850	850	850	850	5,100
Salaries/Wages	4,800	5,200	4,700	7,200	4,400	7,200	33,500
Superannuation	456	494	447	684	418	684	3,183
Total Expenses	12,181	12,619	12,047	19,609	11,893	15,009	83,358
Budgeted Profit	16,889	17,905	20,003	14,043	20,077	15,362	104,278

FIGURE 17-3:
Stay realistic
using budgets.

The trick is to tell your spreadsheet about these relationships so that it calculates them for you automatically. In Figure 17-3, for example, I've got Total Income in Row 7. If I know that purchases average 55 per cent of my selling price, as my formula for January purchases, I would type =B7*55%.

TIP

The neat thing about specifying relationships in this way is that when you change one figure in the spreadsheet, other figures change automatically, too. So, if you raise your sales forecasts, purchases correspondingly go up; if you change wages, superannuation also changes.

MONEY STUFF

A BUDGET OR A PROJECTION?

I tend to use the words 'budget' and 'projection' synonymously, but a subtle difference does exist. A *budget* makes estimates as regards future sales and sets upper limits for expense spending so that profitability targets are met, assuming the sales budgets are met. If you employ any kind of managers, part of their responsibilities often include making sure spending doesn't exceed allocated budgets.

On the other hand, a *projection* looks to the future, often extending three or five years ahead. In your business plan, you may choose to have a 12-month budget, along with annual Profit & Loss projections that extend forward several years. (The first year's budget would likely be identical to the first year's Profit & Loss projection.)

Understanding the psychology of budgets

Forget astrology, numerology, psychometric testing and aura reading. Instead, observe your partner or colleagues or lover as they create their first budget and, within hours, you know more than you may ever wish to know about their personality. The optimists pump up sales beyond reason, the pessimists warn against enormous expenses, and creative types scrawl a few lines and give up. I don't know what kind of person you are, but here are some general tips for creating a budget that works easily and ends up somewhere close to the truth:

>> **Involve different staff members:** The more input, the more realistic the budget can be.

>> **Compare budgets against actuals:** Comparing your hopes and aspirations against the grim truths of real life, as I do in Figure 17-4, shows up your delusions in a flash.

REMEMBER

>> **Allow extra for unforeseen expenses, especially if you're doing a budget for a new business:** Things always cost more than you think. (Head back to Chapter 15 for more about budgeting for business start-up expenses.)

>> **Consider carefully the timing of irregular payments:** Things to remember include quarterly electricity bills, months with five pay weeks and annual insurance premiums.

>> **If you budget for higher sales for this year than last year, make sure you've got whatever it takes to reach that goal:** For example, if you decide to increase the sales budget to $70,000 (compared with $62,000 last year for that month), put changes in place that make this higher budget possible, such as new stock lines, increased advertising or more staff training.

AHEAD OF THE PACK

>> **Have one sales budget for sales staff, and another for finance:** Low sales budgets are hardly going to act as motivators for your sales team. So, keep two sets of sales budgets: One for sales staff and another for yourself or your finance manager. The lower set of sales budgets are what you should use in order to set your expense budget for the year.

>> **Split sales budgets into regions, customers, territories or salespeople:** Because sales budgets are so crucial, split them up as much as possible. For example, if you have a team of salespeople, ask each one to set a sales budget, and provide coaching and support to help your team achieve this.

Realism City Budgets versus Actuals for January			
	Jan Budget	Jan Actual	Variance
Sales — Clothing	34,500	32,000	–2,500
Sales — Jewellery	23,400	25,000	1,600
Sales — Giftware	6,700	6,200	–500
Total Income	64,600	63,200	–1,400
Purchases — Stock	35,530	36,024	494
Gross Profit	29,070	27,176	–1,894
Advertising	1,200	1,100	–100
Bank Charges	75	60	–15
Electricity/Gas	350	370	20
Motor Vehicle	850	963	113
Office Rental	3,600	3,600	0
Postage & Stationery	850	250	–600
Salaries/Wages	4,800	5,462	662
Superannuation	456	519	63
Total Expenses	12,181	12,324	143
Budgeted Profit	**16,889**	**14,852**	**–2,037**

FIGURE 17-4:
Keep budgets real by comparing against actual results.

Developing your budget in tune with your business plan

When you create a budget, take time to ensure it fits with the other elements of your business plan. For example, if your marketing plan proposes that you expand your online advertising by 300 per cent, make sure that you increase the amount you allocate for advertising in your budget accordingly.

When you use budgets properly, they become an instant feedback mechanism for decisions. For example, imagine your first shot at a budget ends up looking pretty gloomy so you decide to cut some of your expenses, and in particular, you decide to reduce the hours for one of your salespeople. However, when you cut back on the hours for this salesperson, this affects your sales budget, which in turn affects the income projections in your financial budget. You may then have to tweak other expenses, adjust pricing policies or consider different strategies to make your business model work.

Looking at Cashflow

Cashflows seem pretty similar to budgets at first glance, but instead of making projections (or commitments) about income, expenses and profit, cashflows make projections about cash in and cash out, and how much money you'll have in the bank at the end of each month.

For an example of what I'm on about, compare the budget in Figure 17-3 with the cashflow in Figure 17-5. Spot the differences:

TECHNICAL STUFF

>> The budget shows sales, whereas the cashflow shows receipts from sales. (If you offer credit to customers, a bumper sales month doesn't necessarily result in a bumper month in terms of cash. A big sales month may actually eat up your cash because you have to pay for additional stock, and you could have to wait up to 60 or 90 days till the cash benefit of those sales comes through.)

>> The budget shows figures before GST (because you never include GST in Profit & Loss results), whereas the cashflow shows figures including GST, including the quarterly tax payment (this payment may also be monthly or bi-monthly, depending on your arrangements).

>> The cashflow includes incomings from loans (in Figure 17-5, this is called 'Receipt of loan from ANZ').

>> The budget shows purchases of stock, whereas the cashflow shows payments made to suppliers.

>> The cashflow includes loan repayments, the budget doesn't.

>> The cashflow shows wages *before* employee tax, but the budget shows wages *including* employee tax. However, the cashflow shows the payment of employee tax going out every quarter.

>> The cashflow includes the purchase of capital equipment (notice the new computer system purchased in March), but the budget doesn't.

>> If you're a sole trader or partnership, the budget wouldn't show personal drawings, but the cashflow would.

>> The cashflow includes three extra lines at the bottom: Starting Cash Balance, Cash In less Cash Out, and Closing Cash Balance.

Realism City Cashflow for January to June							
	Jan	Feb	Mar	Apr	May	Jun	Total
Cash Inflow including GST							
Receipts from Clothing Sales	34,155	37,656	38,748	41,499	37,453	38,427	227,937
Receipts from Jewellery Sales	23,166	25,541	26,281	28,147	25,403	26,063	154,601
Receipts from Giftware Sales	6,633	7,313	7,525	8,059	7,273	7,463	44,266
Total Receipts from Sales	63,954	70,509	72,554	77,705	70,129	71,952	426,804
Plus: Receipt of loan from Bank	–	12,000	–	–	–	–	12,000
Total Cash Inflow (incl GST)	63,954	82,509	72,554	77,705	70,129	71,952	438,804
Cash Outflow including GST							
Payments to suppliers for stock	42,000	39,083	41,037	43,089	45,243	42,981	253,434
Advertising	1,320	1,320	1,320	1,375	6,600	1,485	13,420
Bank Charges	75	75	75	75	75	75	450
Electricity/Gas	–	–	1,155	–	–	1,050	2,205
Loan repayments	5,500	5,950	5,950	5,950	5,950	5,950	35,250
Motor Vehicle	935	935	935	935	935	935	5,610
New Computer System	–	–	19,000	–	–	–	19,000
Postage & Stationery	935	935	935	935	935	935	5,610
Rent	3,960	3,960	3,960	3,960	3,960	3,960	23,760
Net Wages	3,840	4,160	3,760	5,760	3,520	5,760	26,800
Superannuation	900	–	–	1,117			2,546
Total Cash Out (inc GST)	59,465	56,418	78,127	63,196	67,218	63,131	388,085
Payment of GST and PAYG	7,200			6,876			14,076
Starting Cash Balance	**1,500**	– 1,211	24,880	19,307	26,941	29,851	
Cash In Less Cash Out less GST	– 2,711	26,091	– 5,573	7,634	2,911	8,821	
Closing Cash Balance	**– 1,211**	**24,880**	**19,307**	**26,941**	**29,851**	**38,673**	

FIGURE 17-5:
A sample cashflow report.

TIP

The really neat thing about cashflows is that you make predictions about the state of your bank balance and plan accordingly. For example, in Figure 17-5, note that Realism City is going to have a tight month in January, due to big supplier payments and payment of GST, but that things brighten up by the end of June. Given this gloomy prediction, Realism City may be wise to ease back on spending as much as possible during January.

If you're a small business that pays cash for most things, you're going to find that cashflow projections don't bear much relevance, and that a decent budget will be sufficient. However, if you're a business that owes money on letters of credit, has large stock holdings, seasonal sales, very slow-paying customers or extended credit from suppliers, cashflow projections are a lifesaver.

TIP

The easiest way to create a cashflow projection is to use a spreadsheet program or specialised business-planning software. In my example, I opened my budget spreadsheet and saved it under a different name. Then I made all the necessary changes, adding several lines to modify the budget so it became a cashflow projection.

TRUE STORY

GET OVER-SENSITIVE

I used to work for a company that was always teetering on the verge of insolvency. They stayed in business far longer than they should have done because they were fantastic at convincing gullible investors and bank managers to lend them money. Part of the money-lending sell was based on glamorous cashflow projections showing that if only the requisite loan could be found, everything would prosper. The managers would sit in front of the computer, hour after hour, fiddling with projections until they arrived at figures that looked good (but, of course, had little bearing on reality).

This experience taught me how sensitive budgets and cashflows are to relatively small changes. Take your own budget and boost sales by 10 per cent, every month. Chances are things look great. Then take the same budget, but this time pull sales down by 10 per cent, and maybe yank up expenses by 5 per cent. Doesn't look so crash-hot any more, I bet. Often, an adjustment as small as 2 per cent a month in sales or expenses makes a humungous difference to your bottom line.

I'd be kidding you if I said that cashflows are always as simple as I make them out to be. In reality, cashflow projections often require several worksheets, all of which interconnect with one another. For example, a cashflow may have one worksheet for sales budgets, another for predicting when customers are likely to pay, another forecasting when suppliers are to get paid, and a prediction of stock levels. If your cashflow gets this complex, you probably want to get some help from an accountant to create your first template.

TIP

Don't forget to allow for company tax bills when making cashflow projections, for as soon as your business starts making a profit, you're going to be hit with tax bills.

IN THIS CHAPTER

» Deciding whether or not to register for GST, and picking a flavour to suit

» Collecting receipts like a magpie and claiming deductions

» Preparing for tax ahead of time

» Avoiding the classic pitfalls of those new to business

» Budgeting for tax and surviving the second-year roller-coaster syndrome

Chapter **18**

Taming the Tax Tyrant

How do I write a chirpy introduction about one of the most tedious and cheerless subjects in the world? I could tell you that doing your tax is not only a fascinating process, but also a great way of meeting a new lover and a constant source of new insights and inspiration. I could even tell you that this chapter is much more exciting than watching sport and will improve your hair-loss problem.

Sad fact is, I don't think you'd believe me. So, in the interests of honesty, I'm going to skip the chirpy introduction bit and progress to the meat of the matter . . .

Getting a Grip on GST

If you're starting a new business, you can register for GST at the same time as you apply for an ABN. (For more about ABNs or registering your business, refer to Chapter 7.) On the other hand, if your business is already up and running and you want to alter your details to register for GST, contact the Tax Office who will cheerfully take your details and sign you up.

However, I recommend that you don't plunge into the whole GST shenanigans without thinking through your options carefully. Do you have to register? And, if not, would you be better off *not* registering? What accounting basis is best for your business? How often should you lodge reports? I answer all these questions, and a bit more besides, in the next few pages.

Deciding whether to register or not

If your turnover is less than $75,000 a year, you can choose whether or not you want to register for GST. (*Note:* The only exception is if you're a taxi driver, in which case you have to register, no matter how much you earn.)

If you register for GST, you have to charge GST on every sale you make, unless you're selling goods or services that are exempt from GST. However, you can also claim GST on your purchases. Every reporting period, you calculate the difference between GST collected (that is, the GST you charged to customers) and GST paid (that is, the GST you paid to suppliers). If GST collected is *more* than GST paid, you pay this difference to the government. If GST paid is more than GST collected, you claim a refund.

If you *don't* register for GST, you can't charge GST on your customer sales. However, don't think that you can escape paying GST on purchases: Even if you're *not* registered, a tax-registered business still has to add GST on its charges to you. You can't claim this GST back, although you can claim the full amount of the purchase as a tax deduction.

TRUE STORY

For many small businesses, it doesn't make sense to register for GST. My neighbour chose not to. He runs a small lawn mowing business that turns over about $800 a week, an income that falls short of the threshold over which he'd have to register. He chose not to register because that way he doesn't have to charge customers GST, and his prices are more competitive.

Note: Some people might advise you that if you don't register for GST, customers don't want to trade with you. Pish tosh. So long as you have an ABN and your prices are competitive, most customers don't mind either way.

Choosing your cashflow destiny

When you register for GST (refer to Chapter 7 for more details about how this is done), you see an innocent-looking question asking whether you want to account for GST on a cash or accrual basis. Here's what this means:

>> **Cash basis reporting:** *Cash basis reporting* means you only pay GST when you receive payments from customers and you only claim back GST when you make payments to suppliers. Note that you're only allowed to report for GST on a cash basis if your business has a turnover of less than $10 million per year.

If you tend to owe *less* to suppliers than what customers owe you, cash basis reporting works best.

>> **Accrual basis reporting:** *Accrual basis reporting* means you pay GST in the period that you bill the customer or receive a bill from the supplier, regardless of whether any money has been exchanged. This approach means that if you bill customers in March and they don't pay until July, you have to pay the GST in April regardless. Similarly, if you receive a bill from a supplier in March and you don't pay them until much later, you still claim back the GST in April.

If you tend to owe *more* to suppliers than what customers owe you, accrual basis reporting works best.

You can choose to report for GST on a different basis to income tax. For example, you can choose to report for GST on a cash basis and report for tax on an accrual basis or vice versa. Most small businesses opt to report on a cash basis for both GST and for income tax purposes.

You may be feeling bamboozled by all this tax chat. No sweat — the important thing for you to realise is that any selection you make regarding your accounting or GST reporting basis may have a big impact on the cashflow of your business. If you're in doubt as to what's best for you, speak to your accountant first.

Reporting for duty — how often?

If your annual business turnover is $20 million or less, you can choose to report for GST on a monthly, quarterly or annual basis.

I find that reporting every three months is a happy medium between the hassle of monthly reporting and the psychological hurdle of only doing your books every six or twelve months, whereas reporting monthly makes sense if you always receive a GST refund.

The only tricky thing about reporting every three months is that you can end up with a big bill that is hard to manage. For more ideas about managing this cash-flow challenge, see the section later in this chapter 'Budgeting for Tax'.

Coughing up

Here are five tips for making Business Activity Statements as inconsequential in your life as your second cousin's birthday. Here goes:

TIP

>> **Subscribe to accounting software:** If you have more than 20 transactions or so a month, subscribe to accounting software so that you can do your books and generate your Business Activity Statement automatically.

>> **Don't tie yourself in knots:** These cursed government forms aren't something you have to get 100 per cent right. Work through the questions as best you can and, if something doesn't balance by a couple of dollars, don't put yourself through too much heartache.

>> **Learn how to double-check your figures:** Insure yourself against these seemingly lackadaisical attitudes by making sure someone (if not you) compares the figures on your Business Activity Statement against your Profit & Loss report and Balance Sheet (refer to Chapter 17 for more on these reports). Ask your accountant to teach you how, if need be.

>> **Know your limitations:** Why not get someone else to do all your GST stuff (your bookkeeper or accountant are likely victims)? Sure, you will have to pay this person for their efforts, but your time will be left free to do the things that you're good at, such as running your own business.

Staying out of trouble

Everyone dreads an audit, and no-one wants to receive a fine or an unexpected tax bill. Here are some common mistakes auditors look for, if you're unlucky enough to get hauled over the coals:

WARNING

>> You can't claim GST on bank fees, interest, loan payments, private drawings, tax payments or wages.

>> You also can't claim GST on government charges, such as motor vehicle registration, licence renewals or stamp duty.

>> You can't claim the full amount of GST on expenses that are partly personal (motor vehicle and home office expenses are the obvious culprits). However, you can claim the full amount of GST during the year, and then make an adjustment for private use in your final Business Activity Statement.

>> You can't claim GST on invoices from unregistered suppliers. If a supplier isn't registered for GST, treat them as a GST-free purchase.

>> You can't claim GST on any amount over $82.50 unless you have a Tax Invoice.

Growing Some Recordkeeping Smarts

British economist John Keynes once said, 'The avoidance of taxes is the only intellectual pursuit that still carries any reward.' Cynical maybe, but how *do* those big corporations get away with paying not a brass razoo?

I can't explain the bad guy secrets, nor can I give you advice on opening Swiss bank accounts, using tax havens in far-flung Patagonia or hiding wads of cash under the floorboards. Rather, I take a more straightforward and no-nonsense kind of approach, hoping that in the end, you don't pay a cent more tax than you have to.

Treating receipts with respect

Imagine that you go into a shop and buy some printer toner for $60. You pay cash and pop the receipt vaguely into the back pocket of your jeans. Life carries on at its normal crazy pace, your jeans soon go through the washing machine and, before a few days are out, the receipt is nothing more than a few bits of irritating fluff. Sounds familiar?

Now imagine getting a $20 note out of your wallet and, for no particular reason, cutting this note into hundreds of little bits. Pure madness, yes, but no more so than losing that receipt.

REMEMBER

At an average tax rate of around 33 per cent, losing a receipt for $60 is like throwing a $20 bill out the window. Losing a receipt for $150 is like throwing a $50 bill out the window. Why? Because if you don't have a receipt, you can't claim the expense against your tax. Simple logic.

Cultivating your obsessive-compulsive streak

When you receive an invoice or a receipt, check the fine print. As Figure 18-1 shows, the kind of details an invoice should include are the supplier's ABN, an accurate description, the date and the total amount payable. If the supplier is registered for GST, the invoice should also say 'Tax Invoice' at the top, and either a statement that GST is included or a subtotal showing the amount of GST charged. Last, any invoice over $1,000 needs to show your name and address, plus the quantity or volume of the goods or services supplied, such as litres of petrol or hours of labour.

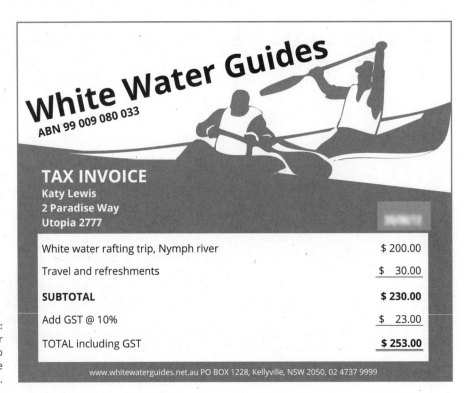

White Water Guides

ABN 99 009 080 033

TAX INVOICE
Katy Lewis
2 Paradise Way
Utopia 2777

White water rafting trip, Nymph river	$ 200.00
Travel and refreshments	$ 30.00
SUBTOTAL	**$ 230.00**
Add GST @ 10%	$ 23.00
TOTAL including GST	**$ 253.00**

www.whitewaterguides.net.au PO BOX 1228, Kellyville, NSW 2050, 02 4737 9999

FIGURE 18-1:
An invoice or receipt needs to include all the right details.

WARNING

Most invoices and receipts have all of these details on them as a matter of course, with the exception of credit card or EFTPOS dockets, which usually just say the total amount and don't include a description. Be careful, because in most situations, credit card and EFTPOS dockets aren't legitimate receipts as far as your tax is concerned, so you need to keep the original receipt or invoice as well. (I guess the tax auditors are trying to cover for all those situations where someone buys $40 of petrol on their credit card and then chucks a Paddle Pop and a bunch of flowers on top.)

The only exception to these rules is for what the Tax Office describes as 'small expenses'. You can use diary entries instead of receipts for small purchases of under $10, so long as the total of these expenses isn't more than $200 over the course of a single financial year.

Riding that (t)rusty chariot

Probably the biggest expense that small business people forget to claim, or claim in a way that isn't to their best advantage, is their motor vehicle. Part of the reason for the general confusion is that several different methods are available for claiming motor vehicle expenses.

I'm not going to go into the detailed methods of claiming motor vehicle expenses here, because chances are by the time you read this, the legislation could have changed. However, I will provide a few pointers:

» If you use your motor vehicle regularly for business purposes, I recommend that you track your business trips using a logbook. Don't worry — you don't need to log all business trips for ever more. Instead, so long as your business use is consistent from one year to the next, you only need to maintain a log book for 12 continuous weeks every five years.

» If you keep a logbook and establish what proportion of your mileage is for business purposes, you can then claim this percentage for all motor vehicle expenses. The outcome is often a pretty handsome tax deduction; not only can you claim expenses such as fuel and insurance, but you can claim interest on motor vehicle loans and depreciation also.

» Remember that you can't claim travel between your home and your office as business kilometres, because this kind of travel doesn't count as business use. However, if you have a legitimate home office, mileage from home for business purposes is deductible. (Sound convoluted? It is. If you're at all unsure what you can claim, check first with your accountant.)

» If you are reading this and thinking that the advice has come too late because you haven't kept a logbook, don't worry. Your accountant will still be able to claim a generous cents-per-kilometre allowance for up to 5,000 business kilometres per year, so long as you can justify your business travel by diary entries or some other method.

TIP

You can switch methods from one year to the next, depending on what method gets you the biggest deduction in any one year. For example, I don't do an enormous amount of business kilometres with my vehicle, so I normally use the cents-per-kilometre method. However, if I have a very expensive year with running costs, I compare the cents-per-kilometre method against the logbook method, and pick the highest one of the two.

Declaring home office expenses

If you work from home occasionally, you're able to claim a proportion of home office *running expenses*, such as cleaning, depreciation on furniture, electricity, gas, internet, mobile phones and repairs.

If you actually run your business from home, you may also be able to claim *occupancy expenses*, which include mortgage interest, home building insurance, rental expense, council rates or water rates.

With any home office expenses, please bear the following warnings in mind:

WARNING

>> Using the dining-room table every blue moon doesn't mean you can claim occupancy expenses. You can only claim occupancy expenses if you run your business from home and have at least one room exclusively devoted to your business. You're best to speak to your accountant to see whether or not you qualify.

>> You usually claim occupancy expenses in a slightly different way from running expenses, by calculating the percentage of floor area taken up by your home office. For example, if your office measures 10 square metres and your house measures 50 square metres, you can claim 20 per cent (10 divided by 50 equals 20 per cent) of expenses.

>> Always get your accountant to double-check any occupancy claims, and in particular ask whether claiming occupancy expenses risks exposure to capital gains tax further down the track. For example, if you buy your home for $800,000 and ten years later sell it for $950,000, and in the years in between you claimed a proportion of mortgage interest and rates as a tax deduction, you may have to pay capital gains tax on part of the $150,000 profit from the sale of your home.

>> When claiming for running expenses, don't be tempted to pull a random percentage out of your hat. Instead, you need to follow very specific rules in order to substantiate your claim. I suggest you go to the ATO website for details, or ask your accountant for further advice.

>> If your income is deemed by the Tax Office to be Personal Services Income (see 'Avoid Personal Services rulings, if you can' later in this chapter for more details) then you may be limited as to what home office expenses you can claim.

Planning Ahead

Don't wait till the financial year has ended before you plan for tax. Instead, start planning in about April. Get your books up to date, generate an interim Profit & Loss report and Balance Sheet (if available), have a think about what your end-of-year profits are likely to be, and make an appointment to see your accountant.

WARNING

In the meantime, a word of warning, especially if your profits look healthy and you know a tax bill awaits: Don't be tempted to splurge on unnecessary expenses. Here's the thing: Just because you can claim something on your tax doesn't mean this is a wise business decision. Even if this purchase is a legitimate tax deduction, you'll only get back 30 cents or so in the dollar. Cash is still going out from your business, leaving the bottom line of your business looking less healthy if you want to sell in the future, reducing your working capital, and leaving you with less room to grow.

Alternatively, if your concern is that your business might make a loss this financial year, speak to your accountant as soon as you can, particularly if you earn income from other sources such as wages. Ask your accountant how you can avoid this loss being classified as non-commercial and, if relevant, how you can carry this loss forward to future years.

Getting an instant deduction

One great tax break for small businesses is the instant asset write-off, which allows your business to purchase capital assets and at the same time reduce your taxable income. The threshold for the instant tax deduction varies each year according to government policies, but generally falls somewhere between $10,000 and $150,000. For example, at the time of writing, if I purchase a new motor vehicle for $25,000 and I intend to use this vehicle exclusively for business purposes, I can write off the whole amount against my tax.

WARNING

However, before running out to buy new equipment, take a moment to understand how this tax break works. The instant deduction is not a cash refund but, rather, is a reduction in your taxable income. For example, if I do buy a vehicle for $25,000, I'll receive a reduction in my tax of approximately 30 per cent (depending on my business structure and marginal tax rates). In other words, although I'll reduce my tax by about $7,500, I'll still be out of pocket by $17,500.

The other thing to be wary of, particularly if you're planning to purchase a vehicle as an instant deduction, is this: To claim the full amount of an asset purchase as a deduction, you must use this asset in your business, and if there is any personal use, the deduction needs to be adjusted to reflect this.

Are you wondering what happens if an asset purchase exceeds the instant deduction threshold? In this situation, you can't claim a straight-out tax deduction. Instead, you have to depreciate the asset, claiming the cost gradually over several years.

Managing stock valuations

If your business carries stock on hand — maybe you're a wholesaler, manufacturer, distributor or retailer — then the value of your stock on the last day of the financial year can have a significant impact on your tax.

TIP

If you're carrying obsolete or difficult-to-sell items, you may be eligible to revalue your stock, valuing your stock at its market selling value or replacement value, rather than at cost.

If you think that adjusting stock valuations may help minimise your tax, talk to your accountant ahead of time, and ensure you conduct a detailed stocktake when the end of financial year rolls by.

Salting funds away into super

After the family home, superannuation is one of the best tax breaks going, and additional super contributions are a good tactic for minimising your end-of-year tax bill. Do speak to your accountant first, however, to seek advice about contribution limits and the best way to manage any additional contributions.

REMEMBER

Setting funds aside for super is particularly important if your business runs under a sole trader or partnership structure, because with this type of business structure, you're not legally bound to make any super contributions. (In contrast, you must pay super on wages you draw from a business that's structured as a company.) Many business people find that because they're not compelled to pay super, they don't.

In my first 20 years as a sole trader, I didn't contribute a single cent into super, ending up aged 43 with only $1,500 saved in super. This was a decision I now regret, especially now that I understand how effective super could have been if I had managed it well as a tax deduction.

Staying Out of Trouble

In the next delightfully cheery section of this delightfully cheery chapter, I talk about all the ways you can end up in trouble with the Tax Office. Skip these next few pages, dear reader, at your peril.

Don't claim what you can't

When writing this section, I asked my friend Steph (who's a tax accountant) what kinds of expenses she'd seen people try to claim against their tax. She laughed outright, and came up with a list of everything from diamond rings to new kitchens. She also offered me this list of the most common deductions that people try to claim, but shouldn't:

>> **Domestic expenses.** Childcare, cleaners at your home, clothes and school fees are the regular suspects.

>> **Entertainment expenses.** No matter how late you're stuck at the office, you definitely can't claim takeaway dinners, beers at the pub, or a night out on the

town with your mates. In some limited situations, you can claim some expenses of wining and dining a client, but the rules are complex, and you're best to check with your accountant.

>> **Expenses relating to income that you're not declaring.** You can't have things both ways. So, if you don't declare the income from playing in a band on the weekends because you argue it's a hobby, you can't claim a tax deduction for guitar strings and amplifier repairs.

>> **Pet food and vet bills.** Sounds nutty, but my friend laughs at how frequently she sees people trying to claim pet food and vet bills as a tax deduction, declaring vehemently that Fluffy the Poodle is a necessary guard dog protecting their business premises.

>> **The personal proportion of expenses that are a mix of personal and business.** The most common culprit here is motor vehicles — if you use a car for both business and personal purposes, you can only claim the proportion that's business. Be careful with holidays and travel also. If you head to the Gold Coast for a fortnight and attend a conference for a weekend during that time, you can't claim the whole trip.

>> **Traffic fines.** Or any fines for that matter. Even if you were speeding to get to a job.

Be able to back up your story

If I had only one piece of advice to give you about how to survive an audit, it would be this: *Be able to back up your story*. As anyone who has ever needed an alibi knows, nothing can substitute for cold, hard evidence.

Many small businesses come adrift with the way they claim expenses that are part-personal and part-business, such as home electricity, internet, mobile phones or motor vehicle. More often than not, people make a rough guess, saying 'Oh, about 20 per cent of home electricity is due to the business' or 'I reckon my car is only 5 per cent personal; the rest is definitely business'.

Although I explain the rules for recording and claiming expenses in detail earlier in this chapter (see 'Riding that (t)rusty chariot' and 'Declaring home office expenses'), the crux of the matter is that every expense you claim needs substantiating with receipts, detailed calculations or log books.

REMEMBER

Be diligent about keeping business expense records. After all, the devil is in the detail and the detail is up to you!

Avoid Personal Services rulings, if you can

If your business earns income from providing services to others, your accountant will need to figure out if this income is categorised as *Personal Services Income*. Your business may not have much control over this classification, because the decision depends on a range of factors including the number of clients you have and the percentage of income from each one, whether you need tools or equipment to do your work, whether you maintain business premises separate from your home, and a few others things besides.

TECHNICAL STUFF

If your business changes from year to year, your classification for tax purposes may change as well. For example, if a consultant works exclusively on a single contract with one client for 12 months, paid on an hourly basis and working at the client's premises, this income would almost certainly be classified as Personal Services Income. However, if this contract finished and the next year the consultant worked for a variety of different clients, their income may well revert to being exempt from this classification.

Personal Services Income legislation prevents people claiming the income tax benefits of being a small business when what they really are is an employee (as in the consultant example I just mentioned). If your income is classified as Personal Services Income, you can't claim tax deductions for things such as mortgage interest or rates on your home office, or wages and super paid to family members who are doing admin work only. Also, if you operate under a company structure, any profits made in excess of salaries are treated as salaries, meaning that you have to pay PAYG on them. In short, all that 'cream' of being self-employed is done away with.

If you think your income may be classified as Personal Services Income, do talk to your accountant. A whole stack of exceptions and qualifications may apply, none of which I have the room to explain here. You may be able to argue that you're operating under unusual circumstances — and aren't we all? — and apply for a Personal Services Business Determination. (See your accountant for how to do this.) Alternatively, you may be able to adjust or diversify your business model.

Monitor shareholder or director loans closely

Company structures can be challenging for owner-operators to understand. If you incorporate your business as a company, the company becomes a legal entity that's separate to you, even if you're the only director and the only shareholder.

One of the biggest differences between being a sole trader and a company is that when you operate as a company, you can't draw money out of the company bank account for personal use. In order to withdraw funds from your own company, the company must pay you a wage, deducting tax and paying super in the same way as for any other employee.

WARNING

If you withdraw funds from your company bank account and don't process these withdrawals as wages, your bookkeeper or accountant will typically record this transaction as a Loan to Director. When end of financial year rolls around, if you owe the company more than the company owes you, this may be deemed to be an 'unfranked dividend' and be taxable at a high marginal tax rate. If possible, you want to avoid this situation.

If you know you've taken money from the company that hasn't been processed as wages, and you're likely to owe the company money at the end of financial year, seek advice from your accountant. They may suggest settting up a formal loan agreement between you and your company. You'll pay interest on this loan and will have to make regular repayments, but this may be a better plan than paying the high tax of an unfranked dividend.

Don't kid yourself about the cash economy

If you sometimes receive money in cash from your customers, you need to declare this income in the same way as you declare any other business income that you receive.

WARNING

Don't be tempted to pocket the cash and delete the invoice, or not raise an invoice at all. The Australian Tax Office is getting smarter all the time in the way it bench-marks income and expense claims for each industry. For example, if you're an electrician, the Tax Office expects you to spend a certain percentage of your income on materials. If you spend more than this percentage, because you're claiming all the purchases you make but you're not declaring all your income, this is likely to trigger an audit.

Budgeting for Tax

Many businesses struggle to cope with the cashflow roller-coaster that GST, PAYG tax and personal income tax bring. Unless you're in a situation where you normally receive GST refunds, you probably find that in the weeks following your most recent Business Activity Statement, your bank balance looks healthier and healthier. You may be tempted to ignore your better instincts and spend some of the cash that you (somewhat mistakenly) feel is yours. But then, by the time you have to pay your quarterly tax bill, your bank account doesn't have quite enough funds to foot the bill.

In this section, I share a few tips about budgeting and planning for personal income tax and GST. The best business managers I know all follow some kind of process the same as or similar to the one I recommend here — and their business performance is much the better for it.

Planning for that difficult second year

If you're a sole trader or partnership, you don't pay tax on your first year's profits until you lodge your first year's tax return. Similarly, if you choose a company structure, the company doesn't pay tax on its first year's profits until it lodges its first year's return.

REMEMBER

For sole traders and partnerships, you get taxed on the profit that you make, not on the money that you draw out of the business. For example, if the business makes $50,000 profit, but part of these profits goes into building up stock, and you only take out $30,000 to live on, you still get taxed on the $50,000.

If you're one of those lucky souls who make a profit in their first year of trading, the tax bill can come as a bit of a shock. This shock can be exacerbated by the fact that you not only have to pay the tax bill for the year just gone (your first year of trading), but you may also have to pay tax for the year you're currently in (your second year of trading).

The double-whammy of last year's tax bill *plus* part or all of this year's tax bill, both falling due within a few months of one another, can be a real killer. For this reason, I suggest you start putting funds aside for tax as soon as you know you're making a profit. Read on to find out more . . .

Putting funds aside

Having some understanding of personal tax is all very well, but you still need to map out a plan for how you're going to come up with the funds. Here are some ideas to help you on your way:

AHEAD OF THE PACK

1. **Subscribe to accounting software.**

    If you want to keep tabs on how much profit you're making, having accounting software up and running is the only efficient way. For more info on this topic, refer to Chapter 16.

2. **At the end of every three months, work out how much profit you've made.**

   Remember that if you're a sole trader or partnership, the amount of profit you've made is the final figure on the bottom of your Profit & Loss report, and not the amount you've drawn out of the business.

3. **Multiply your quarterly profit estimate by four.**

4. **Estimate how much tax you would pay if this were your annual profit.**

   Go to www.ato.gov.au and search for the Simple Tax Calculator.

5. **Divide this estimated tax amount by 52 to arrive at your weekly savings amount.**

   This calculation gives you a rough amount of how much tax you should be putting aside each week.

6. **Set up a direct debit from your business account that transfers your weekly savings amount into an online savings account.**

7. **Repeat this process every three months, adjusting your weekly savings amount as necessary.**

   Sounds hideously pedantic? Never mind. I reckon a wee bit of pedantry goes a long way towards keeping the blood pressure down.

Budgeting for GST and PAYG

In the same way as I recommend you budget for personal income tax (refer to preceding section), I also suggest you budget for GST and PAYG tax (the tax you deduct from employee wages) so that you're not caught short. So, if you're on the hunt for a stress-free existence, read on:

1. **Keep your accounts up to date.**

   Dull, I know. But unless you keep track of your sales and expenses, how else can you figure out where you stand with GST?

2. **Generate a GST report at the end of each month.**

   Notice how the report in Figure 18-2 summarises both GST collected and paid? I used QuickBooks to produce this report, but you can get the same information using any accounting software.

3. **Subtract the amount of GST you pay from the amount of GST you collect.**

   The difference between these two figures is the amount of GST you owe.

4. **Calculate how much tax you withheld from employee wages for the month.**

    Look up how much tax you deducted from employee wages — if any.

5. **Total the amounts that you calculated in Steps 3 and 4 above.**

6. **Transfer the total amount from Step 5 into an online savings account.**

7. **Sleep well . . . no nasty surprises waiting around the corner.**

    With the exception of those four big green bogeymen, of course.

Confirm your GST

Reports can help you confirm your GST. Make sure the GST codes are correct ⬀ and check transactions that don't have a GST code ⬀.

Total sales	$197,564	GST collected on sales	$7,974
Total purchases	$121,888	GST paid on purchases	$4,199
		GST due	$3,775

FIGURE 18-2: Generate reports regularly to find out how much GST you owe.

Fessing up if you're short on cash

A few years ago, a client rang me and confessed that she hadn't lodged her Business Activity Statement for over three years (a pretty scary story, considering she was on quarterly lodgements). When I asked her what had been going on, she told me that she didn't have the money to pay the first activity statement and so she'd put it off. After she'd put the first one off she got into a whole negative spiral just thinking about GST and tax, so she'd stuck her head in the sand and pretended that everything was okay.

TIP

If you're short of cash, lodge your Business Activity Statement anyway, and call the Tax Office to make payment arrangements. So long as you send in the form itself on time, you're not fined a cent. Then, if you can't pay within the next week or so, simply phone the Tax Office on 13 28 66. The Tax Office is surprisingly willing to make alternative payment arrangements, usually suggesting a series of instalments over the following 10 to 20 weeks. You're going to have to pay interest, but the rates aren't too punitive, and you don't get hit with loan set-up fees or penalties.

TIP

KEEP THE TAX BILL DOWN

Need some emergency tips to keep your tax down this year? Here's a handy checklist of things to think about before the end of the financial year rolls by. However, even if your accountant is the kind of person who doesn't tend to initiate these kinds of suggestions, always speak to them first to ensure that your proposed action is a sensible one.

- Consider upgrading existing equipment. Ask your accountant what the current asset threshold is, and what is the maximum you can spend for this purchase to be 100 per cent tax deductible in the year of purchase. Or, even if an asset isn't 100 per cent tax deductible in the first year, ask if this asset can be 'pooled' and how much you can claim as a deduction.

- If you've got spare cash, consider paying some expenses in advance. Insurance, interest, rent and lease payments are all likely candidates.

- Have you got any dud stock? Getting rid of obsolete stock is quite legal.

- Has the purchase value of your stock gone down, not up? If so, you can use the 'replacement value' or 'market selling price', rather than the book value, for these items.

- Are you married or in a de facto relationship? If your partner is on a low income, you may be able to make a superannuation contribution of their behalf and gain a tax offset.

- Got any slack customers who are unlikely to cough up? Write off bad debts before the end of the financial year (this tip only works if you report for tax on an accruals/invoice basis — ask your accountant if you're not sure).

- If you can legitimately put off billing customers till after the end of the financial year, doing so isn't a bad idea (again, this tip is only relevant if you report for tax on an accruals/invoice basis).

- Feeling generous? Now's the time to make those tax-deductible gifts and donations. By the way, if you're part of a couple, the individual with the highest income is the one who should make the donations.

- Be a benevolent dictator and dish out staff bonuses now.

- If you've got old equipment, computers or office gear kicking around the office or factory, consider scrapping the stuff. (Scrapping equipment is only a tax benefit if the gear hasn't completely depreciated yet.)

- Pay money into superannuation, making sure your payment clears through your bank account before the end of the financial year. (The worthiness of this advice entirely depends on your personal situation, and you must speak to your

(continued)

(continued)

accountant for more advice before making extra payments.) If you have a company structure, ask about super salary sacrifice arrangements.

- Make sure all superannuation payments due on behalf of employees are up to date. If you're too late with employee super payments, you can't claim them as a tax deduction at all — not even in the following tax year.

- Stock up on everyday business items such as stationery, printer toner, small tools and furnishings.

- Run away to a tax haven, preferably one with lots of sunshine.

6

The Part of Tens

IN THIS CHAPTER

» **Reinventing yourself**

» **Pulling back on personal spending**

» **Chasing overdue money, no holds barred**

» **Running special offers and making more sales**

» **Swallowing your pride and asking for help**

Chapter **19**

Ten Things to Do If You Hit Hard Times

So, things are looking a little grim? Your bank balance is in the red, you have a pile of bills a mile high, you haven't paid yourself wages in weeks and you're wondering if you're going to make it through this difficult patch.

Just knowing that lots of people have been where you are now, and they've gotten to the other side, can be a comfort. I know of a few businesses that have teetered on the edge of the precipice for months or even years, hanging on with steely determination. Yet somehow they make it back, reinventing themselves and finding success once more. As the saying goes, winners never quit, quitters never win . . .

In this chapter, I share a few tips for how you too can keep clinging on and, with any luck, turn things around as well.

Work Out How Bad Things Really Are

The key to surviving and avoiding a crisis is to understand the early warning signs. The worst thing you can do is stick your head in the sand and pretend everything is okay.

So, come clean and ask yourself the following:

>> Do your Profit & Loss reports show consistent losses, month after month?

>> Are you paying all your bills on time? Or do you stretch some bills out to 60 or 90 days, or even longer?

>> Do you owe money to the Australian Taxation Office?

>> Over the last 24 months, have you taken out any new loans? Do you owe more now than you did 24 months ago?

>> Have you been running up credit card debts?

>> Have some suppliers shifted your payment terms to cash on delivery?

>> Do you have problems obtaining finance?

>> Are you relying on the next big job or sale to pull you out of trouble?

>> Is your business plan out of date or, worse still, non-existent?

>> Do you sometimes skip paying yourself wages?

>> Are you behind on paying employee superannuation?

If you answer 'yes' to two or more of these questions, chances are your business isn't generating enough cash to survive in the long term. Even if you currently have cash in the bank, take these warning signs seriously. You need to take action, right now.

WARNING

If you're trading as a company, don't operate under the illusion that having a company structure gives you automatic protection against creditors. As far as the law is concerned, a company is insolvent as soon as it is unable to pay debts *as and when they fall due.* If a company keeps trading when insolvent, the directors may end up being personally liable for any debts.

Get Breathing Space

If you've got temporary cashflow blues but your core business is still quite solid, maybe all you need is some breathing space. Here are some strategies to help you buy time:

» **Own up:** Contact your creditors and tell them the date you plan to pay them, even if this date is much later than the date bills are due. This straightforward approach often works a treat. You can also suggest that you pay a small amount every week. So long as you keep in contact and stick by your word, most creditors are willing to come to the party.

» **Ask whether you can pay your tax debt in instalments:** The Tax Office is usually quite willing to make a payment instalment arrangement.

» **Approach your bank:** Ask your bank for a temporary overdraft to tide you over.

» **Apply for voluntary administration:** The most extreme solution, applying for *voluntary administration* means that you ask a registered accountant or liquidator to become your business administrator. Usually, the administrator negotiates with creditors, and may be able to secure an agreement to 'freeze' your debts for a certain period (usually one or two years), and work with you to get your business back on the road.

Innovate!

Do you have a sneaking suspicion that your business model is actually a bit of a dud? If things have been slowly sliding backwards for years, or they simply never got off the ground in the first place (maybe the beachwear shop in the Snowy Mountains was a crazy idea after all), then the time has come to reassess your idea. As the Spanish say, 'There's no use trying to plough the sea with a tractor.'

I don't necessarily mean closing your business completely (after all, you probably have lots of lovely tax losses to take advantage of), but I am talking about the need to think laterally and reinvent yourself. Maybe you need a new business partner, maybe you need to move location or maybe you need to do something totally different? A good starting point is to make your way back to Chapter 2 and re-evaluate your business strategy, in particular looking at your competitive advantage and point of difference.

Another possibility is to consider selling your business, particularly if your business carries a substantial amount of debt such as business loans, leases or shareholder loans. If you can find a purchaser who can run your business without the same level of debt, your business might be a viable going concern.

Slash Those Expenses

Sometimes when money gets tight, you have to get tight, too. Be brave, be mean, and think economic rationalism with the following:

MONEY STUFF

TIP

>> **Anything on a plan:** The usual culprits are mobile phone plans, internet plans, electricity and gas. If your current contract period has expired, get on the phone and start negotiating a new plan with bigger discounts.

>> **Lease payments:** If you're leasing anything that's non-essential for your business, consider terminating the lease.

>> **Interest expense and loan repayments:** If you have lots of credit cards, reduce interest expense and monthly repayments by asking your bank to consolidate the debt into a single loan or single credit card with lower interest. Alternatively, if you have large loan repayments every week, ask your bank if you can refinance this loan over a longer repayment period.

>> **Monthly subscriptions:** You know the ones. Everyone from your cloud backups to VOIP, from Netflix to Dropbox. Take the time to unsubscribe from anything that doesn't generate value for your business.

>> **Rent:** You may not have a choice about your rent, but do at least consider how you may reduce this expense. Maybe you can sublet some of your premises or even negotiate with the landlord to reduce the rent. Or, if you're not in retail, maybe you can move to smaller or less expensive premises.

>> **Wages:** Although you may not be able to afford to get rid of any employees who form a vital part of your business income, wages are often the biggest expense for a business. When things get tight, avoid paying overtime (employ casuals instead), work weekends yourself and make sure you're not using skilled labour for unskilled tasks. Last, if you need to lay someone off, don't postpone the deed for longer than necessary — terminating someone's employment is horrible, but if you procrastinate and your business goes down the drain, everyone loses. (For more about terminating employees, refer to Chapter 14.)

REMEMBER

When cost-cutting, don't get stuck in the tiny details of rationing toilet paper or limiting small comforts. Instead, look at your Profit & Loss reports for the last six months, and identify the five highest expenses. Wherever possible, find ways to reduce each one of these expenses by 10 to 20 per cent each.

Pull Back Personal Spending

Another option is to cut back on how much you, other directors, partners or relatives are drawing out of the business. Common culprits that make for high personal spending include the following:

MONEY STUFF

» **Inflated wages:** I'm talking both your own wages here, and possibly wages paid to spouses or relatives as part of tax minimisation strategies.

» **Extra superannuation:** If times are tight, you don't have to put anything into super if you're a sole trader or a partnership. If you're an employee of your own company, you only have to pay the minimum percentage as stipulated by the government (refer to Chapter 13 for more details).

» **Motor vehicles:** Get rid of the fat hire purchase debt and downsize your motor vehicle. Come to that, buy a pushbike. (Yep, I know I'm being drastic.)

» **High-end travel and accommodation:** You know the deal. If your business is really suffering, you're best to make the change in personal lifestyle now, rather than being forced to make these changes later on.

Get Rid of Dead Weight

Almost any small business has at least two or three cost centres. The secret of financial stability is to find out how much each part of your business generates in profit, and make sure that each and every cost centre pulls its weight.

Some examples of cost centres include

» A tradie who does repairs and maintenance but also mows lawns

» A hairdresser with three different shops in three different suburbs

» A distributor with offices in three different cities

» A retailer with products that fall into a handful of different departments

» A wholesaler who sells imported goods but also manufactures goods to sell

If your business has multiple cost centres, I suggest you waste no time in setting up systems that let you analyse how much profit each cost centre generates. Any mainstream accounting software package includes these features. (The terminology varies, and may be called job analysis, category analysis, class analysis or cost centre analysis, but the principle remains the same.)

As soon as you can analyse how much profit (or loss) each cost centre generates, consider getting rid of anything that doesn't pull its weight.

TRUE STORY

A client of mine builds custom kitchens for a living but he also used to sell tiles from his factory unit. When he did the numbers, he found the tile sales generated very little profit and required an extra staff member. The decision was a no-brainer. He got rid of the tile sales, sublet the factory space that was freed up, and got rid of the extra staff member.

Chase Up Overdue Accounts

I talk about debt collection in Chapter 16, but the topic is worthy of a second mention here. Whenever your customers owe you money, think of this money as *your* money — dollars that are much better in your pocket than anybody else's.

TRUE STORY

I visited a client a couple of months ago who was feeling desperate, wondering where on earth she would find the money to pay a $20,000 tax bill. Looking through her financials, I noticed how much money she was owed (some of the overdue accounts went back six months or more). 'Oh, I phone them up,' Ailsa sighed, 'and they promise to send money soon, but still I'm waiting.'

I explained to Ailsa that if an account is due at 30 days, she should start chasing at 40 days and, if the account is still overdue at 60 days, to take more serious action. Ailsa took me at my word and became a fox terrier, chasing after *her* money without being afraid to follow through on her threats. The strategy worked and these days Ailsa's cashflow is much, much better.

Run Special Offers

Special offers and sales are fab if you want some quick cash. However, before you get too drastic, here are a few things to keep in mind:

WARNING

>> **Pick specials carefully:** Run specials on stock that isn't moving. After all, old stock only ties up cash and takes up shelf space. However, don't discount the high-end items that loyal customers associate with your brand.

>> **Do your sums:** If you offer discounts on all of your range — for example, offering 10 per cent off all purchases before 30 September — do your sums cautiously, because you don't want to run the risk of undermining your overall profitability. For example, imagine a surf shop buys boogie boards for $60 and sells them for $100, and they decide to offer a 10 per cent discount for a month. The owners would have to increase sales by more than 30 per cent simply to end up with the same amount of profit as they would have made had they not changed their prices.

>> **Don't become a dollar shop:** Be careful not to offer specials and discounts too often, because you may tarnish your image and sacrifice your brand.

>> **Keep your desperation under wraps:** Try not to wait till you're desperate before offering specials. See the trouble coming, and take action in advance.

For more tips about pricing strategies, make your way to Chapter 8.

Re-Jig Your Margins

Are you continually hovering on the edge of profitability, even when your sales are fairly healthy? If so, take some time to look at your prices and profit margins. Sometimes, tweaking margins by a couple of per cent here or there is all you need to do to turn your tin-pot business into a goldmine.

TRUE STORY

I knew a tyre retailer who was continually struggling to stay in business and, indeed, when I first met the owners of the business, it looked like the bank was about to foreclose. However, looking at their prices, I discovered just a few brands of tyres where price was crucial in order to appear competitive. With this in mind, we bumped up the price of all the other tyres by a modest 5 per cent. The tyre prices weren't affected much (a $150 tyre now cost $157.50), but 5 per cent on their annual turnover of $1,000,000 meant $50,000 extra profit per year. This difference was all they needed to turn their business around. With cashflow finally freed up, they were able to finance additional marketing activities, which in turn increased profitability even more.

In any kind of business, identify the *price-sensitive* products or services (such as milk and bread in a general store). Keep these prices low. Then identify the products that aren't price sensitive (maybe gourmet goat cheese in a general store), and aim for handsome profits on these items. For more about pricing, refer to Chapter 8.

Don't Be a Shag on a Rock

No matter what your social conditioning, remember you're not alone. Lots of people around you can help — all you have to do is be brave enough to ask. I bet you're going to be pleasantly surprised by how willing people are to give you a hand.

Over the years, I've seen struggling businesses helped by friends volunteering time, relatives coming up with generous loans, and business mentors offering their consultancy services for free. I've also discovered how readily business people share their experiences and advice with one another in discussion groups online.

REMEMBER

Next time you're feeling blue and you get a dose of the two-am heebie-jeebies, remember that you're not the Rock of Gibraltar. You're part of a big, dynamic community of people who, at the bottom of it all, are keen to be there for one another.

IN THIS CHAPTER

» **Preparing for sale, years ahead**

» **Identifying the secret weapon that makes your business worth five times more**

» **Compiling the ultimate sales document**

» **Doing the buyers' job for them: Due diligence and more**

» **Finding a buyer**

Chapter **20**

Ten Tips for Selling Your Business

A t risk of recommending you put your feet up before starting to run a marathon, I suggest you start planning the sale of your business before you so much as open doors for trading.

Any business benefits when you, the owner, can stand separately from the business. Plan to build a business that still generates revenue even when you're away, and that doesn't rely solely on your efforts. Otherwise, you're not really creating a business; rather, you're creating a job with a pile of overheads.

Preparation is the key to securing a good price for your business. Plan to sell when the timing is best not just for yourself but also for your industry and the current economic climate. You don't want to be forced into a sale, or simply to sell your business because someone fronts up and offers a half-decent price. Instead, plan to exit with a sense of flair, with money in your pocket and a smile on your face.

Start with a Game Plan

Always try to have an exit plan simmering away, even if you don't plan to sell in the immediate future. Ask yourself: If I were to sell this business today, what could I get for it? When would be the best time to sell? Who would potential buyers be? Can this business run independently of me? What assets or business systems do I have to sell?

AHEAD OF THE PACK

If possible, try to create a formula with your business that you (or someone else) can replicate again and again, so that your business idea can expand. For more on this way of thinking, see if you can get your hands on either copy of one of the best-selling titles *The E-Myth* or *The E-Myth Revisited*, written by author Michael Gerber, and both quite transformative in the way Gerber provides models for turning a simple business idea into a valuable asset.

Prepare Well in Advance

One of the keys to getting a good price for your business is being able to choose the time when your business is at its peak. Too many business owners get forced into selling due to ill-health, personal circumstances or because they're struggling to survive. You can't hope to get a good price in this situation. Rather, aim to time the sale to suit yourself, doing the groundwork at least three years (yep, I said years, not months) in advance. If a buyer can tell that you've been planning this transition for quite some time and that you have well-kept financial records, proper policies and procedures and comprehensive customer records, then you're going to maximise your sale value.

The first step, which is only possible if you plan in advance, is to declare every cent of cash takings. (Sure, you could choose to keep a 'black book' where you record cash takings but, hey, if you offer visible proof that you're happy to be dishonest about your tax, how can a prospective buyer trust you not to be dishonest about other things too?)

The next step is to improve your net profit every which way you can. Remember, for every dollar you increase your bottom line, you may be able to realise up to five times that amount in the increased value of your business. I knew a husband-and-wife team who ran a nursery business with a turnover of $600,000 and average net profits of $50,000 a year. As part of preparing to sell, they bumped up prices by 10 per cent. Sales only dropped a little but, even so, they immediately made an extra profit of $40,000, increasing average profits to $90,000 a year. The result was an instant increase in value of their business of about $80,000.

Your business may not be so fortunate that it can sustain a price increase of 10 per cent, especially in the current economic climate. However, I bet you can find a few ways to increase net profits:

>> Keep your focus on the main game by avoiding new projects and products.

>> Clamp down on any personal expenses that you filter through the business.

>> Look for ways to save money, such as subletting unused factory space or renegotiating telephone contracts.

>> Get rid of old equipment and tools.

>> Go through stock holdings item by item, selling old stock for whatever you can get for it. (Even selling stock for cost is better than giving it away for nothing because the new owner isn't prepared to take it on.)

>> Ask staff, contractors and clients for suggestions and ideas about improving customer service, increasing revenue and reducing costs.

TIP

Although I recommend you pull back on expenses where you can, don't cut corners on things that count towards first impressions. Keep your premises looking clean and free of clutter, with new paint and well-maintained equipment.

Give Your Financials a Make-Over

Any prospective buyer is going to want to have a stickybeak at your Profit & Loss reports, Balance Sheet and Aged Receivables report. (For more information about these reports, and what info they include, mosey back to Chapter 17.)

You're probably thinking, 'All I have to do is click a few buttons in my accounting software and print the reports. No sweat.' Not quite. Your job, in order to get the best price possible, is to make sure these financial reports are in marvellous shape. (*Note:* I'm talking financial reports here, not financial results. For more about financial results, refer to the preceding section.)

First, go through your Profit & Loss reports and identify any irregular expenses. Maybe repairs were high one year because you renovated the office. Maybe you had big workers comp expenses because of an employee claim, or maybe you relocated your warehouse. If possible, separate these expenses and show them below your Net Profit figure, under a heading called Abnormal Expenses.

Give your Balance Sheet a tidy-up too. Check the value of land, equipment and furnishings: If values appear too low, ask your accountant about the possibility of adjusting these figures to show what stuff is really worth. If you can see any accounts on your Balance Sheet that shouldn't be there (such as old loans or personal credit card debts), ask your accountant to get rid of them.

With your Aged Receivables report, remove any debts where you know you have little chance of getting paid. Then go on the warpath, and chase any other debts that are overdue.

Get a Professional Valuation

Almost everyone who tries to sell their business has an unrealistic expectation of how much their business is worth and what the market might be prepared to pay.

Many business owners have spent years investing everything they have into building their business, and don't think of the value of the business in terms of what somebody might be prepared to pay, but rather in terms of what they think they deserve. Others decide the value of their business by thinking about how much they need in order to retire, and then reverse engineer the price from there.

If you search on the internet, you'll quickly find different methods for calculating the value of your business. The most common method is to calculate your average earnings before income tax and depreciation (a figure known by the snappy acronym of EBITDA) and then multiply this figure by anywhere between 1.5 and 6, depending on the industry. However, even this conventional method can be very subjective, if only due to the choice of multiplier.

Instead of trying to value your business yourself, I recommend you seek out a broker who specialises in selling businesses. A good broker should understand different valuation methods, industry standards and current market trends, all of which contribute to a fair price. You will need to pay a fee in order to secure a full valuation, but I reckon this is money well spent.

Go for the Max

One way to maximise the value of your business is to identify a strategic advantage that you own and which some other business — usually one that's bigger than your own — can lever to great benefit. Sometimes this strategic advantage may be worth very little in your eyes but can be worth a great deal in the eyes of a buyer. (*Note:* This strategic advantage method of valuing a business is often overlooked by brokers who tend to rely on more conventional methods.)

Some examples of strategic advantage include:

>> **Customer relationships:** A client of mine managed to get his product into a national retail chain and, over the years, built a great relationship with this chain. My client sold his business, at a substantial premium, to a larger player in the same industry who was having problems getting its product accepted by this chain.

>> **Software design:** Several years ago, another client of mine developed some clever software — at great expense and with many teething problems — that managed medical appointment bookings online. A much larger medical company, with branches in every state, purchased his business primarily to get ownership rights for the software, which they instantly implemented nationally, resulting in substantial annual cost savings for them.

>> **Exclusive supplier deals:** Another client secured exclusive dealership rights to import a certain product from China. My client then sold the business, along with the distribution rights, to a much bigger competitor with outlets all around Australia. Although my client's business was suffering at the time, sustaining losses month after month, the business was sold for a handsome sum, simply because the competitor was so eager to get hold of those distribution rights.

Can you think of some strategic advantage that your business has, which might be worth more to somebody else than it is to you?

Plan for a Few Bills

Regardless of whether you think you're gonna make a motza or sell your business for a song, speak to your accountant before putting your business on the market.

The main expense to be aware of is capital gains tax, which in theory applies for any profit you make on the sale of your business. For example, if you start a business from scratch and, then, five years later you sell the goodwill for $50,000, you may be liable for capital gains tax on that $50,000. You may also have to pay GST on any assets that you sell.

With a bit of foresight, however, you may be able to minimise this tax, maybe by rolling the money into another business, putting funds into superannuation, or selling off shares. You may also be able to reduce or offset your tax by selling shares in your business; for example, by selling 33 per cent each year for three years. Each of these strategies demands careful planning and professional advice.

On the flip side, if you think you're going to sell your business at a loss, a bit of tax planning in advance is wise. For example, you may be able to cut back on next year's tax bill by timing the sale of your business to offset capital gains on other assets or income from a regular job.

MONEY STUFF

Last, don't underestimate how much selling a business costs, not just in taxation but in other costs as well. Typical costs include legal fees for drawing up contracts, valuation fees for property and for stock, lease transfer fees, early loan payout penalties and accounting fees. You may also have to pay out trade creditors and any staff entitlements for holiday or long service leave.

Woo the Buyer

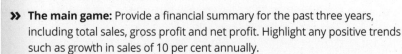

Your next job is to woo the buyer. Not with flowers, wine and sweet nothings (although this strategy may be a winner, depending on the buyer) but, rather, with an impressive document that presents your vital statistics in a seductive manner. You can write this document yourself, hire a writer or appoint a business broker to assist you.

Here's what to include:

>> **The story of your business:** Write a description of your business, when it started, what you sell and who your customers are. If you have a recent business plan (for more about business plans, check out Chapter 6), some of this info is probably already sitting pretty, ready to go.

>> **Current battle tactics:** Share a short synopsis of your marketing plan and marketing strategies.

>> **Lease commitments:** Include a description of your business premises, how much rent you pay each month, and the terms of your current lease. Remember that most commercial leases require your landlord to agree before you can reassign somebody else to the lease. If the lease is close to expiring, the landlord may insist upon a new lease.

MONEY STUFF

>> **The main game:** Provide a financial summary for the past three years, including total sales, gross profit and net profit. Highlight any positive trends such as growth in sales of 10 per cent annually.

>> **A people picture:** Include a summary of all employees, how much they earn and any special skills they have.

>> **Big deals on the go:** Do you have any major contracts with customers or suppliers? Share the details.

>> **Dreams in the making:** Deal-making is exciting stuff, and a dream may captivate a buyer more than reality ever can. Mention any ideas you have for expansion, such as new locations, online sales or new product lines.

>> **Why you're special:** Have you won any awards, received local business citations or do you have a collection of customer testimonials?

>> **The reason you're out of here:** Any buyer wants to know why you're selling, so be honest and to the point.

>> **The bottom line:** What does your asking price include? Obviously, your price includes goodwill, but what about assets such as stock or debtors, or liabilities such as unpaid employee leave or supplier accounts?

TIP

I suggest you have a legally binding Non-Disclosure Agreement (NDA) signed and in place before sharing intellectual property or detailed financial records with any potential buyer. This legal agreement outlines the confidential information, knowledge or materials that you wish to share, and places an obligation upon any prospective buyers not to disclose such information.

Do Due Diligence in Advance

When buyers are interested in purchasing a business and have started the formal negotiation process, they go through a process called *due diligence*. Due diligence involves making sure every single piece of paperwork is in order. Most sellers wait for the buyer to ask the questions, and then do the running to provide the information. Thing is, you always end up being one step behind the eight ball, and every time the buyer finds something that appears to be not quite right, the negotiation process, as well as valuable trust, gets eroded.

A smarter approach is for you to do the due diligence for the buyer and present everything as a single document. (I offer a simple checklist in Figure 20-1.) Put yourself in the buyer's shoes: If you were looking to buy this business, what would cause you to hesitate? The fewer problems that arise, the less chance to negotiate the price downwards, and the quicker the deal can go through.

Checklist for Preparing Your Business for Sale

- ☐ A contract for the sale of the business
- ☐ Profit & Loss reports for the last three years, along with tax returns
- ☐ Audit reports, if available
- ☐ Up-to-date Balance Sheet
- ☐ A list of what customers owe you, and a list of what you owe suppliers
- ☐ Proof of past sales (till rolls, invoice copies, contracts)
- ☐ A list of stock items held, including quantities, purchase dates, cost value and recommended sell price
- ☐ Proof of work-in-progress
- ☐ Employment contracts
- ☐ Copies of leases, both for premises and for equipment. (Oh yes, and make sure the lease is up to date.)
- ☐ Risk management plan and records of OHS compliance activities and fire safety inspection reports
- ☐ A register of staff training activities and copies of staff certificates
- ☐ Proof of software licences, and information about the ownership of any custom software applications
- ☐ A list of assets with current values, as well as a current depreciation schedule
- ☐ Any significant contracts held with customers or suppliers (if you have any agreements that aren't in writing, organise that now, too)
- ☐ Copies of insurance policies
- ☐ Copies of all outstanding quotations, including date of issue for each one
- ☐ Intellectual property register along with proof of intellectual property, such as copies of registered designs or trademarks, recipes or product patents
- ☐ Customer database information (make sure this info is up to date)
- ☐ A list of any customer deposits held, or supplier payments made in advance

FIGURE 20-1:
Checklist for preparing your business for sale.

Be Straight Up with Employees

In the initial stages of preparing to sell your business, keep your plans under wraps. You don't want employees to get wind that you're looking to sell and start looking for work elsewhere.

Later on, when you decide to spread the news that you're up for sale, start by telling staff about your intentions. Present the news in a positive way, reassuring staff that their jobs aren't on the line, and that you're going to be involved in the handover and the whole transition process.

If the new owners choose to retain existing employees when they take over, provide as much information as you can to the new owners, such as employee records, a history of all leave taken, and a summary of existing obligations including personal leave, annual leave and long service leave.

Alternatively, if the new owners do not intend to retain your employees, seek advice from Fair Work or your employer association regarding termination procedures, notice periods required and payouts of leave and other entitlements.

One tricky area can be family employees. Sure, the new owners may be happy to employ your son or aunty or cousin-three-times-removed, especially if that person contributes valuable skills. However, the owner's unreliable son who currently gets a sweetheart deal with their employment is another matter. A good strategy (if those concerned are willing) is to get each family employee to sign two letters: The first letter being an Employment Contract agreeing to stay with the business and agreeing to certain conditions of employment; the second letter being a letter of resignation. The new owners then have the choice between which letter they accept, and whether they inherit family employees with the business, or not.

Spread the Word

Don't assume that the best approach is to advertise your business for sale, listing the business online or via the local real estate agent. By cutting straight to advertising, you risk losing your best prospects.

Instead, have a think about any employees, customers or suppliers who may be interested in purchasing your business. Never underestimate the power of word-of-mouth advertising. After all, these people know and trust you, and probably understand your industry. One of my clients sold his restaurant to a faithful customer who, when the idea of buying the restaurant was suggested to him, simply couldn't resist.

At the same time, consider whether any of your competitors may be interested in buying your business. Are you squirming at the very thought? Don't. Earlier in this chapter (refer to the section 'Go for the Max'), I talk about identifying and capitalising on any possible strategic advantage that you can. Competitors are often best placed to capitalise on a strategic advantage and, for that reason, may offer you a price you won't get anywhere else.

If you don't get any nibbles from people in your network, take the next step and advertise your business for sale. I can't recommend any particular method, because the best strategy depends on your business and the kind of money you're looking for. Traditional advertising media include your local real estate agent, a business broker or a notice up in the shop window. Increasingly, however, people find success listing their business for sale online, in one of the many online directories available.

Ask yourself: 'Who might want to buy my business?' For example, if your business belongs to an industry with trade publications, try the classifieds in these publications (for example, a freight haulage business may find that advertising in trucking magazines attracts the right buyer).

REMEMBER

Throughout the sales process, be patient. In the same way that building up a business takes time, selling a business takes time, too. Often, whichever side of the negotiating table has the most time gets the best deal. If you plan your sale well in advance, you have a much higher likelihood of achieving full value for your business than if you're time-pressured to sell. Hang out for the best deal and, hopefully, you can walk away from this period of your life with a deep sense of satisfaction.

Index

About the Author

Veechi Curtis is passionate about Australian business and the potential that people have to achieve financial independence and realise their dreams.

Born in Scotland, Veechi attended university in Australia, where she completed her undergraduate degree in Accountancy and a Masters in Business Administration. She has been a small business consultant for more than 20 years, training and mentoring hundreds of businesses over this time. She has written for many publications and has also been a columnist for *The Sydney Morning Herald*.

Running a business in theory is very different from running a business in practice. In *Small Business For Dummies*, Veechi draws on her experience of running her own business, as well as her experience serving as a director on the boards of several local business and community organisations.

Veechi is also the author of *MYOB Software For Dummies*, 8th Edition, *Bookkeeping For Dummies*, 3rd Edition, and the international edition of *Creating a Business Plan For Dummies*.

Veechi lives with her partner and her slightly nutty rescue dog in the beautiful Blue Mountains of New South Wales, where she works as Executive Director at Varuna, the National Writers' House.

Author's Acknowledgements

Thank you to the many business professionals who have contributed their expertise and wisdom at some point during the development of *Small Business For Dummies*.

Thanks to the John Wiley editorial team, in particular Charlotte Duff and Ingrid Bond.

Last but not least, thanks to my very silly and wonderful family, who provide me with all the inspiration I could ever need.

Publisher's Acknowledgements

Some of the people who helped bring this book to market include the following:

Acquisitions, Editorial and Media Development

Copy Editor: Charlotte Duff

Project Editor: Tamilmani Varadharaj

Acquisitions Editor: Lucy Raymond

Editorial Manager: Ingrid Bond

Production

Graphics: SPi

Proofreader: Evelyn Wellborn

Indexer: Estalita Slivoskey

The author and publisher would like to thank the following copyright holders, organisations and individuals for their permission to reproduce copyright material in this book.

- © ASIC www.asic.gov.au: **page 113**.

- © Commonwealth of Australia 2021 reproduced by permission: **page 114**.

- © Intuit Australia Pty Ltd 2021: **page 318**. Screen capture from QuickBooks Online used with permission. QuickBooks Online and the QuickBooks Online logo are registered trademarks of Intuit Australia Pty Ltd. Any data displayed in these images is fictitious, and any similarities with any actual data, individual, or entity is purely coincidental.

- Microsoft Excel screenshots used with permission from Microsoft: **pages 85, 144, 145, 153, 155, 159, 161, 167, 168, 172, 173**.

Every effort has been made to trace the ownership of copyright material. Information that will enable the publisher to rectify any error or omission in subsequent editions will be welcome. In such cases, please contact the Permissions Section of John Wiley & Sons Australia, Ltd.